Exclusion and Poverty in
India and Central Asia

Exclusion and Poverty in
India and Central Asia

A Diversity and
Development Perspective

Chittaranjan Senapati

PARTRIDGE

ISBN: Softcover   978-1-4828-8521-7
            eBook   978-1-4828-8520-0

Print information available on the last page.

To order additional copies of this book, contact
Partridge India
000 800 10062 62
orders.india@partridgepublishing.com

www.partridgepublishing.com/india

Contents

List of Tables

List of Figures and Box

Abbreviations

ADB	Asian Development Bank
AIDIS	All India Debt and Investment Survey
ANC	Antenatal Care
APL	Above Poverty Line
BMI	Body Mass Index
BPL	Below Poverty Line
BTI	Bertelsmann Stiftung's Transformation Index
CAC	Central Asian Country
CARs	Central Asia Republics
CDS	Current Daily Status
CIS	Commonwealth of Independent states
CSO	Civil Society Organization
DISE	District Information System for Education
DLHS	District Level Household Survey
DRDA	District Rural Development Agency
ECA	European and Central Asian Countries
EFA	Education for All
GBAO	Gorno-Badakhshan Autonomous Province
GDP	Gross Domestic Product
GER	Gross Enrolment Ratio
HDI	Human Development Index
HDR	Human Development Report
HIV	Human Immunodeficiency Virus
HPI	Human Poverty Index
ICDS	Integrated Child Development Services

IDA	Iron Deficiency Anaemia
IDP	Internally Displaced Persons
ILO	International Labour Organisation
IMR	Infant Mortality Rate
LBW	Low Birth Weight
LCL	Low Cost Latrines
LFPR	Labour Force Participation Rate
LSAR	Living Standard Assessment Report
MCD	Minority Concentration District
MDG	Millennium Development Goal
MEI	Multidimensional Exclusion Index
MGNREGA	Mahatma Gandhi National Rural Employment Guarantee Act
MMR	Maternal Mortality Ratio
MNC	Multinational Corporation
MPCE	Monthly Per Capita Consumption Expenditure
MPI	Multidimensional Poverty Index
MRP	Mixed Recall Period
MSDP	Multi-Sectoral Development Programme
MSP	Minimum Support Price
NAR	Net Attendance Ratio
NDB	National Data Bank
NER	Net Enrolment Ratio
NFHS	National Family and Health Survey
NGO	Non Governmental Organisation
NHDR	National Human Development Report
NSDP	Net State Domestic Product
NSS	National Sample Survey
NSSO	National Sample Survey Organization
OBC	Other Backward Classes
OD	Open Defection
ODF	Open Defection Free
OOP	Out of Pocket Expenditure
PESA	Panchayat Extension in Scheduled Areas
PF	Provident Fund

PRSP	Poverty Reduction Strategy Paper
RBI	Reserve Bank of India
RCH	Reproductive and Child Health
RGNF	Rajiv Gandhi National Fellowship
RSBY	Rastriya Swastha Bima Yojana
RTE	Right to Education
SC	Scheduled Caste
SRS	Survey Registration Scheme
SSA	Sarva Shiksha Abhiyaan
ST	Scheduled Tribe
TFR	Total Fertility Rate
TRIFED	Tribal Cooperative Marketing Development Federation of India Limited
TSP	Tribal Sub-Plan
U5MR	Under Five Mortality Rate
UEE	Universalisation of Elementary Education
UNDP	United Nations Development Programme
UNESCO	United Nations Education Scientific and Cultural Organisation
UNHROHC	United Nations Human Rights Office of the High Commissioner
UNICEF	United Nations Children's Fund
UPSS	Usual Principal and Subsidiary Status
URP	Uniform Recall Period
VAD	Vitamin A Deficiency
WFPR	Workforce Participation Rate
WPR	Worker Population Ratio

Foreword

Dr. Chittaranjan Senapati has written a very interesting book on "**Exclusion and Poverty in India and Central Asia: A Diversity and Development Perspective**". In this book he has discussed the problems of social exclusion in market economy in India and Central Asian countries. This comparative study basically deals with the diversities and ethnic connotations to inclusive policies and development in these countries.

The study has contemporary relevance and is useful to policy makers, academicians, government officials and general readers at large. It explains how to understand the context, scale and extent of exclusion, various concepts of deprivations, social statistics related to exclusion, causes and consequences of exclusion, in India and Central Asian countries. The study facilitates understanding of the economic, political and social processes of exclusion that will be useful to develop policies of economic and political inclusion in these countries.

The study reveals the commonalities and major differences among five Central Asian countries with India, regard to the design and implementation of social policies. This domain of knowledge will be mutually beneficial for all these countries in economic, political and socio-cultural spheres.

Tahir Asghar
Professor
Centre for Russian and Central Asian Studies
School of International Studies
Jawaharlal Nehru University,
New Delhi

Acknowledgement

I would like to extend thanks to Jawaharlal Nehru University and University Grants Commission for giving me all the support to accomplish this work. I am also very thankful to Prof. Tahir Asghar, School of International Studies for writing foreword of this book. I would also like to extend thanks to the libraries in JNU, New Delhi, different institutes and professors / researchers in Almaty, Kazakhstan during my academic visit to pursue this piece of work.

Chittaranjan Senapati

Chapter 1

Introduction

"No society can surely be flourishing and happy, of which the far greater part of the members are poor and miserable."

Adam Smith (1776): The Wealth of Nations

Change is universal law in world and in human life. Change from traditional to modern, change of technology and economic system for betterment of life is predominantly acceptable to all rational human beings. The change of economic systems in India and Central Asia in 1990s was historical for the people as well as regimes. The change is inevitable and change is life, but the early years of economic reform has neglected social sector both in India and Central Asia, as a result of which poverty has increased in India and Central Asian countries. The early 1990s political decision has been dominated by a narrowly conceived version of economic policy of both India and Central Asia. This preoccupation has sometimes been detrimental to the quality of both Indian and Central Asian societies, and the structure of social protection. Indeed, in some cases the pursuit of a strict economic orthodoxy has left various sections of the community marginalized and alienated. Both the societies confront a number of challenges as profound as the economic changes of the past. The general argument in favour of new economic policy and adoption of globalization were that (1) it would improve the quality products and services to people at affordable prices, (2) large global business corporations increase employment opportunities, and (3) poverty will finally disappear from the global village.

Theodore Levitt observed, "technology was producing a new commercial reality - the emergence of global markets on a previously unimagined scale of magnitude." The world would be dominated by standardized products and universally

1

appealing brands. The three benefits of globalization mentioned above are yet to happen (Levitt 1984).

The introduction of the New Economic Policy 1991 of the Government of India and Central Asian Republics (CARs) were aimed at opening up the economy to global competition. According to C. Rangarajan, "the New Economic Policy comprises the various policy measures and changes introduced since July1991 in India. There is a common thread running through all these measures. The objective is simple to improve the efficiency of the system." The justification for the New Economic Policy 1991 was that "the country had lived beyond its means in the eighties. A correction is thus called for the stabilization policies coupled with the structural reform policies should ultimately result in accelerated growth which is the best answer to poverty." Thus, the New Economic Policy is supposed to operate within the limits of growth with social justice; politics of India and structural reforms are to be taken up with a human face.

According to Justice B.P. Jeevan Reddy, "unfortunately, this decision to practically reverse our economic philosophy-abandonment of the economic doctrine followed till 1990-1991 – was taken by the government without a national debate on the desirability or otherwise of a sudden and substantial change in the nation's economic policies. Indeed we were in no position to question it – that is until the collapse of the South East Asian Tigers."

It is also observed that poverty is the most visible face of the developing world and it has been made worse by globalization. And this is happening when it is being realized the world over that removal of poverty is a moral imperative.

According to some observers, many scams happening since the New Economic Policy 1991, are partially attributed to the Policy, if not a direct outcome of the Policy itself. Most particularly, the ever increasing uncertainties in the lives of common people reflected in indicators such as decreasing jobs in the organized sector, decrease in the trade union membership, job losses in the organized manufacturing sector, and increase in the cost of healthcare and education are linked to the after effects of the New Economic Policy 1991.

In 1964 ILO members adopted Convention No 122 on employment policy which states that, with a view to stimulating economic growth and development, raising levels of living, meeting manpower requirements and overcoming unemployment and under-employment, each member (state) shall declare and pursue, as a major goal an active policy designed to promote full, productive and freely chosen employment.

The said policy shall aim at ensuring that (a) there is work for all who are available and seeking work. (b) such work is as productive as possible (c) there is freedom of choice of the employment and the fullest possible opportunity for each worker to qualify for, and use skill and the endowments in a job for which he is well suited, irrespective of race, colour, sex, religion, political opinion, national extraction or social origin.

This convention was ratified at a time when unemployment levels are high in India and also in many other nations. One has to presume that the Government is now committed to pursue an active policy designed to promote full, productive and freely chosen employment.

From the commitments of the Government of India, it can be deduced that the following rights of workers have been recognised as inalienable and must accrue to every worker under any system of labour laws and labour policy.

The processes of globalisation and technical change has influenced our economy and society in complex ways including raising expectations of consumption and remuneration for skilled knowledge workers, creating greater demand for some information skills and services, causing unemployment amongst those with few qualifications, and destabilizing some traditional ways of life and increasing social exclusion. Existing traditions, norms and symbols of these societies have questioned and evaluated by younger generations and by people from different ethnic and religious backgrounds.

Many challenges we will face in the future require an increased commitment to the goals of social policy. This requires recognition of interdependence and the corresponding need to ensure that welfare state, communities, families and individuals are able to achieve social policy goals (Giddens 1994).

There are two characteristics of exclusion particularly relevant to define social exclusion. First, the deprivation caused through exclusion in multiple spheres showing its multidimensionality. Second, it is rooted in the societal relations, and societal institutions — the process through which social groups are excluded from participation in the society.

3

The same rights and opportunities denied to socially excluded groups because they are not able to fulfil their potential, are made available to others in their society. An estimated 891 million people in the world experience discrimination on the basis of their ethnic, linguistic or religious identities alone (DFID 2005). In this process social exclusion causes poverty. Broadly, we can find out causes of poverty in two ways:

1) It causes the poverty of particular group, which registered higher rate of poverty materially. It makes them poor by denying access of resources in terms of income, health, education, markets and public services. Even this socially excluded people are denied the opportunities to increase their income and escape from poverty. Economy may grow and general income level can rise but excluded people are likely to be left behind. Poverty reduction policies often fail to reach them unless they are targeted.

2) Social exclusion reduces the productive capacity of a society as a whole. It obstructs the efficient operation of market forces and restrains economic growth. Some people with good ideas may not be able to raise the capital to start up a business. Socially excluded groups in many times participate in labour market but in unequal terms. In labour markets the powerlessness of excluded groups easily get exploited due to their disadvantaged position.

1.1 Methodology of the Study

The social exclusion aspect is focussed in the present study both in India and central Asian context. In Indian context, the social exclusion has its roots in historical divisions along the lines of caste, tribe and religion. These inequalities are more structural in nature and have kept entire groups trapped, for which they are not able to take advantage of opportunities that economic growth offers. Culturally rooted systems perpetuate inequality that afflicts disadvantaged groups. In fact, this inequality prevents these excluded groups breaking out from traps.[1] In Central Asia, social exclusion is a matter of historical process since long time infiltration of different ethnic groups to this region.

---

[1] Coined by anthropologist Oscar Lewis, the term 'culture of poverty' refers to a unique value system of the poor. It was Lewis's belief that the poor are socialized into believing they deserve to be poor, leading to low aspirations, low effort and inability to escape poverty.

A lot of literatures are available to define poverty and its measurements in different dimensions. But poverty in this study would be measured in social exclusion criteria. There are broadly four approaches to measure and conceptualise poverty. They are monetary, capability, social exclusion, and participatory (Caterina Ruggeri Laderchi, Ruhi Saith, and Frances Stewart, 2006). While a monetary approach measures increasing money incomes, economic growth or income redistribution, a capability approach emphasises on the provision of public goods and welfare measures. As far as social exclusion approach is concerned, it draws attention to the need to break down exclusionary factors, and introduction of inclusive policy measures like redistribution and anti-discrimination policies. Although, anti-discrimination policies do not directly influence an aggregate income-based poverty measure, they can be a criteria to assess the nature of the poverty. On the other hand attention to human capability like health and education is very important to impact on social exclusion, poverty and participation.

In India and Central Asian countries have a common general intuition like poverty which exists and different groups of people are not attaining a "minimum" level of well-being. It depends partly on the prevailing standards of societies of India and Central Asian Countries (CACs). Therefore, measuring relative poverty can be more appropriate than absolute poverty. Although there will be complications in measuring income based poverty in the absolute or relative term, but it will be convenient to compare measurement across societies. Gary Fields (2001) identifies four questions on it:

1. Is the basis income or consumption, and how comprehensively will either one be measured?
2. What is the income-receiving unit: individual, family, per capita, or adult equivalent?
3. Will there be a single poverty line or will there be separate ones for urban and rural areas or different regions of the country?
4. Is the poverty line income determined scientifically, politically, subjectively, or as a matter of convenience?

However in India and CARs (Central Asian Republics) poverty head count ratio is standard scale to measure poverty line. Although it is not free from criticisms, this poverty measure will be used in this study.

The study is based primarily on secondary data collected from several sources NSSO (National Sample Survey Organisation) reports, Census reports, reports of various Ministries and published government documents. The incidence of poverty and other socio economic indicators are made available on NSSO reports, NFHS (National Family Health Survey) reports and DISE (District Information System for Education) reports. The present study uses all the sources of data. Mostly the data of post reform period has been compared by social and religious groups. Besides the qualitative information gathered from discussion with subject experts was used to obtain an understanding of the issues.

A field visit to Almaty (Kazakhstan) was undertaken to collect study materials and meet scholars related to the subject. However, the conceptual and theoretical understanding was developed from the extensive review of literature. Comparative analysis of India and Central Asia was undertaken in order to capture the process of social exclusion in these countries. Needless to mention, similar to India, Central Asia has various diversities.

In order to understand the situation of Central Asia, international sources were consulted such as World Bank, United Nations Organization, Statistical Database, the government websites of Central Asian countries Kazakhstan, Kyrgyzstan, Tajikistan, Turkmenistan and Uzbekistan. Minority Rights Group International (United Kingdom) and Centre for Analysis of Social Exclusion, London School of Economics.

The book is not intended as a policy document, although some of the empirical findings lend themselves to policy conclusions. Data for this study primarily came from multiple survey reports such as National Sample Surveys (NSSs), NFHS. Besides this/ these, numerous government reports and database of various ministries have been consulted.

1.2 Review of Literature

Buvinic summarises the meaning of social exclusion as follows "The inability of an individual to participate in the basic political, economic and social functioning of society." Later he adds that it involves the denial of equal access to opportunities imposed by certain groups in society upon others (Buvinic 2005). This definition captures three distinguishing features of social exclusion: it affects culturally defined groups, is embedded in social relations between them and results in deprivation or low income for those excluded (Haan 1997 and Sen 2000). It is critical to take note of the particular form of exclusion in the Indian context, where inscriptive rather than achieved characteristics are the basis of exclusion.

The former is not amenable to alteration as a consequence of individual agency and cannot therefore be regarded as a matter of personal responsibility.

Amartya Sen has drawn worldwide attention to the dimensions of social exclusion. He draws distinction between situations in which individuals are kept out and circumstances of inclusion on unfavourable terms. Either type can generate adverse effects (Sen 2000). Sen differentiates between active exclusion – blocking opportunity through deliberate policy interventions on the part of the government – and passive exclusion, which does not rely on these interventions, but may lead to similarly negative outcomes.

Sen draws attention to various dimensions of the concept of social exclusion and this distinction is drawn between the situations where some people are kept out and where some people are being included. He describes the two situations as 'unfavourable exclusion' and 'unfavourable inclusion' (Sen 2000). The 'unfavourable inclusion' with unequal treatment may carry the same adverse effects as 'unfavourable exclusion'.

Sen views Social exclusion as a multi-dimensional concept that covers economic, social and political aspects: it deals with the failure to attain adequate levels of various functioning that are deemed valuable (Sen 1985). Social exclusion is a relative concept in the sense that an individual can be socially excluded only in comparison with other members of a society: there is no 'absolute' social exclusion, and an individual can be declared as socially excluded only with respect to the society.

What is social exclusion and how does it differ from concepts such as poverty and disadvantage? Muddiman quoted (Muddiman 2000) in the social exclusion unit of cabinet office of London views "the theorists of social exclusion stress its multidimensional nature. Social exclusion, they argue, relates not simply to a lack of material resources, but also to matters like inadequate social participation, lack of cultural and educational capital, inadequate access to services and lack of power". In other words, the idea of social exclusion attempts to capture the complexity of powerlessness in modern society rather than simply focusing on one of its outcomes.

Duffy views social exclusion as a broader concept than poverty, encompassing not only low material means but the inability to participate effectively in economic, social, political and cultural life and in some characterisations alienation and distance from mainstream society (Duffy 1995). Within this framework, the term social exclusion has also been most generally used to refer to *persistent and systematic* multiple deprivations as opposed to poverty or disadvantage experienced for short periods of time (Walker 1997). In this respect, the concept of exclusion is also important because it captures the *processes* of disempowerment and alienation, whereas other descriptions focus largely on the outcomes of such processes.

Arjan de Hann (1997) describes two defining characteristics of exclusion are equally relevant namely the deprivation caused through exclusion (or denial of equal opportunity) in multiple spheres – showing its multi dimensionality. Second feature is that it is embedded in the societal relations and excluded from full participation in the society in which they live. It recognises the diverse ways in which social exclusion can cause deprivation and poverty. Consequences of exclusion thus depend crucially on the functioning of social institutions and the degree to which they are exclusionary and discriminatory in their consequences. Social exclusion has impact on an individual's access to equal opportunity if social interactions occur between groups in power. The groups focus thus recognised the importance of social relations in the analysis of poverty and inequality (Buvnic 2005).

Todman suggests that social exclusion refers to processes in which individuals and entire communities of people are systematically blocked from rights, opportunities and resources such as housing, employment, healthcare, civic engagement, democratic participation and due process that are normally available to members of society and which are crucial to social integration. Social exclusion prevents individuals or groups from participating fully in the economic, social, and political life of the society in which they live.

Dreze and Sen (1991) and Burgess and Stern (1991) view individuals who do not achieve certain standards of functioning related to health, nutrition, education as could thus be considered 'socially excluded'. Such studies assessing indicators of health, nutrition, education have been carried out in a number of developing countries, though not under the rubric of 'social exclusion.'

Appasamy *et al.*, (1996) in an ILO study in India, define social exclusion in terms of exclusion from a few basic welfare rights. They concentrate on the dimensions of health, education, housing, water supply, sanitation and social security. Attempts are made to identify percentages of individuals with no access/inadequate access to each of these rights. Analysis is disaggregated by State, location (urban and rural), gender, age, income level, asset-base, religion and caste.

Nayak (1994) focuses in India on a) exclusion from basic goods due to (income) poverty; b) exclusion from employment – including a discussion of the difficulties in conceptualising employment as in the West; c) exclusion from rights – particularly the right to a secure childhood in the context of child labour and d) exclusion on the basis of caste which the author recognises as an exclusionary dimension of central importance in India.

In a World Bank study, Mearns and Sinha (1999) explore the issue of social exclusion and land administration on Orissa in India. They look at a number of factors that constrain access to land for the poor and women.

While all these studies are explicitly looking at exclusion from something, given the absence of the concept of the welfare state and formal employment in developing country contexts, the original sense in which the concept was developed is not applied. Most studies although labelled as 'social exclusion' are thus quite similar to earlier multidimensional poverty studies performed in the respective countries. Poverty research that earlier looked at landlessness now looks at exclusion from land; those that looked at gender, caste or race based discrimination now look at exclusion on the basis of gender, caste or race; those that looked at access to health, nutrition, education now look at exclusion from basic rights or basic capabilities.

The UNDP report (2011) proposes a new approach for quantifying social exclusion. The approach is reflected in the Multidimensional Social Exclusion Index, which captures the complex nature of social exclusion. It is based on the multidimensional poverty methodology of Alkire, Sabiana and Foster (2011) which has been employed in UNDP's 2010 Global Human Development Report. The index assesses the status of people and their households along three dimensions: economic exclusion, exclusion from social services, and exclusion from civic participation. The social exclusion index employs 24 indicators – eight for each dimension – that reflect the ways in which people are denied access to labour markets, education and health systems, as well as to civic and social networks. An individual is defined as socially excluded if he or she is deprived in at least nine indicators. Since a dimension contains only eight indicators, to be considered socially excluded a person must be deprived in at least two dimensions. The index reflects both the share of people that experience at least nine out of 24 deprivations, and the depth (how many deprivations socially excluded people experience on average).

This methodology shows that social exclusion is pervasive in Central Asia region. According to the analysis, one out of every three persons is socially excluded. Seven out of 10 is socially excluded in Tajikistan. Furthermore, the report confirms the hypothesis that economic indicators of social exclusion only partly explain this phenomenon. Two other factors – lack of access to social services, and lack of access to civic and social networks – contribute equally to social exclusion.

In an article, Babajanian (2006) reviews the concept of social exclusion and applies it to an analysis of some of the key aspects of poverty in Tajikistan. It demonstrates that the application of the social exclusion framework can allow a more in-depth understanding of poverty than the commonly used monetary or income based framework.

In a paper Spoor (2011) views unique form of measuring social exclusion, namely through the Multidimensional Exclusion Index (MEI), which broadly follows the methodology as developed by Alkire and Foster (2007), for their Multidimensional Poverty Index (MPI). The MEI measures exclusions from economic life; social services; and civic life and social networks. Rural social exclusion is widespread in the region; it is (like rural poverty) largely worse than in urban areas in the countries for which the MEI has been measured. While rural-urban inequities were already present during the socialist era, the unbalanced, urban-biased, and "growth-pole" oriented development strategies have worsened them substantially.

A large number of empirical studies have been conducted on the issue of poverty. Some studies use primary and secondary data to examine the extent of, and disparity in, poverty among social groups, and factors that contributed to chronic poverty among excluded sections of society. An attempt has been made to review the important studies focusing mainly on the different aspects of poverty among social groups in India.

A study by Krishna, Kapila, Porwal and Singh (2003) in Gujarat found that SC, ST and OBCs were poorer compared to other households. The study found that size of landholding and level of education has positive correlation with reduction of poverty among SC, ST and OBCs.

A study by A. de Haan and Dubey (2003) made the observation that the incidence of poverty was considerably higher among SCs/STs compared to non-SCs/STs. A vast majority of SCs/STs in rural areas were agricultural wage earners. The poverty ratio was higher among STs in rural and SCs in urban areas. The pace of decline was more rapid among non-SCs/STs compared to others during 1983-2000.

Meenakshi, Ray and Gupta (2000) argue that caste and poverty seemed to go hand-in-hand — an outcome of historic discrimination based to economic factors. It was evident that incidence of poverty varied substantially between rural and urban areas and also between the various social groups. Poverty was more rampant in SC/ST households than others irrespective of deprivation measures. A study by Mehta and Shah (2001) revealed that chronic poverty seemed to be disproportionately higher among SC/STs compared to "Others" both in rural and urban areas. It has been noted that, on an average, one out of two persons belonging to SCs/STs was poor compared to the average of less than one of three non-SCs/STs. The persons belonging to STs in rural and SCs in urban areas were engaged as casual wage labourers in the agricultural and non-agricultural sectors. Agricultural labourers were identified as most susceptible to chronic poverty.

Thorat and Mahamallik (2005) found that the incidence of poverty was quite significant among STs followed by SCs compared to "Others" in rural areas from 1983 to 1999-2000. The disparity was marginally higher between STs and Others compared to that between SCs and Others. The incidence of rural poverty declined at 3.2 per cent per annum at the All-India rural level from 1983 to 2000. It declined at an annual rate of 2.9 per cent among SCs and 2 per cent in respect of STs during the same period. The former experienced a steeper decline than the latter. The poverty gap between SCs/STs and non-SCs/STs increased although the levels of poverty declined among all social groups in varying degrees. They concluded that the decline in the incidence of poverty was accompanied by a rise in poverty disparity between SCs/STs and non-SCs/STs in the 1990s.

Mutatkar (2005) in a study notes d that the incidence of poverty was historically significant among SCs/STs compared to non-SCs/STs in rural and urban areas. A great majority of STs in rural and SCs in urban areas were in absolute poverty. The study also recorded that poverty declined at faster pace among "Others" compared to SCs/STs from 1983 to 2000. The decline seemed to be slower in respect of STs compared to SCs.

A micro level study (Krishna, Kapila, Porwal, and Singh 2005) in northeast Gujarat observed that SCs, STs and OBCs tended to experience, a higher incidence of poverty. They recorded that compared to the General category a higher percentage of SCs, STs, and OBCs escaped from poverty in the last 25 years — 15 per cent SC households, 12 per cent ST households, and 10 per cent OBC households escaped from poverty compared to 7 per cent General Category households. The SC, ST and OBC households, however, continued to be poorer

11

on an average compared to General Category households — 83 per cent SCs, 79 per cent STs and 83 per cent OBCs were poor 25 years ago, compared to just 32 per cent General Category households. Further, since the liability of debt bondage hangs most heavily upon households at the bottom of the local social hierarchy, the ability of SC, ST and OBC households to escape poverty in future is also impaired to a considerable extent.

A study by Mehta (2006) in Gujarat shows that the incidence of poverty was much higher among SCs/STs than the general population, both in rural and urban areas. In rural areas, the incidence of poverty among STs (27.5 per cent) was more than double that of the general population in the state. The STs were the most vulnerable to poverty in the state compared to SCs.

For all the social groups, the poverty estimates were significantly lower among rural rather than urban counterparts. The decline in the general incidence of poverty during 1993-94 to 1999-2000 was more than double in Gujarat (8.5 per cent) than in the rest of India (4.1 per cent). The pace of decline in poverty among SCs, followed by STs, was more than that of "Others" and their counterparts in India during the same period. The decline in poverty was significantly higher in respect of SCs *vis-à-vis* STs, both in rural Gujarat and India (Mehta 2006). A study by Krishna (2006), covering 36 villages in Andhra Pradesh recorded that poverty was higher, on an average, among SCs STs and OBCs compared to "Others" (Krishna 2006).

1.2.1 Factors Contributing Poverty among SCs/STs

A study by Thorat and Deshpande (1999) argues that the labour market segmentation and uni-directional discrimination against the lower castes prohibited occupational mobility, which further aggregated production inefficiencies and stagnation of skills and wages. The entire social system under the Hindu social order in India resulted in creation of a major group of poor concentrated in a single caste group and over time increased the gap in the economic welfare of the two extremities. The highest echelons of the Hindu social order, enjoyed high returns on their work while the groups in the lower strata endured lower wages and remained impoverished. They have concluded that the caste-induced labour market discrimination can be treated as one of the basic reasons for productive inefficiency and deprivation of the lower caste groups. Identifying some correlates of poverty status, Meenakshi, Ray and Gupta (2000) show that the educational level of the head of the household and access to land were important correlates of poverty status. The level of education of the heads of SC/ST households was at least one year less than that of the heads of non-SC/ST households. The SC households typically fared worse than the ST households. Similarly, poverty rates declined with larger landholding size; the decline was economically significant only between medium and large-sized land-owning classes (Meenakshi, Ray and Gupta 2000). A study by Mehta and Shah (2001) found that the multiple deprivations suffered by historically marginalised groups such as SCs, STs, etc., made it harder for them to escape poverty as different forms of disadvantages tended to be mutually reinforcing. The key factors of chronic poverty are low productivity of land and labour, lower earnings and wage rates among SCs/STs, especially in Orissa, Madhya Pradesh and Bihar (Mehta and Shah 2001).

A study on Orissa's poverty, viewed lack of efforts from people is the cause of poverty in Orissa despite abundance of mineral resources. Deprivation in terms of lack of access to education, income, market, etc., was compounded by deprivation on the basis of social identity while social mobilisation to address these inequalities was limited (A. de Haan and Dubey 2003).

A study by Krishna, Kapila, Porwal and Singh (2003), covering 20 villages in Gujarat, observes that different social groups simultaneously experienced both relief from poverty and also? into poverty. The study identifies a combination of factors as being responsible for households falling into poverty, namely, ill health and heavy health-related expenditure, heavy customary expense on marriage and death feasts, and high interest payment on credit and also debt bondage to creditors (Krishna, Kapila, Porwal and Singh 2003). On the other hand, the growth rate of Net State Domestic Product (NSDP), growth of employment in private and government sectors, diversification of income sources mainly through dairying operations and informal employment and industrial growth emerged as important factors eradicating poverty in the state (Krishna, Kapila, Porwal and Singh 2003:5176). However, the study did not find much difference in the reasons for relief from and decline into poverty by social groups; rather the same factors seemed to have affected all households regardless of caste, religion or social status (Krishna, Kapila, Porwal and Singh 2003)

A micro level study by Dasatharamaiah and Ramanaiah (2006), describing the household level socio-economic features, found that SCs/STs had larger household of size, higher infant mortality, illiteracy, *kacha houses* and poor availability of sanitation and drinking water facilities. Most of them were agricultural labourers. The limited diversification in occupation and cropping pattern made it quite difficult for them to improve their socio-economic well-being.

A higher incidence of poverty among STs, was attributed to landless farmers, limited access to forest resources, no crop diversification, low input usage, informal wage labour, lack of social infrastructure, geographical isolation, inadequate investment in agriculture and lack of human capital development. The most important determinant of poverty was lack of remunerative employment, especially in respect of STs and SCs (Mehta 2006).

A study by Krishna (2006), based on the empirical evidence from Andhra Pradesh, argues that poverty needs to be addressed simultaneously with different set of factors — one set to assist them to escape and another set to prevent descent. The study found that ill health and high expenditure on healthcare, social and customary expenses (funeral and marriage), high interest on debt, drought and large family size were some of the factors contributing to a higher incidence of poverty. Industrial growth and education had only marginal effect on poverty reduction. A large number of villagers were educated, but only a small proportion had been able to secure jobs. Diversification of agriculture through improvement in technology proved to be the most rewarding pathway out of poverty. A study by Ramanjaneyulu (2007) argues that high incidence of poverty among STs, followed by SCs, was attributed to poor social inputs such as education, health, sanitation, etc. A co-relationship existed between poverty and social indicators.

The Multidimensional Poverty Index (MPI) provides a fuller measure of poverty than the traditional dollar-a-day formula. The MPI consists of three dimensions - health, education and standard of living. These are measured by ten indicators such as child mortality, nutrition, years of schooling, child enrolment, electricity, drinking water, sanitation, flooring, cooking fuel and assets (UNDP 2010).

Earlier, research on poverty emerged in three important dimensions. First, the entire focus was on identifying cause of poverty and the continuous academic debates on fixing poverty lines. The second dimension represented a more practical group of studies investigating into what causes poverty and are the poorest group. Finally, the third dimension dealt with the alleviation measures.

Biradar (2012) is also concerned about the location of poverty among social groups. With the analysis of NSSO data he argues that the concentration of poverty is among the Scheduled Castes and Scheduled Tribes. Sen (1981) views it is difficult to attribute specific causes of poverty because it is the cause and effect of the development process. Poverty is the failure of endowment, production, exchange and consumption.

In all these studies the usual focus was to study various dimensions of poverty, determinants of poverty, factors contributing poverty, extent and disparity of poverty among social groups, and factors that contributed poverty among sections of society. In the following section, an attempt has been made to study extent of exclusion among socially excluded groups in last two decades. Thus various human development indicators were analysed in the process.

The literature on poverty in Central Asia is evolutionary in nature. It highlights the major sections of society living in poverty and social and structural causes leading to poverty.

In a study, Christine and Revenga (2000) notes that the survey methods for living standards had methodological bias towards the rich and extreme poor. Though survey methods are still evolving hence suggests the measures for better reflection of poverty within society. Central Asian surveys categorize people in the form of social groups defined on the basis of their occupations, age and gender. The presence and lack to trace the informal economy is another major factor. They identify and analyse structural changes, labour market especially unemployment, low wages and inequality as important causes for poverty.

Kandiyoti (1999) in an article highlights the limitations of survey techniques in the transition process. The study is based on field survey in Uzbekistan; it explains ambiguities surrounding basic concept as household, employment, access to land, income and expenditure. The author brings out the missing links between the present methods of data collections largely influenced by western and soviet conceptualization of concepts. It results in the failure to capture the process undergoing and hiding poverty. He showed the disjuncture between official source of income and actually people living on. He suggested the need of understanding poverty in local, regional and cultural context.

Falkingham (1999a, 1999b and 2002) in a book examines impact of transition and poverty on the living standard of people in Central Asia especially in Kyrgyzstan and Tajikistan. The causes identified are declining wages, decrease in employment, high dropout and declining health standard. It suggests increased employment opportunities; improve social safety net and protect the region's human capital as possible measures for reducing poverty.

Tilly (2007) had discussed politics of exclusion as reason of production and reproduction of poverty. It explores the causal link between social exclusion and poverty and the process of exits from poverty. How the production process of inequality among different social categories leads to production of poverty. Tilly argues lack of favourable category or connection limits the possibilities of escaping from poverty. Exclusion and the political, economic and social systems produce poverty through their traditional interaction. The present poverty reduction approach focuses on facilitating crossing the existing boundaries like income. Instead Tilly suggests there is need to have new systems of production to overcome the poverty, in which previously poor people can acquire collective control over newly productive resources. This is likely to benefit whole categories of poor people directly and rapidly than facilitated crossing of existing boundaries.

Jha et. al (2009) has explored the argument that current poverty level may not necessarily good guide. The article discusses the limitations for tracing the real poor with the present methods of poverty measurement. Thus author suggests to examine the measurement through 'vulnerability to expected poverty' which is risk of being poor faced by the section of population. Determinants of vulnerability identified are locality as rural-urban, household size, head of the household, ethnicity in certain states like Kyrgyzstan, dependency ratio, unemployment and asset distribution. Through its analysis it showed that sizable fraction of population in the Central Asian countries considered non-poor has the risk of vulnerability across different segments of population.

World Bank (2000-2011) through reports on Living Standard Assessment Reports (LSAR) and Poverty Reduction Strategy Papers (PRSP) has contributed significantly to poverty reduction measures. It gives detail survey reports on living standards assessment for four states except Turkmenistan. The common features for these four states are geographical distribution of poverty, education, underemployment, low wages, and presence of large informal economy. Their degree of effect and impact on poverty varies. In Kazakhstan rural areas are most important affected area. In Kyrgyzstan rural, children, youth and ethnic minorities are living under poverty. Tajikistan has child and youth poverty as major concern while in Uzbekistan gender, ethnicity and wage differentials are important drivers and discriminatory policies and institutions resulting into poverty. The report World Bank (2003) on Uzbekistan's living standard assessment notes that unexplained differences are persisting between different nationalities or ethnic groups. Viewing the ethnic diversity of the population and increases in migration in Central Asia, an analysis of the source and reasons for existence of differences and policies to promote ethnic equity in labour markets is needed (World Bank 2003).

Largely, the literatures on poverty in Central Asia came from state based surveys, World Bank, United Nations. All reports have only passing references to ethnicity as factors. The recent study Social Exclusion Survey 2009 in Europe and Central Asia (UNDP 2011) also recognizes the ethnicity as important factor. Besides ethnicity, gender is an important determinant of social exclusion in Central Asia.

Though data on ethnicity is collected; same is not analysed. The major focus areas of discussion are occupation, rural-urban and various provinces (Oblasts). Though the book (Christine and Revenga 2000) recognizes that ethnicity is a high risk factor in the region and lack adequate space in literature and discussion of poverty.

The ethnic minority groups due to numerical weakness lack adequate attention. Hence does not have detailed analysis of such situation, from the perspective of social exclusion as analytical tool to understand poverty. As poverty is not just about material deprivation but deprivation of social relations as well. Such denial of recognition for legitimate space to ethnic dimension raises many unanswered questions and shows the scope for further research. While understanding poverty during transition, labour market, per capita income, services of health and education are major drivers in Central Asia.

1.3 Research Gaps and Limitations of the Study

The review of literature reveals that most of the studies have not attempted to describe the social exclusion of SCs/STs and Muslims with regard to employment, asset ownership, poverty, education and health. The Planning Commission's recent report (Planning Commission 2011) is the first attempt in this regard. There is lack of studies in Central Asia related to ethnic based exclusion. This study has thrown some light on the issues and recommended some inclusive policies for all these countries under study. The deprivation at international context and comparison of multi-ethnic countries between India and CARs is the key feature of the present study.

It is essential to understand the root cause of poverty and other dimensions to address the issues of social exclusion. A higher incidence of poverty among SCs/STs may be due to several economic and non-economic factors. It can be hypothesised that the economic factors such as lack of productive assets like land and human capital, lack of access to decent works, entry barrier to rural non-farm activities, low wages, indebtedness, under-utilisation of government funds allocated for poverty alleviation schemes etc., may be contributing to the poverty and social exclusion especially in the case of SCs/STs. Similarly, non economic factors such as attitude of privileged, lack of freedom, dignity and inferiority feeling excluded groups, are also equally important factors leading to further impoverishment of SCs/STs. An attempt to address the above exclusion issues may certainly help the policy makers and development practitioners in deciding the type of the policy intervention needed to tackle the long-standing problem of exclusion and ensure India has inclusive society. The study has undertaken vast areas of research where disaggregation of national statistical system data on the basis of social excluded groups is scant in India and CARs.

1.4 Structure of the Book

The book focuses on four select groups that face exclusion in India. They are Scheduled Castes (SCs), Scheduled Tribes (STs), Other Backward Castes (OBCs) and Muslims. Whereas in case of Central Asia, the exclusion of ethnic minority groups in five central Asian countries, Kazakhstan, Kyrgyzstan, Tazkistan, Turkmenistan and Uzbekistan are discussed.

The research attempts to address following issues: (a) conceptualise the nature and dimensions of the "social exclusion-linked deprivation and poverty" of socially disadvantaged groups particularly in Indian and Central Asia societies; (b) social exclusion occurs where a person's well being is such that they are unable to participate in society. So the overall aim of the study is to formulate social-economic policy to tackle exclusion; to improve the well being of all Indians and Central Asians in particular; c) poverty, which is closely associated with the processes of exclusion in the past, is generally reflected in a higher magnitude of poverty among the social groups in India and Central Asia societies. The purpose is to capture the impact of historical exclusion in term of group disparities between them and rest of the societies. With this theoretical back drop it tries to provide empirical evidence on the practice of exclusion and discrimination and denial of rights to the disadvantage group in civil, social, cultural, political and economic spheres, leading to lack of income earning capital assets like agricultural land, employment, education and social needs like housing, water, electricity, food and health security and clothing. This powerlessness leads to human rights violation of the disadvantage groups.

Exclusion operates along multiple and interrelated dimensions. Because addressing them all would be an insurmountable task, this book does not attempt to do so. It does focus on exclusion because of castes or religion. Even in the case of caste, tribe and minority, the literature is vast, multidisciplinary, and so prolific that it appears to grow every day. The evidence contained in this book builds on this vast database obtained from government sources. The book is by no means an attempt to provide a comprehensive survey of the evidence or even a review of all the issues involved. The fact that each of these groups is highly heterogeneous and that outcomes and processes differ by state and by type of caste or tribe makes the task even more challenging.

The book is organized into seven chapters, in addition to this overview each one dealing with an excluded group: STs, SCs, OBCs, Muslims and Women. The objective is to provide an analysis of how the socio-cultural groups have fared along various development indicators during a period of rapid economic growth in the national economy. In seeking these objectives, the chapter one describes the introduction to the book and analyses the research design and the process followed for the study. An exhaustive literature review has been undertaken to identify the exclusion issues analysed and research gaps in previous studies. Chapter two is an overview of conceptual frame works, theories of social exclusion, its applicability to India and Central Asian countries and main findings of the book. Chapter three describes the profiles excluded groups in India and CARs. Chapter four examines the poverty concept, various estimation methods adopted in poverty counting. Moreover, the poverty level of various social groups has been analysed. The rights and entitlements of social groups have been the focus of fifth chapter. Inclusive policies for the disadvantaged groups have been the focus of the sixth chapter. The last chapter is concluding chapter and policy implications.

The book is not intended as a policy document, although some of the empirical findings lend themselves to policy conclusions. Data for the book come primarily from multiple rounds of national-level household survey data (NSS, NFHS and DLHS) the database of various Ministries. Large national data sets, while allowing for national-level and to some extent, state-level generalizations, do not allow analysis of outcomes below the state level or within group differences and processes.

Chapter 2

Overview: Conceptual Framework and Key Findings

Section I

2.1 Concept of Deprivation

Deprivation and social inequalities have been topics of discussion for decades. Of late, it has caught the attention of social science researchers and policy makers. More specifically, the 12th five year plan (2012-2017) has emphasised on social inclusion. Deprivation is the prevention of relations between groups and society. Deprivation implies a "status of material and social harm" which affects a group in society. There is no unanimity on deprivation concept. The concept of deprivation has some common characteristics with poverty. Townsend (1979) viewed different concepts of deprivation such as material, social and multiple deprivations. Material deprivation indicated limited access people have to material resources. Access to resources enables people to play proactive roles in society. Social deprivation communicates people's roles and association, membership in social institutions and social interactions. Lastly, multiple deprivations relate to the occurrence of several forms of deprivation such as poverty, low income, poor housing, poor health, low education and unemployment etc.

The social deprivation is a contributory factor of social exclusion. These factors include disability, poverty, poor education and low socio-economic status. The socially deprived may experience a deprivation of basic capabilities due to a lack of freedom, rather than merely low income (Bassouk 2003). This lack of freedom may include reduced opportunity, political voice or dignity (Pierson 2002). Pierson has identified five key factors of social exclusion – poverty, lack of access to jobs, denial of social supports or peer networks; exclusion from services and mainstream society.

While the concept of deprivation is a static concept, social exclusion has important dynamic aspects. A group is socially excluded if deprivation prolongs for a longer period. Thus, deprivation has to be measured in a time frame (Atkinson 1998).

Arjan De Haan (2000) has argued that social exclusion facilitates the understanding of deprivation. Deprivation is multi dimensional phenomena and deprivation is part and parcel of social relations. Social exclusion has entered into debates on deprivation and policies that combat deprivation.

In the Indian context, exclusion and deprivation revolves around institutions that discriminate, isolate, and deprive certain groups on the basis of identities like caste, religion and gender. Social exclusion denotes a group's rights to resources in comparison to other members of society. Thus, the concept of social exclusion is linked to deprivation. Deprivation has two basic determinants: the lack of recognition by other members of society and the aggregate alienation experienced by the group (Thorat 2004a).

Social exclusion manifests itself in the lack of an individual's access to functioning as compared to other members of society. The concept is closely related to deprivation. Runciman (1966) formulated the idea that a person's feeling of deprivation in a society arises out of comparing its situation with those who are better off. Runciman defined deprivation as "the magnitude of a relative deprivation is the extent of the difference between the desired situation and that of the person desiring it". This intuition was used by Sen (1976), Yitzhaki (1979) and others, in order to obtain a measure of deprivation in the uni-dimensional space of income. Building on this concept, deprivation is viewed as a multi-dimensional distributional phenomenon characterized by two basic determinants: (a) the lack of identification with other members of society and (b) the aggregate alienation experienced by an agent with respect to those with fewer functioning failures.

The exclusion is resulted in incidence of poverty, limited access to education and health services and poor ownership of assets for certain social and religious groups. The empirical evidence of the exclusion is discussed in subsequent chapters.

With this, below is an attempt to review the literature on social exclusion. In the following section, a context for the empirical evidence of social exclusion is provided dwelling on the basic framework of social exclusion.

2.2 Social Exclusion: The Concept

In academic literature of the more recent times, Richard Lenoir introduced the term 'social exclusion' (1974) in the context of France. He defined the socially excluded as those who did not have access to welfare programmes run by the state. Thus all socially misfit individuals such as mentally challenged, physically disabled, aged, drug users and delinquents. Reference to exclusion is also traced Adam Smith's writings. He mentioned the inability of some people to "appear in public without shame" as a form of deprivation (Sen 2000). In all such references, social exclusion is widely perceived as domain of sociologists. When economists introduced development discourse on exclusion, they dealt with poverty and deprivation.

In the seventies and eighties globalisation and privatisation, resulted in reduction of public services, targeted assistance and deregulation of the labour market. These changes brought rising unemployment in Europe and weakened social networks (Bhalla and Lapeyre 1999). Currently, the term 'exclusion' has extended beyond the French definition to include the unemployment, weakened social relations. It has recognised that employment is not mere income, but also about social networks, and a sense of dignity that the unemployed were 'deprived. The approach gradually became popular in other countries in Europe and was adapted by the European Union.

The relevance of social exclusion has been incorporated into the development domain in a number of ways. It has been used in the social science literature to distinguish it from concept of poverty and rules of exchange and practices that keep groups out. Worldwide, excluded groups are ethnic or religious minorities. By virtue of their different cultural practices, they are considered as "separate group." Social exclusion as a concept perceives the individual as an entity embedded in society and groups. The focus is thus not on outcomes such as consumption, income, health or education alone, but on factors that restrict individuals from achieving the outcomes (Haan 1997). Amartya Sen (1998) terms these as "relational roots of deprivation" whereby membership in a particular group (women, religious minorities, lower castes and indigenous people) limits the "functionings" of individuals to use their capabilities. The term social exclusion is rather relative rather than absolute concept. Exclusion takes place when people lack capacity of doing well-defined things.

2.3 Dimensions of Social Exclusion

Social exclusion exists in various spheres and in many forms. However, race and caste have dominated the debate on social exclusion. As discussed earlier, social exclusion is lack of access to resources and consequent inability to utilize them. It is further aggravated by denial of opportunities which enhance access to resources. Thus, besides caste and race, religion, gender, position in social hierarchy is all volatile to social exclusion. Stratification of human populations occurs at various levels and in many forms. It has a reflection of power dynamics which exist between people and also between groups. This drives some caste and religious groups to be more advantaged as against others. Similarly, the gender roles are likely to put women at certain disadvantages vis-à-vis men. Applying this with lack of access to education and employment, incomes, land ownership and political participation are all driving factors of social exclusion.

Social exclusion is the impact of a process of discrimination on the basis of cultural, social or racial identity. Such discrimination can generate exclusionary processes. Discriminatory processes are reinforced by religion, tradition and social practices – as exemplified by India's caste system - and reflected in social attitudes, behaviours and prejudices.

Discrimination is clearly a particular kind of exclusion and it can take on an active or passive form. Active exclusion through discrimination will see agents systematically refusing to hire or accept the participation of members of a social group despite their formal qualifications. The consequences of discrimination can lead to deprivation.

The exclusion can be of three types: social, political or economic. Denial of rights to participate in social institution conveys social exclusion. Rejection of rights to participate in political activities explains the political exclusion. Similarly, the economic exclusion indicates lack of access to forms of livelihood. It is an important factor as it leads to exclusion in terms of low consumption levels, education and health care. The location of public goods, its accessibility and ability to pay are a few factors leading to exclusion; it is much true in the context of education. The exclusion from land is a critical issue in many developing countries and more over, it is widely associated with poverty and insecurity. Land is not only a source of livelihood but also of social integration in a broader sense. This is more relevant to the developing nations where land is the prime source of employment and livelihood.

2.4 Features of Exclusion

Exclusion is Multi-dimensional: The idea of exclusion links together both social rights and material deprivations. So it encompasses not only the lack of access to goods and services but also exclusion from security, justice, representation and citizenship. The central idea is that exclusion has much to do with inequality in many dimensions such as, economic, social, political and cultural. This broad framework not only helps to identify the most important mechanisms and dimensions of exclusion which vary from one situation to another, but it also provides a basis for an interdisciplinary approach.

Exclusion Focus on Process: Exclusion may describe a state but its particular advantage is that it focuses on the process rather than on other dimensions. It is very important to identify the process and factors which lead to the process of exclusion. It talks about two situations: one is permanent exclusion in which groups live on the margins of society and the other is created and recreated by the operation of social and economic forces in the society.

Focus on Social Actors: There are processes which include and exclude but there are also social actors who both include and exclude. An important aspect of social exclusion is to identify these actors and understand how and why they exclude others. Actors are social groups, state, political parties, enterprises, local authorities, religious bodies and opinion leaders.

2.5 Economic Exclusion

Economic exclusion marginalizes individuals in the distribution of economic resources. From the human development perspective, this hinders the development of people's capabilities, which would have helped them to satisfy their needs and exercise their rights, enabling them to make choices to attain the living standards and quality of life that they value. Economic exclusion limits people's access to the labour, financial and housing markets, as well as to goods and services. This leads not only to income poverty, but also to reduced access to services such as education, health care and social insurance—ultimately resulting in a loss of capabilities. The feedback loops are crucial. For example, exclusion from the labour market leads to the loss of critical social benefits – such as health care, pension and disability insurance – which increases the risk of long term exclusion. Furthermore, economic exclusion resulting from poverty and material deprivation reduces opportunities for education and participation in social networks. Economic exclusion contributes to a culture of poverty characterized by feelings of powerlessness, discouragement and despair.

The main elements of exclusion from economic life are income poverty, unemployment, and lack of access to assets and capital. These are discussed in chapter three.

2.6 Exclusion from Social Services

Social services offer opportunities such as employment, education and health care have inherent value and are important for social inclusion. The same applies to other social protection measures (social insurance, social assistance, and social safety) access to housing and support infrastructure. Exclusion from social services refers only to quality, accessibility and affordability of such services by different groups.

2.7 Exclusion from Public Participation

The key concept for inclusion in public processes is *participation*. Exclusion from civic and social life and networks therefore refers to denied participation in different aspects of political, cultural and civic activity. These include engagement in the electoral process, the right to elect and be elected, freedom of expression and association, access to justice and information, and public and political security. Exclusion from civic and social life and networks occurs not only through formal institutions but also through lack of access to informal structures and opportunities. Informal social networks and formal civic institutions are complementary avenues for participation in public life.

Two aspects of civic, cultural and political exclusion are noteworthy when looking at social exclusion: the development of political culture and social capital. Political culture refers to the nature of rule or authority, role of individuals or groups in public life and political role models. Political culture is reflected in political participation beyond turnout at elections, and levels of public confidence in state institutions. Social capital is based on norms of reciprocity and mutual trust (Putnam et al. 1993) increased through social networks and individuals linked through them. Research suggests that societies with higher level of social capital stand a better chance of becoming democratic and stable. Social capital is especially important for low and middle-income transition countries that face the triple challenge of democratization, economic development and avoidance of violent conflict (Kuzio 2001).

2.8 Social Exclusion in India

Social exclusion is a universal phenomenon which has existed over time and space. However, in India, social exclusion has been predominantly used in understanding caste based discrimination. The social exclusion in India has its roots in India's historical divisions along lines of caste, tribe, and gender. These inequalities are more structural in nature and have kept entire groups trapped, unable to take advantage of opportunities that economic growth offers. Century old practices perpetuated inequality, and, culture of poverty among disadvantaged groups. These inequalities prevented the groups to come out of poverty.

There are various forms of social exclusion experienced by Dalits in India. After partition of the country in 1947, the religious minority Muslims experienced social exclusion in various spheres of life. They were deprived of education, health services, housing and employment. The practice of caste and religion based exclusion involves failure of access and entitlements not only to economic rights but also civil, cultural and political rights. It has been described as living mode exclusion, exclusion in political participation, social and economic opportunities (UNDP 2004a).

Unlike the West, where the concept of social exclusion was evolved and promoted by policies and programmes, same in India was aggravated by social practices. Moreover, India has historically been multi-religious, multi-lingual, multi-cultural and multi-ethnic country. The caste hierarchy in India neglects those at the bottom of the social ladder; a class society ignores those from the lower classes; minority religions experience discrimination from majority religious groups. Some ethnic and cultural societies are marginalized because they deviate from core culture or ethnicity. The problem of exclusion becomes much more acute in view of scarce resources. Even in advanced economies, exclusion, both on the basis of race and class is a well-known phenomenon. The African Americans in the United States of America face racial prejudice even today and incidence of poverty among them continues to be very high. Even now, religious and cultural minorities in developed countries are experiencing social exclusion.

India has uniquely large social diversity with at least three large social folds, related to religion, ethnicity and caste, often linked to differences in well-being and of which the manifestations are regionally specific. Hinduism is the largest religion, but Muslims constitute 13.4 per cent of total population. In absolute numbers, Muslims add up to 140 million populations (Census 2001). A large proportion of the population belongs to the various groups of *Adivasis* or Scheduled Tribes (8.6 per cent), they tend to live in remote areas and have much higher incidence of poverty (Xaxa 2001), lower rate of labour migration[2] and vulnerability to forced displacement.[3] Finally the country is marked by a well known and described caste system which divided the Hindu population into five groups. Of these, Scheduled Castes (16.9 per cent) suffer from high level of socio–economic deprivation.

In India, social exclusion has been for all minorities but much more so for Muslims. Their exclusion from social, cultural, economic and political processes, poses various problems. Given the present regime of upward growth of the economy, it is essential for the state to recognize the need of abandoning caste, religion, region and ethnicity based social exclusion. Social exclusion has to be addressed for future technological advancement, economic growth and development of the country.

The GDP growth rate was 5.5 per cent per annum during the period 1997–8 to 2001–2, which accelerated to an average of 7.7 per cent per annum during the period 2002–3 to 2006–7 in India (Government of India 2008a). However, the non-inclusive character of the growth process has been a major concern for Indian policymakers, including the Planning Commission. It stated that 'a major weakness in the economy is that the growth is not perceived as being sufficiently inclusive for many groups, especially the SCs, STs and minorities. There are evidences that not all religious communities and social groups have shared equally the benefits of the growth. Among these, the Tribals, Dalits and Muslims, the largest minority community in the country, are deprived the most. The historical factors such as partition of the country on the basis of religion in case of Muslims and remoteness of Tribals aggravated poverty, poor education, and economic backwardness which culminated in social exclusion.

---

[2] Minority data are analyzed in de Haan and Dubey, 2006. It is important to point out that the poorest also migrate. Similar data for china are not available though observations suggest that minority groups may have faced barriers to migration because of distance and language.

[3] Minority Rights Group International conclude that "while 85 per cent tribals live in poverty, they receive little or none of the wealth extracted from the land" (http// www.minority rights. Org/4047/reports/the advasi of india.html).

The contributory factors to social exclusion and its link to other factors like poverty and deprivation in India are explained below (Figure 2.1). Moreover, women are another deprived group. They face a range of multiple challenges ranging to access to employment, health care, improper working environment, numerous social restrictions, employment security, wage parity etc. Women have been largely excluded due to social and cultural practices.

Figure 2.1: Contributory Factors to Social Exclusion, Poverty and Deprivation

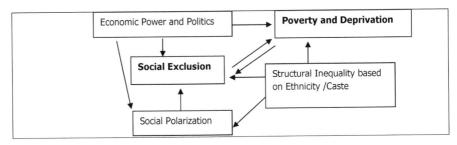

Source: Authors' analysis

Section II

2.9 Social Exclusion in Central Asia

Understanding the concept of social exclusion is critical for assessing the transformations in the post-socialist countries of Central Asia[4]. The changes in the post colonist socialist system have redefined people's lives, values and behaviour. During such transition many people were deprived of their ability to live healthy and productive life, though large section of people had better freedom of choice. In Central Asia, income-based measures of poverty are insufficient for capturing the depth and breadth of the deprivations in the region. Thus, analysing the transformations through the broader prism of human development becomes critical.

---

[4]   CIS (Commonwealth of Independent States) and Georgia: The countries in this sub-region fall into three Groups: Central Asia (Kazakhstan, Kyrgyz Republic, Tajikistan, Turkmenistan, and Uzbekistan), Western CIS (Russian Federation, Belarus, Republic of Moldova and Ukraine), and Caucasus (Azerbaijan, Armenia, and Georgia).

It is a general phenomena that, the exclusion increases, if we move from urban centres to rural areas. Similarly, in Central Asia, population living in rural areas experiences four times more exclusion that of the urban areas (UNDP 2011). Living in rural areas is a massive disadvantage due to lack of job opportunities, lack of access to basic social services as health, transport and goods results into setting up the trend of rural to urban migration. Such phenomenon often causes more harm than benefit in long run to the society. It is observed that, the employment opportunities social exclusion was relatively high among the communities where by one or two companies had been dominated since 1989. This is an important issue. Government should work to increase employment opportunities especially for people living in mono company towns, to reduce social exclusion.

The governments of Central Asian countries should address the three dimensions of social exclusion — exclusion from economic life, social services, and civic life and networks in an integrated manner. Central Asian government needs to adopt strategy of multiple interventions rather than focusing on reducing only income poverty. Facilitating the accessibility of quality essential services as water, sanitation, housing, health, education and transportation can initiate such multiple intervention mechanism. It can play essential role to breaking the intergenerational cycle of social exclusion.

Employability and inclusive markets matter to the social exclusion. An important way to promote employment opportunities for groups at risk of social exclusion and a mindset change in society to improve the employability of the labour force through improved vocational education, active labour market policies and social economy. Inclusive institutions, education and labour market policies would gradually change the drivers of social exclusion and raise tolerance in society.

The concept of social exclusion in Central Asia context has been re-articulated over time. Within the discourse of citizenship, social rights and social justice, the status of 'being socially excluded' is not merely understood as a lack of access to goods, but as a lack of access to rights. If poverty is defined in relation to income or material deprivation, social exclusion is defined in relation to social rights such as the right to work, housing, health services and education (Lister 2004). Following social exclusion chain can explain the real scenario.

Figure 2.2: Chain of Social Exclusion

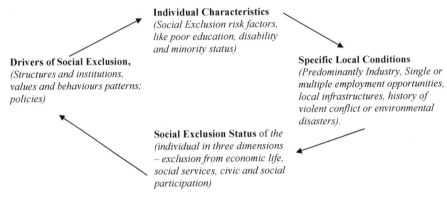

Individual Characteristics
(Social Exclusion risk factors, like poor education, disability and minority status)

Drivers of Social Exclusion,
(Structures and institutions, values and behaviours patterns; policies)

Specific Local Conditions
(Predominantly Industry, Single or multiple employment opportunities, local infrastructures, history of violent conflict or environmental disasters).

Social Exclusion Status of *the (individual in three dimensions – exclusion from economic life, social services, civic and social participation)*

Source: UNDP (2011)

2.10 Dimensions of Social Exclusion in Central Asia

By the first half of the 1990s, the transition recession had taken its toll in Central Asian countries. Central Asian countries resumed positive growth only in the second part of the decade. However, the growth was not accompanied with increased employment opportunities. Human development in Central Asia followed a similar pattern, falling in the early 1990s but rising in the latter part of the decade. Countries experienced a significant increase in income inequality within and across sub-regions. In larger context, the three major dimensions of social exclusion, from economic life, social services and social networks will be elaborated below to understand the dynamics of social exclusion in Central Asia.

2.11 Exclusion in Economic Life

Economic exclusion limits people's access to the labour, financial and housing markets, as well as to goods and services. This leads not only to income poverty, but also to reduced access to services such as education, health care and social insurance—ultimately resulting in one's loss of capabilities. The cumulative effect of exclusion from the labour market leads to the loss of critical social benefits which increases the risk of long term exclusion. Furthermore, economic exclusion resulting from poverty and material deprivation reduces opportunities for education and participation in social networks. Economic exclusion contributes to a culture of poverty characterized by feelings of powerlessness, discouragement and despair. The main elements of exclusion from economic life are income poverty, unemployment, and lack of access to assets and capital. These elements will be discussed in turn.

2.11.1 Income Poverty

Income poverty is an obvious aspect of economic exclusion, but it implies much more than limited consumption. Poverty increases people's vulnerability to social exclusion in other areas of life. For example, children of parents who are struggling to make both ends meet often drop out of school to get a job. Income poverty limits the opportunity to participate in public life, particularly in periods of structural transformation when the old 'non-monetary' channels of inclusion, such as free access to childcare, have disappeared without affordable market-based alternatives.

In the early 1990s, poverty increased on a significant scale in Central Asia. This happened in part because the relatively low poverty levels of the 1980s had been financed by international borrowing. Thus, falling poverty in the 1980s did not reflect sustained gains in competitiveness and economic efficiency, but rather deficit spending (Gaider 2007). In subsequent years, countries have had to service the debt, which together with the transition recession and the Russian crisis—helped to explain why in 2005, a significant portion of the region's population – approximately 142 million people – were living below the 4.30 Purchasing Power Parity dollar per day poverty line (UNDP 2011).

Geographically isolated regions and rural areas, particularly those that are far from urban centres, were largely the poorest, pointing to a structural form of spatial economic exclusion. Everywhere, poverty dropped substantially between 1998 and 2003, most notably in national capitals (Table 2.1). Although the percentage of poverty was high in 1998 it has recorded declined in 2003 in Central Asian countries.

Table 2.1: Spatial Distribution of Consumption Poverty (1998-2003) (per cent)

Name of Country	1998			2003		
	Capital	Other Urban	Rural	Capital	Other Urban	Rural
Kazakhstan	7	25	40	2	14	31
Tajikistan	73	90	92	54	73	76
Uzbekistan	24	50	60	4	43	55

Source: World Bank (2005: 242-4)

However, in some countries, small-and medium-sized towns and cities are nearly as poor as rural areas. This is partly due to land reform, which in some cases provided agricultural land to rural dwellers, while citizens in 'other urban' areas (such as in 'mono-company' towns) very often lost their main source of employment, and did not have access to land. As a result, they had no opportunity to practise subsistence farming; on the other hand the sharp food price increase of 2008 had affected them greatly.

2.11.2 Unemployment

Employment provides more than a wage. When people are excluded from formal employment, they are not only cut off from income and related benefits, but also from broader opportunities. Poor employment opportunities are a major contributor to exclusion from economic life.

The first years of transition saw sharp increases in unemployment, straining the social fabric. The labour market offered new opportunities, but also demanded new skills, resulting in mismatches between the skills employers needed, and those which people possessed. These mismatches were more prevalent in certain sectors and age groups. In some cases, this process has led to the marginalization of whole groups, further amplifying societal strains. In the region, economic exclusion often occurs because of labour informality, inactivity and under-employment. Informality has broader implications for social exclusion, eroding the tax base, institutions and societal norms.

It is important to understand how transition has affected the position of women and men in the labour market. Under socialism, countries had often strongly encouraged women to work, in part by offering company-sponsored childcare. However, women were often the first to be laid off during the transition recession of the early-mid 1990s.

Table 2.2: Percentage of Employment Status *(As on November 2009)* (per cent)

Working Status	Kazakhstan		Tajikistan	
	Male	Female	Male	Female
Employed	61	39	47	24
Unemployed	8	5	5	4
Pensioners	14	20	7	9
Children and Students	6	6	10	8
Inactive	11	30	31	55
Total	100	100	100	100

Source: UNDP (2011)

The impact of the 2008-09 global crises is more nuanced. Women have faced a lower risk of being laid off, both because male dominated sectors such as construction have been among those most severely hit by the crisis, and because firms could save more by firing men, who tend to receive higher remuneration. But this gender 'advantage' is dubious, as women must generate higher incomes to support their households. The inactivity among female was higher than male according to the Social Exclusion Survey (Table 2.2).

Table 2.2: Percentage of Employment Status *(As on November 2009)* (per cent)

Working Status	Kazakhstan		Tajikistan	
	Male	Female	Male	Female
Employed	61	39	47	24
Unemployed	8	5	5	4
Pensioners	14	20	7	9
Children and Students	6	6	10	8
Inactive	11	30	31	55
Total	100	100	100	100

Source: UNDP (2011)

2.11.2.1 Access to Assets and Capital

Transition has led to a skewed distribution of wealth. Many households have faced higher utility bills after privatization because hefty government subsidies for utility companies were cut. Unable to pay the higher tariffs, many poor households were disconnected from utility networks. In many cases, privatization resulted in 'privatizing the profits and nationalizing the losses' of state-owned enterprises, leading to a massive appropriation of capital. Particularly in Central Asian counties, economic wealth is now very concentrated, often in the hands of a small group of individuals. This massive asset inequality emerged in a very short period of time—after decades of state ownership. Because of an inherited legal framework that was not designed to regulate private monopolies, together with gaps and inconsistencies in newly adopted legislation, asset inequality has remained an obstacle to fostering inclusive growth.

2.11.3 Exclusion from Social Services

Social services offer a wide range of opportunities critical for human development. Like employment, education and health have intrinsic value and are important for social inclusion. Social protection services provide assurance of better human development. These services can range from basic facilities as housing, infrastructure and transport to social assistance for targeted groups. The exclusion from such services can take various forms for different groups ranging from lack of accessibility and affordability to level of quality of such services.

In the 1990s, the quality of social services and utilities deteriorated rapidly in Central Asia. Employer provided social services disappeared and extended state provision or market-based alternatives had not yet come to replace them. The level of incomes and pensions was too low to generate sufficient demand for market-based social services provision. Attempts at decentralizing responsibilities to local administrations without providing them adequate resources have further weakened the social infrastructure, in particular in rural areas and small towns. Capital-city centred models of growth and opportunities for employment abroad additionally undermined finances and governance capacity at local levels, which was already weak at the beginning of transition. All this contributed to exclusion from social services, either through reduced access or through reduced affordability.

Privatization of public utilities (water, sanitation and electricity) has often contributed to exclusion. While increasing efficiency, privatization failed to live up to expectations. There was no effective regulatory framework and genuine competition. State owned monopolies were often replaced by poorly regulated private monopolies. Public subsidies for utilities (heating, water and electricity supply) subsequently fell sharply, placing cost-recovery out of reach even though prices of services increased substantially after privatization. In the cases when subsidies were retained, they disproportionately benefited the more affluent segments of the population, contributing to the exclusion of the poor. Moreover, social disruption and the destruction of physical infrastructure in war-affected areas and countries, notably Tajikistan, made the sustainable delivery of social services and the effective maintenance of public utilities nearly impossible, with serious implications for social exclusion.

2.11.3.1 Education and Training

Pre-school years are immensely important for child development and for equality of opportunity. Both are vital for preventing the social exclusion of children, particularly for children from vulnerable groups who face the highest risk of exclusion (UNDP 2011). While pre-school facilities had been widespread in the region before transition, they were employed unevenly. In rural Central Asia, children were traditionally kept within the extended family until school age. Recent data on pre-primary enrolment rates show just seven per cent in Tajikistan afford to attend pre primary school education depriving large number of children (UNICEF 2009a).

Rural-urban disparities exist in pre-school education, as well as in enrolment rates by income quintile. There is also an increasing gap between 'elite' kindergartens and 'mainstream' (usually underfunded and overpopulated) facilities. As a result, instead of equalizing opportunities through a 'fair start for all', pre-school and early childhood services themselves contribute to early exclusion and segmentation, particularly for minorities and marginalized groups. Poverty and prejudice contribute to extremely low enrolment rates of children in pre-school education, augmenting the barriers they face later at school.

The region as a whole has high levels of primary school attendance, which is compulsory from six or seven to fourteen or sixteen years of age. However, household survey data tend to show lower enrolment rates than those based on administrative data, presumably because there are incentives to keep reported rates high to access resources and maintain staffing levels. Rates tend to be lower in rural areas for poor households and for some ethnic groups.

2.11.3.2 Affordable Health Care

Given the intrinsic value of health from the human development perspective, access to health care is critical for social inclusion. Both financial and structural reasons account for health care exclusion. Countries in the region face severe budget constraints, as well as difficulties in implementing reforms that balance quality services, access for all, and efficiency.

As a result, inequalities in access to health care and in terms of health outcomes have been growing throughout the region. While in general, public expenditures on health have been maintained both as a percentage of GDP and in terms of expenditure per person, they are still low, particularly in Central Asia (UNICEF 2009b). The gap is increasingly being filled by private spending. In countries where public expenditure on health is less than three per cent of GDP, private spending in 2006 represented at least fifty per cent of overall health expenditure, except in Kazakhstan (UNICEF 2009b). This increases the risk of exclusion from health services for poorer households.

Two broad groups facing acute health exclusion are older people and people with mental illness. The elderly face challenges in terms of appropriate long-term care services which are neither fully hospital-based nor reliant on informal family and kinship care (World Bank 2007a).

Exclusion from health care, education and employment can be found widely among people living with HIV (UNDP 2008). In Central Asia an estimated 1.5 million people were living with HIV in 2008, an adult prevalence of 0.7 per cent. This is higher than in all other regions of the world except the Caribbean and Sub-Saharan Africa.

2.11.3.3 Social Protection

Social protection systems (social assistance, social insurance benefits, social services, social work, and counselling services) can be crucial sources of last-resort support to the extreme poor as well as to the excluded, or to those at risk of exclusion. Social services reforms have affected service delivery and outcomes. During early transition, serious disinvestment occurred and elements of social services were placed on a market basis. Some countries delayed reforms, maintaining formal equality of access to services alongside a *de facto* deterioration in provision. Social protection schemes in many countries in the region have been 'captured' by particular interests or groups (Cerami and Stubbs 2010), leading to slower reform and under-coverage of those groups that possess less political power.

2.11.3.4 Pension Benefits to Elderly

Pensions constitute an important source of incomes for elderly groups and the performance of pension systems has important implications for social exclusion. The old pay-as-you-go (PAYG) system appears financially unsustainable in countries with ageing populations. Low and declining rates of social insurance contributions, exacerbated by high levels of informal employment, low employment rates and high youth unemployment make prospects bleak in many Central Asian countries. Low replacement rates provide further disincentives for formal sector employment and for contributors to join the system.

Several groups are at risk of being completely excluded from pension benefits. Most migrants lack social insurance both in the native and immigrant countries. Even if they are insured, pension contributions made in one country are not usually transferable to another, raising the prospect of working migrants ending up with no pension when they reach retirement age. This will pose a considerable challenge for countries with a high share of migrants. The large share of the workforce in informal-sector employment, over fifty per cent, is set to be left out of the pension system. Women working in the household, the self-employed in agriculture, and discouraged job seekers all face similar risks of pension exclusion. Low pension levels are a major factor contributing to the risk of income exclusion for elderly people throughout the region. The size of the pension is often too low to guarantee a decent standard of living, and there appears to be significant differences between pension levels for men and women even within Central Asia. Social protection systems remain inflexible in Central Asian region.

2.11.3.5 Housing and Living Conditions

With a high rate of dwelling ownership, housing deprivation in the region is more related to the quality of housing and access to basic infrastructure than to the unavailability of housing as such (except for Roma communities). Problems of overcrowding, quality of housing stock, and access to basic utilities are most pronounced in rural areas, among poorer sections of the population, and among some minorities. Housing deprivation is experienced most acutely by Central Asia, as well as—more broadly—by refugees, IDPs. The homeless suffer from extreme housing exclusion. Given that homelessness is a relatively new problem in the Central Asia region, there are no reliable statistics available for the study.

2.11.3.6 Access to Energy

In recent years, access to reliable and affordable energy has become a key issue for social exclusion. The major challenge however is more related to affordability and availability of service and less to access. The region is characterized by almost universal connection to the electricity grid—the only exception is Tajikistan, where six per cent of households reported being without electricity in the Social Exclusion Survey (UNDP 2011). According to the World Bank, the reliability of supply is generally a greater issue than connectivity. In Kyrgyzstan (except in the capital), Tajikistan, and Turkmenistan, only a minority of users had electricity 24 hours a day (World Bank 2005). In terms of social exclusion, the cost of energy plays a large role, since poor and vulnerable households spend a high proportion of their income on energy.

2.12 Exclusion from Social Networks and Civic Participation

The key concept for inclusion in civic processes is participation. Exclusion from civic and social life and networks therefore refers to denied participation in different aspects of political, cultural and civic activity. These include engagement in the electoral process, the right to elect and be elected, freedom of expression and association, access to justice and information, and public and political security.

Exclusion from civic and social life and networks occurs not only through formal institutions but also through lack of access to informal structures and opportunities. Informal social networks and formal civic institutions are complementary avenues for participation in public life.

2.12.1 *Civil Society Participation in Central Asia*

Citizens are keen to form networks among next of kin, or in their communities. Clearly, throughout the region, post-independence states continued to rely on strong pre-existing social organizations.[5] For example, the politics of clan and kinship play an important role in the Central Asian political landscape, in Uzbekistan and Turkmenistan, while individual and civic activism is rather limited (Collins 2006).

---

5   Social organizations are largely involuntary, promoting communal norms and values, unlike the individualist and voluntary associations that de Tocqueville and others have argued are the basis of Western and democratic civil society.

Furthermore, traditions of 'tribal democracy' among nomadic peoples in countries such as the Kyrgyz Republic contrast with traditions of hierarchy and authority that characterize the settled agricultural society of Uzbekistan. As such, civic engagement is rather active at the community level in Kyrgyzstan, while in Uzbekistan the *mahallas* (self-governance institutions) provide an important community framework for action. Nevertheless, involvement in Civil Society Organizations (CSOs) has remained relatively weak in the region (Rose-Ackerman 2001). The sector, for example, employs less than two per cent of the population.

People of Kazakhstan are disappointed with politics. Thus, Kazakhstan has lowest participation in political parties. Women are strongly underrepresented in political life in all Central Asian countries. People refrain from politics and political activities because of bitter past experiences and the perceived fear that changes may bring negative consequences (UNDP 2011). The example of social exclusion (Table 2.3).

Table 2.3: Social Exclusion in Kazakhstan and Tajikistan

Various Exclusions	Kazakhstan	Tajikistan
A. Social Exclusion Headcount	32	72
B. Intensity: Average number of deprivations among the social excluded	10.5	11.1
C. Intensity: Average share of deprivations (the number of deprivations as a percentage of 24)	44	46
Social Exclusion Index A * C	14	33
Contribution of dimensions to social exclusion index		
Economic exclusion	34	39
Exclusion from social service	34	34
Exclusion from participation in social life and networks	32	27

Source: UNDP (2011), P 38

2.12.2 *Level and Depth of Social Exclusion in Kazakhstan and Tajikistan*

UNDP survey (2011) shed light on social exclusion in the region. The following table captures social exclusion in terms of headcount and intensity. It also presents the multidimensional Social Exclusion Index which integrates the headcount and intensity of social exclusion.

The data clearly indicate that social exclusion is not determined by economic factors alone. All three dimensions contribute equally. Access to social services contributes slightly more than the other two. This reinforces the message that in order to tackle social exclusion, all three dimensions must be addressed equally instead of focussing solely on poverty reduction.

The survey (UNDP 2011) has revealed that in the economic dimension, social exclusion is largely a result of the lack of access to finance, housing, household amenities and information and communications technologies, while income poverty and unemployment seem to play a smaller role.

In Central Asia, age is an important contributor to social exclusion. The data indicate that the elderly experience the highest levels of social exclusion. Similarly, living in a rural location significantly contributes to the social exclusion headcount, and the most extreme forms of social exclusion are predominantly found in rural locations. Unemployment and low education also contribute significantly to social exclusion. Low education levels tend to raise the risk of unemployment.

2.13. Drivers of Social Exclusion:

Three groups of drivers are part of the social exclusion chain underpinning this book. These are (a) structures and institutions, (b) values and behavioural patterns and (c) policies.

2.13.1 Structures and Institutions as Drivers of Social Exclusion and Inclusion

Institutional drivers refer to how public and private institutions and legislation contribute to exclusion through discriminatory practices — or how they neglect to provide opportunities for inclusion. Institutions — public or private — can either exclude people from social services directly, or they can aggravate social exclusion by failing to respond to those who are at risk of exclusion, due to simple oversight, lack of commitment, or inadequate resources.

2.13.2 Legacies of the Past

Pre-transition (and post-transition) heritage contributes to social exclusion. The socialist system was built on the promise of an egalitarian society. As a result, it promoted the universal right to education, health care, and comprehensive social protection. This system attained universal or near-universal access to basic education and health services, as well as achieved dramatic declines in illiteracy (nearly eradicating it in urban areas). However, it fell short in the civic participation aspects of human development (Ivanov and Peleah 2010).

State socialism generated its own patterns of social inclusion and exclusion. Socialist society was inclusive of those who professed to share its principles—providing some genuine opportunities for social mobility. Creation of independent states in 1990s affected the economy of the countries. The overall situation of economy of these states has reached positive growth around the year 2000, but it still failed to address the issues of widespread unemployment, large concentration of poverty in rural areas. This has led to internal (rural to urban and region to region) and external (country to country) labour migration. The economic exclusion often led to multiple deprivations reducing purchasing power in the changed economic structure of market economy.

Independence has weakened institutional structures and capacity which, to some extent, has been offset by the strong tradition of family or 'clan' ties and community structures. These had always played an important role in the Soviet period, but became more important, if not more transparent, during transition. These clan structures works in dual manner, positively providing support through informal networks but simultaneously dominating political and economic power through non transparent means. Such influence of clan networks is most explicitly observed in appointing political and economic positions and responsibilities. The failure to develop competitive, centralised and institutional mechanism for such appointment has raised the risk of exclusion among large section of population.

The tradition of clan structures and patronage, as well as social relations based on hierarchy and authority, together with the preference for strong executive bodies rather than legislative bodies (inherited from the Soviet period) makes stakeholder participation and civic control and accountability difficult. Together with the slow reform process in budget allocation and planning this legacy weakens the quality and availability of social services, and hence contributes to exclusion from social services at the local level.

2.13.3 Drivers of Social Exclusion and Inclusion Policies

The link between policies and social exclusion is indirect, and hence difficult to attribute and quantify. The analysis of present economic growth models, approaches towards regional imbalance and fiscal decentralization, can help to understand the role of policies as drivers of social exclusion and inclusion mechanisms. All of them contribute to the dynamics of social exclusion.

In Central Asia, models of economic growth, fiscal decentralization, social policies and approaches to regional imbalances have contributed to the dynamics of social exclusion. After independence, most of the Central Asian countries followed spatially unbalanced or 'growth pole' based growth (UNDP 2011). In some cases, the unbalanced, capital city centred growth models created new exclusionary structures. In addition, centralized planning left a large number of mono company towns as a legacy. These excluded whole communities from economic as well as social and civic opportunities and continued to have very limited economic alternatives. Two countries Turkmenistan and Uzbekistan followed semi-closed systems relying heavily on import substitution.

In transition economies, the following sectors have stood out as drivers of growth over the past two decades.

Extractive industry and mining: The hydrocarbon sector emerged as an engine of growth in a number of ECA countries, notably Azerbaijan, Kazakhstan, and Russia. However growth was minimal, with employment gains mostly limited to highly specialized skilled labour. Hence, without a strong spillover into other sectors, this growth model contributes to more exclusive and capital intensive growth, which creates economic enclaves and leaves a large fraction of the population excluded from economic participation.

Agriculture with a primary cash crop: Agriculture has the potential to foster social inclusion, primarily by decreasing rural poverty. Cotton tops the list of export commodities in Uzbekistan. Together with strong import substitution, it financed the development of other industries, notably the natural gas sector (Cornai et al. 2003). It has also played an important role in Turkmenistan and Tajikistan. Unfortunately, agriculture led growth was not pro-poor and also faces serious sustainability issues in many parts of Central Asia. Poverty remains more widespread in rural than in urban areas in most countries. To realize the social inclusion potential of agriculture, effective policies are needed to develop local markets and facilitate access for producers to markets. Land reform and the diversification of agricultural output are important to make these gains sustainable.

Service sector, construction and real estate: These cyclical sectors contributed significantly both to the rapid growth in the early 2000s, and to the decline during the global crisis. Soaring bank lending contributed to this, especially in Kazakhstan. The speculative developments in the real estate sector led to a bubble, with painful consequences for social inclusion. The initial spike in demand for construction services attracted investment and labour into the sector, which boosted internal migration and drained resources from other sectors, notably agriculture. These effects persisted, undermining social inclusion.

Finally, data on spatial poverty show that growth models in Central Asia relied heavily on exclusive 'growth poles' promoted social exclusion rather than inclusion.

2.13.4 Values and behavioural patterns

Behavioural and value-based drivers are caused by discriminatory attitudes and cultural practices that regulate norms and behaviour in society and among groups. Social exclusion can result from, and persist in, social traditions and values among different social groups of the population. Thus, individuals, families and communities, as well as state institutions can promote exclusion among vulnerable groups. Behavioural and value-based drivers in Central Asian countries are strong enough to perpetuate exclusionary patterns and have the potential to undermine inclusive projects. Addressing these drivers require long-term approaches that focus on mindset changes within society as well as require changes in social and cultural norms.

2.13.5 Minorities

Social exclusion of ethnic minorities can stem from various sources. Participation in social, cultural, political and economic processes can be put at risk for several reasons, but often because of prejudice and misconceptions, exacerbated by fears and insecurities, especially in periods of crisis and uncertainty.

However, when ethnic groups and minorities become the subject of state-sponsored programmes and benefits due to their ethnicity, they could become the subject of exclusion and non-acceptance by other communities that face similar socio-economic problems but do not benefit from such state support.

The analysis has shown that legacies of the past twenty years still dominate people's perceptions and shape social exclusion outcomes today. The political and economic transformation has led to new forms of governance and massive institution building, posing new challenges to institutional capacities. These developments have significant implications for social inclusion. For example, effective institutions and improved rule of law were found to be important for mitigating individual risks with the potential to prevent social exclusion from occurring. Low wages in local government could make it difficult to improve the quality of governance an essential ingredient for inclusive local development. Old and new prejudices can increase social isolation. Non-existent or unenforced anti-discriminatory legislation can encourage intolerance and make inclusion of minorities even more difficult. Labour market institutions are another important channel through which social exclusion risks materialize in the region. Unemployment agencies matter for decreasing social exclusion, which strengthens the case for improving active labour market policy interventions in Central Asia.

Table 2.4: Groups and Reasons of Social Exclusion in Central Asia

Country	Excluded Group	Reasons
Kazakhstan	• Uzbeks (2.9 per cent) • Kazakhs economically excluded (gradually moving towards better) • Russians politically excluded	• Poverty • Discrimination on the basis of Clan (sub ethnic), Ethnicity and Class • Religion and Gender
Kyrgyzstan	• Uzbeks 14.3 • Russian 7.8	• Gender • Ethnicity • Religion
Tajikistan	• Poverty: GBAO, Rasht Valley, and some isolated and non-cotton growing districts in Sughd in Khatlon. • Ethnic Minorities	• Poverty • Ethnicity • Religion
Turkmenistan	• Russian • Uzbek • Kazakh	• Poverty • Ethnicity
Uzbekistan	• Farmers • Autonomous region of Karakalpakstan (2.20 per cent)	• Profession • Regional

Source: Bertelsmann Stiftung, BTI 2012

The analysis reveals that unbalanced, capital city-centred growth models have created new exclusionary structures in some countries. These have been exacerbated by the legacy of centralized planning that left mono-company towns with very limited economic alternatives and excluded whole communities from economic and social and civic opportunities. Moreover, the large share of the population working in informal jobs and in insecure labour conditions has also led to higher social exclusion outcomes.

Decentralization policies, though intended to improve efficiency, can also undermine social inclusion. Assigning spending mandates to local governments needs to be accompanied by resource transfers and capacity building to ensure that decentralization policies do not exacerbate sub-national inequalities.

Behavioural and value-based drivers related to gender or culture are strong enough to maintain exclusionary patterns and can even cause inclusive projects to fail. Often such cultural and behavioural norms are intricate to separate. They form an unconscious part of daily living and hence need more comprehensive and long term policy to tackle them and needs to transform the mind set of the society as whole.

Chapter 3

Profile of Excluded Groups in India and Central Asia

Section I: Profile of Social Groups in India

In Indian context, Scheduled Castes (SC), Scheduled Tribes (STs), Other Backward Classes (OBCs), Muslims and women are largely excluded groups, although the extent of exclusion and causes of exclusion are different. Thus the focus of analysis is turned towards to the profiling of each social excluded group.

3.1 Profile of Scheduled Castes

The SCs constitute 16.9 per cent (12th Five Year Plan) of India's population. In the past, they have been marginalised, socially exploited and denied basic rights and entitlements. The socio-economic development of SCs has been a high priority from the very start of the planning process. People belonging to SC communities are spread all over the country, with 80 per cent of them living in the rural areas. They constitute more than a fifth of the population of Uttar Pradesh, Punjab, Himachal Pradesh and West Bengal. Punjab has the highest proportion of SCs to the State population. More than half of the SC population is concentrated in the five States *viz* Uttar Pradesh (35.1 million), West Bengal (18.4 million), Tamil Nadu (11.8 million), Andhra Pradesh (12.3 million) and Bihar (13.0 million) (Census 2011).

Recognising that the SCs have historically suffered grave social disabilities and educational and economic deprivation, the Constitution provides special provision for advancement of their interests. Expansion in education in general was a major thrust of the Eleventh Plan and this was accompanied by several schemes aimed specifically at educational development among SCs especially women and girl children.

3.2 Profile of Scheduled Tribes

The population of STs in India stood at 84.33 million as per the Census of 2001. STs constitute 8.2 per cent of the total population of the country with 91.7 per cent of them living in rural areas and 8.3 per cent in urban areas. The proportion of ST population to the total population had also increased from 6.9 per cent in 1971 to 8.2 per cent in 2001. In fact, 68 per cent of the country's ST population lives in seven States only (Census 2001)[6].

3.3 Profile of Other Backward Classes

Other Backward Classes (OBCs) comprise the castes and communities which are found common in the lists of the Mandal Commission Report and the lists of the individual state governments. The NSSO survey conducted during 2004–05 (61st Round), estimated that the OBC population constituted 41 per cent of the total population. The Constitution does not make any specific provisions for OBCs, but Article 15 of the Constitution empowers the States to make any special provision for the advancement of any socially and educationally backward classes of citizens. It also empowers the state to appoint a commission to investigate into the conditions of socially and educationally backward classes (Article 340).

After 64 years of independence the OBCs obtained separate recognition and job reservation of 27 per cent in services of Government of India and public sector undertakings. The states and union territories (UTs) were free to decide the quantum of reservation based on the OBC population in their states and UTs. All state governments and UTs administrations were also directed by the Supreme Court of India to set up a permanent body and to draw up their own lists and decide the quantum of reservation as per their demography.

---

[6]   These seven states are Madhya Pradesh (14.5%), Maharashtra (10.2%), Orissa (9.7%), Gujarat (8.9%), Rajasthan (8.4%), Jharkhand (8.4%) and Chhattisgarh (7.8%).

3.4 Profile of Religious Minority – Muslims

According to the Census of 2001, 18.4 per cent of our population belongs to minority communities in India. Muslims constitute 13.4 per cent of the country's total population. In absolute numbers, Muslims constitute nearly 140 million populations. In terms of percentage, they account for 72.8 per cent of the total minority population. The Sachar committee (Government of India 2006) studied the condition of Muslims and made the following observations:

a) Muslims have the highest rate of stunting and second-highest rate of underweight children.

b) 25 per cent Muslim children in the 6–14 years age group have either never attended school or have dropped out.

c) Only one out of every 25 undergraduate and fifty postgraduate students in premier colleges is a Muslim.

d) NCAER figures show that only about four per cent of all Muslim students are enrolled in *madarasas*.

e) Workforce participation rate among Muslim women is only 25 per cent in rural areas, 29 per cent of Muslim women participate in the workforce as compared to 70 per cent of Hindu women.

f) 61 per cent of the total Muslim workers are self-employed as against 55 per cent of Hindu workers. 73 per cent of Muslim women are self-employed as compared to 60 per cent for Hindus.

g) Only about 27 per cent of the Muslim workers in urban areas are engaged in regular work as compared to 40 per cent SC/ST, 36 per cent OBC and 49 per cent Hindu upper caste workers.

h) Less than 24 per cent of Muslim regular workers are employed in the public sector or in government jobs as compared to 39per cent regular SC/ST workers, 37 per cent Hindu upper caste and 30 per cent OBC workers.

i) The share of Muslim male workers engaged in street vending is 12 per cent as against the national average of less than 8 per cent.

j) The share of Muslims in public order and safety activities at the central government level is only about 6 per cent. Hindu upper caste workers have a share of 42 per cent and both SCs/STs and OBCs have 23 per cent share each.

k) The share of Muslims among defence workers is only 4 per cent.

Section II: Profile of Central Asia

Central Asia is the core region of the Asian continent. It is situated between Caspian Sea in West and China in the East, Russia in North and Afghanistan in the South. In modern contexts, all definitions of Central Asia include these five republics of the former Soviet Union: Kazakhstan, Kyrgyzstan, Tajikistan, Turkmenistan and Uzbekistan (UNDP 2011) having a total population of 63.4 million as of 2011 (Table 3.1). In terms of population, this is almost equivalent to Gujarat state of India. At present about 48 per cent of population of Central Asia lives in urban areas, but majority of them are immigrants mostly Slavs[7]; whereas Turkic origin population dominates in rural areas.

It covers an area of 40 lakh Sq. Kms. Each state in Central Asia has its distinct language and culture though they trace similar origin in Turkic language and Islam as religion. The five Central Asian States are at the initial stages of their statehood and undergoing the process of nation building. All of them have declared their independence in sudden change; hence the political leadership is in difficult situation. The challenges were multiplied because of lack direct experience of governance with limited resources (Akiner 1997). The region is relatively unknown and unexplored for the remaining world. Perhaps enough studies have not been undertaken on these countries. Moreover, the studies in regional languages are largely unknown to outer world.

Among all the Central Asian countries Kazakhstan is the largest country followed by Turkmenistan and Uzbekistan in terms of geographical size. Contrarily, in terms of population Uzbekistan is bigger than Kazakhstan. Uzbekistan has high density of population. Kazakhstan has better economy thus per capita income is higher than other countries (Table 3.1). Russians and Uzbeks are the two dominant ethnic groups in Central Asia.

---

[7] a member of a group of peoples in central and eastern Europe speaking Slavic languages

Table 3.1: General Profile: Central Asia

Country	Area km² (In Lac)	Population (2011) (In Millions)	Population density per km²	GDP per capita (2011) (in US D)	Major Ethnic Groups
Kazakhstan	27.24	16.6	6	10,694	Kazakh, Russian, Uzbeks
Kyrgyzstan	1.99	5.5	27	1,070	Kyrgyz, Russian, Uzbeks
Tajikistan	1.43	6.9	51	831	Tajik, Uzbeks and Russians
Turkmenistan	4.88	5.1	10	4,658	Turkmen, Uzbek and Russians
Uzbekistan	4.47	29.3	62	1,572	Uzbek, Russians, Tajiks

Source: (World Bank 2012) for Column 3; and Columns 2, 4, 5, 6 are Author's Compilation[8].

The region was under soviet rule till 1991 so it has many political, economic and cultural characteristics similar to Soviet Russia. The collapse of Soviet Union and their independence in 1991 was important shift at institutional level. This shift is from welfare or socialist to market economy. Traditionally the Central Asian society is culturally divided between nomad and settled people of desert, steppes and river valleys. The nomads were residing in steppes and desert while settle population in oasis and river valleys. The further subdivision was based on clan, tribe and regional affiliations. The emergence of present territorial states can be traced to the national delimitation of 1930s. The creation of new republics was first step of social engineering which was later carried out. The objectives of social engineering were to bring about political, social and economic integration of the region. Mass education and women empowerment were the major outputs of the social engineering process. Communist regime, the process of *Russification* and ethnic engendering are influential factors in the present social formation (Peimani 1998).

Central Asia is a land of diversity. It has as many as 125 types of ethnic groups. On an average each country has 25 types of communities. Uzbeks are the dominant

---

8   The statistics is derived from the respective country's official websites.

ethnic group (35.14 per cent) followed by Kazakh (19.97 per cent), Russian (14.19 per cent) and Tajiks (9.32 per cent) (Table 3.2).

Table 3.2: Ethnic Composition Central Asia

Sr.	Ethnic Group	Per cent
1	Kazakh	19.97
2	Russian	14.19
3	Uzbeks	35.14
4	Ukrainians	1.44
5	Tajiks	9.32
6	Kyrgyz	7.14
7	Tatar	0.53
8	Turks	0.25
9	Germans	0.34
10	Others	11.04
	Total	100

Source: Author's Calculation[9]

Ethnic identities have played important role in formation of national identities. All the Central Asian countries were under Soviet Russia rule. Thus dominance of Russian language and culture was the strategy of assimilation. This process resulted in creation of *Russified* elites and rise of nationalism (Peimani 1998).

In the last two decades, Central Asian Countries have faced economic transition, the major shift was marked from socialist economy to market economy. Market economy has created new inequality, unemployment and concentration of wealth by few. Similarly, the region has faced political transition in the post soviet era; it has seen formal policy of building democracy, new constitution and parliamentary system. Despite all this Central Asian states have developed authoritarian model of governance in the form of secular, national unitary states (Panarin 1996). Central Asian states have their own dual economy, an emerging modern sector in the cities based on market place and residual traditional economy in rural areas.

---

[9]   The figures are calculated by summation of each ethnic group in five Central Asia Republics. The latest data was used for calculation due to unavailability of same year data. The census data used are Kazakhstan 2009 Census, Kyrgyzstan 2009 Census; Tajikistan 2000 Census; Turkmenistan 1995 Census and Uzbekistan 1996 Census.

At present it can be said that the Central Asian states have passed through difficult stage. Now, the fear of collapsing of state economies might have shaded down to certain extent. They have adapted different techniques and way out for their present survival. These include foreign investment, exploring natural resources, focusing on certain aspects of development. With this backdrop we turn our focus to each state of Central Asia

3.5 Kazakhstan

Kazakhstan has population around 16.6 million (2012) and population density is 6.1. Around 54.1 per cent lives in urban and 45.9 per cent resides in rural areas. Kazakhstan has largely young population. Around 22 per cent population is in the age group of 0-14 years and 70.2 per cent is between 15-64 years (Smailov 2011). Kazakhstan has around 29.7 per cent dependent population while 70 per cent are in the working group.

Kazakhstan has the largest land area among the five Central Asian Republics (Table 3.1). The population of the country decreased during the 1990s due to outmigration of ethnic Russians and other groups. The ethnic composition of the state constitutes of Kazakhs (63.1per cent), Russians (23.7 per cent) and other ethnic groups account for 13.2 per cent of the population (Smailov 2011). Kazakhstan has around 125 ethnic groups. Kazakhstan achieved the independence from Soviet Republic in 1991. The dissolution of Soviet Union resulted in the strained relationship with ethnic Russian minorities. Kazakhstan is unitary state with Presidential form of government under the Nurzultan Nazarbayev since 1991. The country is divided into fourteen administrative divisions (oblasts), two municipal cities.

3.5.1 Economy of Kazakhstan: Kazakhstan has the largest economy in Central Asia. It has rich natural gas and oil resources along with mineral and metals (BP Statistical Review 2009). It has around 74 per cent of land suitable for agricultural while giving employment to 20 per cent of its population. Wheat, cotton, wool and leather are major products of export (Embassy of Republic of Kazakhstan). Current GDP per capita shrank by 26 per cent in the nineties.

However since 2000, Kazakhstan's economy has seen rapid growth as a result of increased oil and natural gas prices in the world market. GDP grew by 9.8 per cent in 2000 up from 1.7 per cent growth rate noticed in 1999(World Bank 2012). Kazakhstan has recorded highest GDP (13.5 per cent) growth in the world for the year 2001; the trend for high GDP growth rate (10.6 per cent) continued till 2006 (World Bank 2012). Business with booming Russia and China as well as neighbouring CIS nations have ensured this amazing growth. On economic front the country has relatively better industrial base than other Central Asian countries. Agriculture forms important sector of economy and farming is a source of income for large section of population. Animal husbandry contributes significant share in agriculture income of country.

3.6 Kyrgyzstan

Kyrgyzstan gained its independence from former Soviet Union in August 1991. The country has population of around 5.3 million less than population of Himachal Pradesh (6.8 million) of India. The main ethnic groups of the country are Kyrgyz (71 per cent), Russian (10.3 per cent), Uzbeks (14.2 per cent), Germans, Tartars, Ukrainians, Dungans, Tajiks, Kazaks, Koreans, Jews and others (NSCKR 2010). The main religion is Sunni Muslim with minorities of Russian orthodox and Roman Catholic. The country is small and poor with predominantly agricultural economy (2.3 per cent of GDP in 2011). The Kyrgyz economy suffers badly after the collapse of Soviet Union because the country was dependent on Soviet economy for its export market and budget subsidies. Poverty and income inequalities have increased substantially. In last two decades, Kyrgyzstan has remarkable progress in transition to market economy.

Kyrgyzstan had authoritarian regime till 2010. Recently the Presidential system was replaced with Parliamentary. The country has a coalition government at present. Kyrgyzstan has history of ethnic tension between Kyrgyz and Uzbek caused due to land resources. The minority Uzbek population is mainly concentrated in South Kyrgyzstan.

3.6.1 Economy of Kyrgyzstan: Kyrgyzstan is a mountainous country with a dominant agriculture sector. Cotton, tobacco, wool, and meat are the main agricultural products (Ministry of Agriculture, Kyrgyzstan). Industrial exports include gold, mercury, uranium, natural gas, and electricity. The economy depends heavily on gold exports. Following independence, Kyrgyzstan was progressive in carrying out market reforms, such as an improved regulatory system and land reform. Kyrgyzstan's economy faces the major challenges of shadow economy, wide spread corruption, low foreign investment (BTI 2012 Kyrgyzstan).

3.7 Tajikistan

Tajikistan declared its independence in September 1991 after the break-up of Soviet Union. The estimated population of the country is 6.1 million, which is slightly less than Himachal Pradesh in India. Nearly three quarters of population live in rural areas. After independence, almost half of ethnic Russian population migrated outside the country. The demographic composition is ethnically diversified. Country has two thirds Tajik and one third Uzbeks. Tajik is official state language, but Russian remains the main language of business. The main religion is Islam mostly Sunni Islam. Tajikistan was the poorest of the soviet republics. Its economy collapsed after independence due to loss of its markets and subsidies from Moscow. Tajikistan is primarily an agrarian country. More than 80 per cent population is dependent on agriculture. Tajikistan's population has been impoverished and living standards have plummeted. Over 60 per cent (2009 estimate) population is estimated to living below poverty line.

3.7.1Economy of Tajikistan: Since independence, Tajikistan gradually followed the path of transition economy, reforming its economic policies (BTI 2012 Tajikistan). Tajikistan exports cotton and aluminium and revenue from export contribute significantly. The economy is highly vulnerable. Tajikistan's economy grew substantially after the war in 1997. The GDP of Tajikistan expanded at an average rate of 9.6 per cent over the period of 2000-2007 (World Bank 2012). This improved Tajikistan's position among other Central Asian countries (namely Turkmenistan and Uzbekistan). The 2008 global financial crisis has hit Tajikistan hard both domestically and internationally because it already has a high poverty and many of its citizens depend on remittances from expatriate Tajikistanis.

3.8 Turkmenistan

Turkmenistan is situated at the centre of Central Asia. The country achieved independence in 1991. The official state language is Turkmen, which belongs to the Turkic language group. Present-day Turkmenistan covers territory that has been at the crossroads of civilizations for centuries. Turkmenistan has undiversified economy and government has monopoly over major sectors in economy. Though some reforms as currency convertibility are adopted in 2008, the process of market reforms is not stable (BTI Turkmenistan 2012). Turkmenistan's GDP growth rate is highly unstable ranging from 3.2 per cent to 14.7 per cent (World Bank 2012). It possesses the world's fourth largest reserves of natural gas resources.

Most of Turkmenistan's citizens are ethnic Turkmens with sizeable minorities of Uzbeks and Russians. Kazakhs, Tatars, Ukrainians, Armenians, Azeris, Balochs and Pashtuns form the minority groups. Sunni Islam is practiced by majority people. Turkmenistan is the ethnically most homogeneous state of the Central Asian republics. The minority Uzbek population resides in east along with significant Russian, Kazakh, Tatars and other ethnic minority population. In Turkmenistan ethnic minorities, Kazakhs and Uzbeks experience socio economic exclusion, poverty and social discrimination (BTI Turkmenistan 2012).

Table 3.3: Macroeconomic Indicators in Turkmenistan

Population below poverty line	30% (2004 est.)
GDP Composition by Sector	Agriculture: 7.6% Industry: 24.4% Services: 68% (2012)
Labour force	16.35 million (2012 est.)
Labour force - by occupation	Agriculture: 48.2% Industry: 14% Services: 37.8% (2004 est.)
Unemployment rate	60% (2004 est.)
Household income or consumption by percentage share	Lowest 10% having share of 2.6% Highest 10% having share of 31.7% (1998)

Source: CIA World Fact Book (2013)

3.8.1 Economy of Turkmenistan: It is largely a desert country with intensive agriculture in irrigated oases and sizeable gas and oil resources.

Although agriculture accounts for roughly 8 per cent of GDP, it continues to employ nearly half of the country's workforce. The majority of Turkmenistan's economic statistics are state secrets. Analysis of Turkmenistan situation has been handicapped by data constraints.

The population below poverty line is around 30 per cent and unemployment rate is 60 per cent. Service sector contributes highest 68 per cent to GDP followed by industry 24.4 per cent.

3.9 Uzbekistan

Uzbekistan is most populous Central Asian republics. Nearly half of the population of Central Asia lives in Uzbekistan (Table 3.1). Uzbekistan borders Kazakhstan to the north and west, Kyrgyzstan and Tajikistan in the east and Turkmenistan and Afghanistan to the south. Uzbekistan declared its independence in August 1991 following the collapse of the Soviet Union. Uzbekis are Turkic-speaking people with an ancient and distinctive culture. According to United Nations (2012), Uzbeks comprise a majority (80 per cent) of the total population. Other ethnic groups include Russians (5.5 per cent) Tajiks (5 per cent) Kazakhs (3 per cent), Kara kalpaks (2.5 per cent) and Tatars (1.5 per cent). Other minorities include Koreans, Meskhetian Turks, Kyrgyz, Turkmens, Ukrainians, Armenians, Uyghur and Jews. However, the Uzbekistan country report furnishes Russian population is around 3.25 per cent (2009 census). The ratio of rural to urban population has changed drastically since 2005.

Urban population increased from 36.1 per cent to 51.7 per cent (United Nations 2012) while rural population decreased from 63.9 per cent to 48.3 per cent in the same time. Uzbekistan has 99 per cent literacy rate in adult population. The country has presidential form of government. Uzbekistan has rich resources such as natural gas, gold, uranium and other heavy metals.

Uzbekistan's economy is dependent mainly on commodity production, including cotton, gold, uranium, and natural gas. The state and elite section of society controls the key economic resources. Uzbekistan has necessary legal framework for adaptation of market reforms in place. Reforms are limited to small and medium sectors of economy. State policies result into excess regulation of major sections of economy resulting into less foreign direct investment (BTI 2012 Uzbekistan). Though such strict control has helped the steady growth and recovery of economy since 1995. Uzbekistan has around 66 per cent of population in working age population (15-64 years) and around 28 per cent of population below 14 years (World Bank 2012).

Russians in Uzbekistan represent 5.5 per cent of the total population. Large Russian population has migrated from the country since its independence. Russian population has significant presence largest ethnic group (8.4 per cent 1989 Census) in the state during Soviet period. After the dissolution of the Soviet Union, significant emigration of ethnic Russians has taken place, mostly for economic reasons.

At least 10 per cent of Uzbekistan's labour force works abroad (mostly in Russia and Kazakhstan). Due to legacy of Soviet Union socialist welfare policies Uzbekistan has a high (99.3 per cent) adult literacy rate.

Table 3.4: Macroeconomic Indicators of Uzbekistan (in percent)

Population Below Poverty Line	26.0 (2008 estimated)
Labour Force	16.35 million (2012 est.)
Labour Force - by Occupation	agriculture: 44.0 industry: 20.0 services: 36.0 (1995)
Unemployment rate	1.0 (2012 est.) 1.0 (2011 est.) *Note: officially measured by the Ministry of Labour, plus another 20.0 underemployed*
Household income or consumption by percentage share	Lowest 10.0 per cent having share of 2.8 per cent highest 10 per cent having share of 29.6 per cent (2003)

Source: CIA World Fact Book (2013)

3.9.1 Economy of Uzbekistan: Since gaining independence, the Government of Uzbekistan has gradually moved to a market-based economy. Uzbekistan is a dry, landlocked country; Uzbekistan has around 44.9 million hector land of which around 9.5 per cent (4.3 million hector. is irrigated land (FAO 2003). Agriculture is traditionally strong and stable contributor in Uzbekistan's economy. After the independence in the decade of 1995 -2007, its contribution remained between 23-32 per cent in the GDP of the country (World Bank 2010). More than 60 per cent of the population lives in densely populated rural communities (CIA World Fact Book 2013). In agriculture sector cotton is traditional export commodity, while gold, Hydrocarbons and natural gas contribute significantly in the export earnings. Until 2012, Uzbekistan had posted GDP growth of over 8 per cent per year (World Bank 2012) for several years. Growth slipped in 2012 as a result of lower export prices due to the continuing European recession (World Bank Uzbekistan 2012). The population below poverty line is 26 per cent and labour force participation is highest in agriculture 35 per cent (World Bank 2007b).

During the initial stage of transition period from 1989-1996 all Central Asian states underwent several economic changes. These were agrarian economy, de-industrialization and structural changes in employment. Major changes were occurring in the labour force and employment in the society. Agrarian economy indicated increased agricultural employment in Central Asian countries except Kazakhstan and Tajikistan, whereas industrial employment reduced in Kazakhstan, Kyrgyzstan and Tajikistan. The process of de-industrialization has affected Kazakhstan, Kyrgyzstan and Tajikistan more than Uzbekistan and Turkmenistan (Rumer and Zhukov 2003). Poverty and social exclusion has inextricable relationship.

Poverty is the greatest determinant of social exclusion. People are excluded because they are poor and have limited access to the resources. While discussing social exclusion poverty deserves special mention. Thus, poverty is discussed in the following chapter.

Chapter 4

Poverty in India and Central Asia

Section I

Poverty is the opposite of development. It implies the lack of development or underdevelopment. Poverty in Indian policy making circles is operationalised as income poverty, which is the result of low consumption expenditure of households. Chronic poverty on the other hand is multidimensional deprivation in which households are trapped due to social and economic processes. Hulme (Hulme et.al 2004) argues that poverty is chronic when it is multi-dimensional and long-durational.

It is generally recognized that poverty has both material and non-material dimensions. Because of their obvious tangibility, many development practitioners find it easier to understand and address the material dimensions of poverty. The exclusion of the poor from participation in different aspects of political, cultural, and civic activity and access to opportunities and activities is a major non-material dimension of poverty that also needs to be recognized and addressed. Though the incidence of poverty has declined over time in India and more so in recent years, the incidence of poverty among SCs and STs is higher than the national aggregate by 8.5 (SC-rural) and 19.4 (ST-rural) percentage points. The gap across social groups in poverty has reduced somewhat over time, though it is still present. Across religious groups, poverty among Muslims is also rampant and more so in urban areas. There is a high concentration of Muslims in the urban areas, as a result of which they become more visible (Planning Commission 2011).

4.1 Poverty and Social Exclusion

People who are socially excluded are also generally poor, particularly if poverty is defined in a multi-dimensional way. There are, however, several key differences between the concepts of poverty and social exclusion: (i) the majority of people in a society may be poor but majority are not excluded; (ii) in most cases social exclusion implies inequality or relative deprivation, whereas poverty need not; (iii) social exclusion implies the processes of exclusion, institutional processes and actors responsible for exclusion, whereas poverty does not.

An individual is socially excluded, if he or she does not participate in key activities of the society in which he or she lives (Burchardt et al. 2002). It is likely that many poor households in remote rural areas are socially excluded. Exclusion from access to resources, opportunities, information and connections draw people into severe poverty traps. Social exclusion in remote rural areas is probably to be differentiated by lack of opportunities of jobs, education, and markets, and also lack of information on rights and government policies. Migration is the main cause of exclusion and discrimination suffered by residents of remote villages in labour, housing, credit and other facilities (Kathuria 2012). In a study Kathuria has identified reasons of exclusion of poor from various types of services. According to her, land holding and lack of political affiliation are the causes of exclusion from agricultural services. Caste and gender are the causes of exclusion from political activities.

The concept of poverty is complex dynamic and multi-dimensional. It varies across time, space and social stratification. It has different faces, shapes and magnitudes.

In common terminology, poverty denotes inability to earn livelihood and basic facilities such as food, clothing, shelter, health care and education. Social exclusion creates barriers to income poverty reduction. In Indian context, the social excluded groups, SCs, STs, and Muslims constitute a large section of the poor. All recent studies and surveys have indicated that poverty among Muslims is very high (Government of India 2006). The communities suffer poverty in all three indicators of prevalence, depth and severity of poverty both in rural and urban areas. The OBCs too suffer from poverty though it is lower than the poverty levels among SC and ST population (Biradar 2012). The deprivation of various socio-religious groups is analysed in following chapter.

Poverty is the design of the social order such as wage disparity, rigid division of labour, labour immobility, knowledge deprivation and strict social sanctions against any violation. Therefore, the design of situating poverty is an interesting issue. With this argument here is an attempt to explain connotations of poverty.

4.2 Connotation of Poverty

Poverty implies a condition of life characterised by deprivation in some aspects and perceived as undesirable by the persons concerned or others. It is a multi-dimensional concept. Generally there is consensus among scholars about poverty being conceived and defined as absolute or relative. Absolute poverty implies an individual's lack of access to adequate quantities of goods and services to satisfy his basic needs. Relative poverty in contrast, implies that a person's access to the basic needs of life is relatively lower as compared to some reference group.

Poverty is a major factor contributing to the vulnerability of so many Indians. Poverty is rife in India. In 2004-05, as many as 302 million persons (27.5 per cent) were living below the poverty line in India (Singh 2009). According to Human Development Report (HDR), 2003 of the United Nations Development Programme (UNDP), India has the largest number of poor among the countries of the world and is home to one-fourth of the world's poor with 42 per cent of Indians surviving on $1.25 a day. However, poverty has many aspects and according to the Multi-dimensional Poverty Index which measures poverty in three dimensions – education, health and living standards. Around 55 per cent of Indians, some 600 million people - are considered to be in poverty. Reducing the poverty headcount ratio to half of the 1990 level by the year 2015 is the foremost Millennium Development Goal enshrined in the Millennium Declaration of the United Nations. In the case of India this implies that the poverty headcount ratio should come down to 18.6 per cent by the year 2015 (Planning Commission 2011).

Many studies have dealt with the concept of poverty and its measurement. Approaches to measuring poverty can be classified into two categories, namely, "welfare" and "non-welfare" approaches (Ravallion 1994). The first approach emphasises the measurement of economic well-being or standard of living by considering income or consumption levels. The second approach has been developed in non-economic parlance. The "non-welfarist" approach has been further classified into the "basic needs approach" and the "capability approach". The first approach focuses on the multi-dimensional outcomes that can be monitored. The outcomes are usually linked to the concept of functioning, a concept developed by Amartya Sen (Sen

1997). The functioning approach has similarities with basic needs approach but is not synonymous with the it. Basic needs are required for individuals to achieve some functioning. Basic needs are food, clothing, shelter, water and sanitation (Streeten *et al.* 1981).

The capability approach was advocated by Amartya Sen (1985, 2005) and Martha Nussbaum (2000). This approach has over the past two decades provided the foundation for a model of development that is both human and sustainable. It has focused on participation, human well-being and freedom as central features of development, possessing the capability to achieve basic functioning is the freedom to live well and not to be poor or deprived. Sen (1999) describes poverty, therefore, as lack of capabilities that otherwise enable a person lead a life he values, encompassing such domains as income, health, education, empowerment and rights. There are, however, some measurement and comparison problems in the non-welfarist approach (Duclos 2002).

Poverty is the outcome of disadvantages. Chambers identified five clusters of disadvantages, namely, lack of assets, physical weakness, isolation, vulnerability and powerlessness as the characteristic features of the poor (Chambers 1983). The poor perceive three priorities in life, namely, survival, security and self-respect, the last being their highest priority (Chambers 1988). The consumption/income approach used to define poverty has come under criticism. It has been suggested that in the analysis of poverty, Common Property Resources and State Provided Commodities should be taken into account, and the concept of poverty should be broadened to include lack of assets, dignity and autonomy. By considering the above multi-dimensional phenomenon of poverty, Baulch (1996:2) has proposed the following pyramid of poverty concepts, covering multiple disadvantages. Line one represents the narrower definition of poverty, whereas line six represents broader definition of poverty (Figure 4.1).

Figure 4.1: A Pyramid of Poverty Concepts

PC 1
PC + CPR 2
PC + CPR + SPC 3
PC + CPR + SPC + Assets 4
PC + CPR + SPC + Assets + Dignity 5
PC + CPR + SPC + Assets + Dignity + Autonomy 6

Source: Biradar (2012)

Notes: PC: Poverty Concept; CPR: Common Property Resources; SPC: State Provided Commodities

Another recent approach, the social exclusion approach, emphasizes the importance of institutions and norms that exclude certain groups from a variety of social networks and also the importance of social solidarity in sustaining livelihoods. Since the "non-welfarist" approach to poverty has been associated with several practical difficulties, the "welfarist" approach" as a proxy for income or consumption levels, is widely used (Biradar 2012).

According to the welfare approach, poverty, in the Indian context, is officially defined in terms of the nutritional baseline measured in calorie intake or normative value of consumption expenditure. Accordingly, poverty is treated as being synonymous with the under-nourishment. The normative value of consumption expenditure or calorie intake is converted into a food basket measured through monthly per capita expenditure and is considered to be the poverty line. Therefore, the Planning Commission of India has defined poverty as the state of those who cannot meet the per capita monthly expenditure of ₹ 356 in rural and ₹ 539 in urban areas in 2004-05 (2004-05 all-India price level). This per capita expenditure is believed to be sufficient to derive a daily intake of 2,400 calories in rural and 2,100 calories per person in urban areas. Although, the per capita monthly expenditure is considered for the official poverty line in India, it keeps changing over time. The person who does not meet the calories norm falls below the poverty line and is said to be poor.

4.3 Poverty Estimates

Several attempts have been made in India to estimate the incidence of poverty and trends thereof. The estimates are however not comparable because of differences in the methodologies used to define the poverty lines and size of samples taken. The common poverty estimate measures are as under. In India, the official estimates of poverty are provided by the Planning Commission on the basis of consumption expenditure data collected by the NSSO. Planning Commission has recently released poverty estimates for the year 2011–12. Apart from the Planning Commission's estimates, various other poverty estimates are available at following box

Box 4.1: Poverty Estimates

A. Planning Commission: 27.5 per cent (based on MPCE of ₹ 356 for rural India, and ₹ 539 for urban India)
- NSS 61st Round consumption expenditure data (2004–05)
- The 30 days reference period for all items of current household consumption in NSS
- Different poverty line basket for rural and urban India

B. Tendulkar Committee: 37.2 per cent (based on MPCE of ₹ 447 for rural India, and ₹ 579 for urban India)
- NSS 61st Round consumption expenditure data (2004–05)
- Mixed reference period (365 days for low frequency items, and 30 days for remaining items)
- Mixed reference period equivalent of urban poverty line basket was used as the poverty line basket for both rural and urban areas.

Based on Tendulkar Committee methodology after adjusting for inflation, the incidence of poverty for the year 2009–10 was estimated to be 32 per cent (Abhijit Sen 2000).

C. National Commission for Enterprises in the Unorganized Sector: 77 per cent of the population was surviving with a per capita daily consumption expenditure of ₹ 20 or less and were termed as poor and vulnerable.
- NSS 61st Round (2004–5)

D. Surjit Bhalla: Poverty estimates were based on NSS 64th Round, 2007–8
- 14 per cent based on Planning Commission poverty line
- 27 per cent based on Tendulkar Committee poverty line
- Mixed reference period (365 days for low frequency items, and 30 days for remaining items).

E. Planning Commission (2013): For 2011-12, for rural areas the national poverty line using the Tendulkar methodology is estimated at ₹ 816 per capita per month and ₹ 1,000 per capita per month in urban areas. Thus, for a family of five, the all India poverty line in terms of consumption expenditure would amount to about ₹ 4,080 per month in rural areas and ₹ 5,000 per month in urban For 2011-12, for rural areas the national poverty line using the Tendulkar methodology is estimated at ₹ 816 per capita per month and ₹ 1,000 per capita per month in urban areas.

Thus, for a family of five, the all India poverty line in terms of consumption expenditure would amount to about ₹ 4,080 per month in rural areas and ₹ 5,000 per month in urban areas. These poverty lines would vary from State to State because of inter-state price differentials. These poverty lines would vary from State to State because of inter-state price differentials.

Source: Planning Commission 2011

In India, the poverty estimates are based on a large sample survey of consumer expenditure conducted by the NSSO. The NSS 28th Round (1973–74) consumer expenditure data was used and the poverty lines for rural (₹ 49.09 per capita per month at 1973–4 prices) and urban (₹ 56.64 per capita per month at 1973–74 prices) areas were obtained. Since then, the methodology as formulated by the Task Force has been used in estimating the incidence of poverty by the Planning Commission. The focus of this methodology was on the purchasing power required to meet the specific calorie norms with some margin for non-food consumption needs. The state specific rural and urban poverty lines are updated by using the Consumer Price Index of Agricultural Labourers for rural areas and Consumer Price Index for Industrial Workers in the case of urban areas.

4.4 Monthly Per Capita Consumption Expenditure (MPCE) across Social Groups

Across social groups in 2004–05, STs had the lowest average MPCE. This is based on Uniform Recall Period Consumption (URP)[10] in rural India, while in urban India SCs had the lowest average MPCE (relatively fewer STs reside in urban areas, while SCs are more numerous in urban areas). As expected, in both rural and urban India, the average MPCE was the highest for 'Others' (in rural India it was 1.6 times that of STs, while in urban India it was 1.7 times that of SCs).[11] It was observed that in rural India, the proportion of MPCE on food items was more or less similar. In urban India, the proportion of MPCE on food items was the highest for SCs, while it was the lowest for 'Others' (Table 4A.1). To sum up, MPCE was lower for STs and SCs than for other social groups.

The following table reveals the huge rural–urban differences in average MPCE in the case of all social groups taken together. The average MPCE in urban India was almost twice that in rural India. This rural–urban disparity was the highest in the case of STs (average MPCE in urban India being twice that in rural India), and lowest in case of SCs and OBCs (average MPCE in urban India being 1.6 times that in rural India for both social groups). The analysis clearly reveals tribals' in rural areas were poorer among all and tribals' spent maximum on food items (Table 4A.1).

---

[10] URP Consumption: Uniform Recall Period consumption in which the consumer expenditure data for all the items are collected from a 30-day recall period.

[11] Comparison of MPCE across social groups is not possible between different survey periods because in the 1993–4 survey OBCs were included as a part of 'Others', while in the 2004–5 survey OBCs were considered a separate social group.

In fact, the rural–urban difference in MPCE persisted, and in fact increased, by 2007–8. The average MPCE in urban India was 1.9 times that in rural India. The rural-urban disparity was the highest in case of STs in 2007–8 (Table 4A.2).

Across social groups, the average value of MPCE was the highest for the 'Others' in 2007–8. In rural India, the average MPCE for the SCs, STs, and OBCs was respectively 30 per cent, 40 per cent, and 20 per cent lower than that of 'Others'. A similar disparity could be observed in the case of urban India (Table 4A.3).

It was observed that the social groups which had the lowest value of average MPCE spent the highest proportion on food items. In rural India, it was agricultural labour households which had the lowest value of average MPCE, and in urban India it was the casual labour households. Across social groups, SCs and STs had the lowest average MPCE in rural and urban areas, respectively. An analysis of the pattern of consumption expenditure during the post liberalization period (between 1993–94 and 2004–05) clearly suggested that the biggest gainers were the urban elite belonging to the upper castes.

4.5 Trends in Poverty

Reducing the poverty headcount ratio to half of the 1990 level by the year 2015 is the Millennium Development Goal of India. It implies that the poverty headcount ratio should come down to 18.6 per cent by the year 2015. Considering the present poverty rate this seems achievable (Planning Commission 2008).

The incidence of poverty in India came down from 55 per cent in 1973–74 to 27.5 per cent (as per URP) in 2004–5 (Planning Commission 2008). During this period, the absolute number of people living below the poverty line declined from 320 million to 300 million. In addition, the rural-urban difference in the incidence of poverty declined between the years 1983 and 2004–05 (Table 4.1). It is estimated that though poverty is declining the absolute number of poor is still high.

Table 4.1: Incidence of Poverty in Rural and Urban Areas, 1983, 1993–94 and 2004–5

Year	Rural		Urban	
	Per cent of Poor	Number of Poor (Million)	Per cent of Poor	Number of Poor (Million)
1983	45.7	252	40.8	71
1993-94	37.3	244	32.4	76
2004-05	28.3	221	25.7	81

Source: 11th Five Year Plan, Planning Commission, Government of India, Early calculation from NSS 64th Round, Consumer Expenditure Survey Data.

Note: Poverty based on URP.

The numbers discussed above use the URP method of estimating the headcount ratio of the poor. The MRP method is used for two points of time 2004–05 and 2007–08. Between these two time periods, there was a decline in the percentage of people living below the poverty line.[12] The percentage of people living below the poverty line (as per MRP) declined from 22 per cent in 2004–05 to 15 per cent in 2007–08.[13]

4.6 Poverty across Social Groups

The incidence of poverty was more acute among the SCs and STs. Despite the fact that the incidence of poverty among the SCs and STs declined in 2004–5 as compared to 1993–4, it was much higher than the national average (Table 4A.4).

---

[12] Comparison of incidence of poverty between 2004–5 and 2007–8 is undertaken according to consumption expenditure measured by MRP. Poverty lines for rural and urban India in 2007–8 are calculated by deflating the 2004–5 poverty lines using consumer price index for agricultural labourers in rural areas and consumer price index for industrial workers in urban areas. The poverty lines thus arrived at for 2007–8 are Rs 429 per capita per month for rural areas and Rs 639 per capita per month for urban areas.

[13] Please refer to http://pib.nic.in/newsite/erelease.aspx?relid=26316 for incidence of poverty by MRP for the year 2004–5. For the year 2007–8, the incidence of poverty by MRP is calculated from the NSS database (64th round, consumer expenditure survey)

The high incidence of poverty among SCs and STs could be observed in 2007–08 as well, the estimates of which are based on MRP (Table 4.2).

Table 4.2: Incidence of Poverty (MRP) by Social Groups, 2007-08 (Per cent)

Social Group	Rural	Urban	Total
Scheduled Castes	20.6	22.8	43.4
Scheduled Tribes	25.3	20.6	45.9
Other Backward Classes	12.0	19.0	31.0
Others	6.3	7.3	13.6
All Social Groups	14.9	14.5	29.4
Hindus	14.3	13.0	27.3
Muslims	13.3	23.7	37.0

Source: Calculated from NSS Database, 64th Round Consumer Expenditure Survey.

Note: Poverty based on Mixed Recall Period. These figures are not comparable with those in above table, since those are based on uniform recall period.

Firstly, poverty among SCs and STs, as shown here (Table 4A.5), is declining consistently. It is due to shifting by the group to non agricultural activities. However, the proportion of casual labour among the group is quite significant. Secondly, unlike earlier, proportion of poverty has not reduced much between the periods 1999-2000 to 2004-2005. Thirdly, much difference is not marked, while comparing the figures of two estimates for the year 1999-2000.

4.7 Poverty across Religious Communities

For the country as a whole, the incidence of poverty (URP) among Muslims was higher than Hindus. Close to 32 per cent of Muslims in the country were below the poverty line (Planning Commission 2011). It implies that one in every three Muslims was below the poverty line. However, in urban India, the incidence of poverty among Muslims was much higher than their population share. The relative deprivation of the Muslims in urban areas continued in 2007- 8, with close to one-fourth of the Muslims living below the poverty line. One-third of the Muslims in India were below the poverty line.

4.8 Poverty Gap

The poverty gap is a measure of the extent of poverty and is defined as the distance between the poverty line and income of the poor. In other words, the poverty gap in consumption expenditure indicates to what extent the consumption of the poor falls short of the poverty line. During 2007–8, the poverty gap in both rural and urban India was higher among SCs and STs. This implies that on an average, the consumption expenditure of the poor belonging to the SCs and STs was farther below the poverty line as compared to other social groups. Among religious communities, the poverty gap was higher among Hindus and Muslims in both rural and urban India (Table 4.3), whereas the severity of poverty was higher among SCs and STs. The poverty gap was higher in urban India compared to rural India. For Urban India, the poverty gap in 2007-8 was 19 per cent. This implies that average income of the urban poor was 19 per cent lower the poverty line. Analysis of poverty in 2007-8 (based on MRP) revealed the differences in the nature of poverty between rural and urban India. While the incidence of poverty was marginally lower in urban India, the poverty gap was higher. This indicates higher consumption inequality in urban India.

Table 4.3: Poverty Gap, 2007-08 (Per cent)

Social Group	Rural	Urban
Scheduled Castes	16	21
Scheduled Tribes	18	21
Other Backward Classes	14	19
Others	12	19
All Social Groups	15	19
Hindus	15	20
Muslims	14	19

Source: Calculated from NSS Database, 64th Round Consumer Expenditure Survey.
Note: Poverty based on MRP.

4.9 Poverty among Muslims

A survey by NCAER revealed that three out of every 10 Muslims were below the poverty line and survived on less than Rs 550 a month (2004-05) compared to Rs 338 in rural areas. Even among the poor, urban Muslims were better off. The survey revealed that Tribals were the most vulnerable group with nearly 50 per cent below the poverty line followed by Dalits and Muslims (poverty rates 32 per cent and 31 per cent respectively) according to the Indian Human Development survey undertaken by NCAER (Desai et al. 2010).

In a recent study combining statistical data with ethnography (Jafferlot and Gaynor 2012), several scholars studied the condition of Muslims in Indian cities. Muslims, Parsis and Jews are the urbanised class in India (Vakulbharanam et al. 2007). Their urban poverty is higher than rural poverty and urban poverty of Hindus. The Sachar committee (Government of India 2006) showed that the Muslim community in India suffered from severe deprivation in education, employment, health services, public infrastructure and access to financial services, similar to the condition of SCs and STs. The exclusion of Muslims can be traced back to historical context, loss of princely states to the British, the partition of the country, and rise of Hindu nationalism. The frequent communal riots have resulted in concentration of Muslims in small localities.

According to the Twelfth Five Year Plan, "the poverty ratio for Muslims was 33.9 per cent in urban areas, due to high concentration of Muslims in populous states Uttar Pradesh, Bihar and West Bengal. In rural areas, the poverty ratio for Muslims was high in states such as Assam, Uttar Pradesh, West Bengal and Gujarat," The 12th Plan has focussed on a targeted approach to address the poverty of the community.

At present, Muslims contribute only 11.2 per cent the country's GDP while dalits and adivasis contribute about 16.5 per cent. This is because of lack of education as well as community members still being engaged in traditional occupations. The share of Muslims and SC/STs in the workforce is about 18 per cent each compared to 8 and 14 per cent in modern services (Shariff 2012).

The comparison of NSSO data of 2004-05 with 2009-10 shown that literacy levels of Muslims improved slowly (5.9 per cent in rural and 5.3 per cent in urban areas) compared to Dalits and Tribals. Dalits improved by 8.5 points in rural areas and 5.1 points in urban areas and Triabls' literacy increased to 11.3 points in rural areas and 8.6 points in urban areas. Owing to slower growth in education, Muslims are lagging behind.

4.10 Rural Poverty in India

Poverty is a serious social problem in India. It is more acute in rural areas. The percentage of persons below the poverty line in 2011-12 has been estimated as

25.7 per cent in rural areas. The rural poverty was 41.8 per cent in 2004-05. It was 50.1 per cent in 1993-94. In 2011-12, India had 270 million persons below the Tendulkar Poverty Line as compared to 407 million in 2004-05. More specifically there is reduction of 137 million persons over the seven year period. The per capita income in rural areas is ₹ 816 for 2011-12 (based on MRP). Following the Tendulkar methodology, the rural poverty has been estimated at 25.70 constituting 2166.58 lakh persons (Planning Commission 2013).

In spite of several efforts the incidence of poverty continues to be persistent in India, especially in rural areas (World Bank, 2000a; Dev 2000; Sundaram 2001). The incidence of rural poverty has declined somewhat over the past three decades as a result of numerous poverty alleviation programmes and migration to urban areas.

The post-economic reform period evidenced both progress and setback in poverty reduction. Rural poverty increased from 34 per cent in 1989-90 to 43 per cent in 1992, and then fell to 37 per cent in 1993-94. The poverty ratio in India was 51.3 per cent in 1977-78 and it declined to 22.5 per cent in 2004-05 with a 56.82 per cent over a period of 30 years (Table 4.4).

Table 4.4: Reduction in Poverty over the Period

Year	NSSO Round	Poverty Ratio (per cent)	Reduction in Poverty (per cent) over the period of five years
1977-78	32	51.30	Not Applicable
1983-84	38	45.65	11.01
1987-88	43	39.09	14.37
1993-94	50	37.27	4.66
1999-2000	55	26.09	30.00
2004-05	61	22.5	15.10

Source: Muthalagu (2007),
Note: Based on Mixed Recall Period Consumption

In the last three decades, the regional differences in poverty reduction have been quite substantial. The decline in incidence of poverty in the states was in the range of 12-50 percentages points in rural areas (Singh 2009). The inter-state variations in the rural poverty reduction have been attributed to the variations in agricultural productivity improvement. The green revolution and the land- reform measures of state governments were the measure factors of rural poverty reduction.

Given the rural and the urban poverty lines, rural poverty rates are, in general, higher than their comparable urban counterparts. However, in recent years urban poverty has also increased in some states (Pathak et al. 2013). This is an area for further exploration. The following is an attempt to study the urban poverty in India.

4.11 Urban Poverty

The planning commission (2012) using the Tendulkar committee's poverty lines document that the urban HCR decreased from 25.4 per cent (814.1 million people) in 2004-05 to 20.9 per cent (764.7 million people) in 2009-10, but no one takes these estimates seriously. Essentially, we will have to wait for Rangarajan Committee's report for a consensus on methodological issues of poverty and an acceptable count of urban poor thereafter.

While analysing the distribution of consumption expenditure for various poverty lines to examine which of these groups had a higher prevalence of poverty. The comparison of data from the 61st (2004-05) and 66th (2009-10) round of the NSS consumption expenditure survey found a clear pattern for caste and occupational groups. Among caste groups in urban areas, poverty was highest among SCs, followed by OBCs, STs and others. Among occupational groups, urban poverty was highest among those involved in casual labour, followed by the self-employed (Motiram and Naraparaju 2013).

The use of NSS data shows that the incidence of poverty declines with city size. The larger the city size lesser is the poverty. This is also supported by other authors (Motiram and V . Vakulabharanam 2012 and Kundu and Sarangi 2007). While analysing slum data, Gupta et al. (2009) use NFHS data for 2005-06 to examine eight large cities[14]. They defined the poor in relative terms, as those falling in the lowest quartile of wealth index. Defined this way, poverty varies from, 7 per cent in Mumbai to 20 per cent in Nagpur (Vakulbharanam et al. 2007). As expected, the prevalence of poor is much higher in slums as compared to non-slums (except in Indore). According to the Census 2011, 41.7 per cent dwellers in Delhi are poor.

Using the NSS All India Debt and Investment survey, Jaydev et al. (2011) show that urban SCs are at the bottom of the urban wealth ladder, with urban STs having

---

[14]   Chennai, Delhi, Hyderabad, Indore, Kolkata, Meerut, Mumbai and Nagpur

a marginally higher median wealth followed by the OBCs and non-Hindus. The so called forward caste Hindus are almost like an urban wealth enclave too and overlap little with other caste groups. Starting from low wealth base the urban SCs have registered a higher growth rate in median wealth compared to other groups (especially the urban STs). It is clear that urban poor are disproportionally concentrated in casual labour and self employment. The percentage of persons below the poverty line in 2011-12 has been estimated as 13.7 per cent in urban areas. The ratio for the urban areas was 25.7 per cent for the country as a whole in 2004-05. It was 31.8 per cent in urban areas in 1993-94. Reviewed in 2011-12, India had 270 million persons below the poverty line according to Tendulkar Committee as compared to 407 million in 2004-05, showing a reduction of 137 million persons over the seven years period.

Hereafter, Ministry of Housing and Urban Poverty Alleviation will – identify poor on the basis of social, economic and occupational vulnerabilities. As of now, a family of five earning below Rs 5000 a month are put in the brackets of urban poor.

The ministry is working on a strategy to define the urban poor according to vulnerabilities. Under the mechanism, families will be split into two groups – those automatically included, the other automatically excluded – on the poverty bracket. Those automatically included in the poverty bracket will be the homeless and jobless. Automatically excluded will be families with a pucca house, motor vehicle or electronic appliances such as air conditioner or refrigerator. Moreover, the identification of urban poor will be based on the recommendations of Hashim committee. According to recommendations, those living in slums will automatically be eligible for benefits under the slum rehabilitation scheme.

4.12 Incidence of Poverty in Rural and Urban Areas

It needs to be stated that the proportion of persons below the poverty line (using the uniform recall method of calculating the poverty) has fallen steadily in both rural and urban areas through the 1980s, 1990s and 2000s. Even more importantly, there has been a very sharp reduction in poverty between 2004-05 and 2007-08 (using the mixed recall period method). In 2004-05 overall poverty has stood at 21.8 per cent but by 2007-08 it has declined sharply to 14.9 per cent in rural 14.5 per cent in urban areas (Table 4.5).

Table 4.5: All India Incidence of Poverty in Rural and Urban Areas (URP&MRP)

Year	Rural	Urban
1983	45.7	40.8
1993-94	37.3	32.4
2004-05	28.3	25.7
2007-08	14.9	14.5

Source: The statistics from 1983 to 2004-05 (based on URT) is obtained from 11th Five Year Plan where as the statistics for 2007-08 (based on URT) was obtained from NSSO survey 64th Round. Hence data is not comparable.

The following section is devoted to the issue of measurement of poverty in India.

4.13 Poverty Measurement in India

Poverty measurement in India has faced severe criticisms. The Planning Commission, had accepted Tendulkar Committee's methodology for poverty measurement, although this methodology was not free from criticisms. Subsequently, the Rangarajan Committee was constituted to suggest new a measurement of poverty. The committee's report was made public in 2014.

4.14 Evolution of Indian Poverty Lines

In India, poverty measures are based on consumer expenditure surveys conducted by NSSO and are measured as Head Count Ratios (HCR) – the ratio of the number of poor to the total population.

From the late-1970s to the mid-1990s poverty measures relied upon a methodology proposed by the Task Force 1979 (Government of India 1979), which derived poverty lines from an assumed minimum requirement for calories, separately for the rural and the urban sector.[15] The chosen poverty line for each sector, applied uniformly to all states, was actual monthly expenditure level of the households around two calorie norms. Therefore, the approach implied that the poverty lines were partly structural (based on the calorie norm), and partly behavioural (based on the observed expenditure patterns). Even for this methodology, criticisms arose due to state-level variations in cost of living. Afterwards, the Tendulkar

---

[15] The calories consumption is fixed at 2400 calories per capita per day in the rural sector and 2100 calories per capita per day in the urban sector.

methodology was adopted and poverty for each state was measured. The new approach was applied to the NSS sample survey for 2009-10 for updated poverty measures. Later still the Rangarajan committee was constituted to develop new poverty-measurement methods. The methodology changes can be summarised as under:

First, the new approach no longer anchors the poverty lines to any form of calorie intake. Perhaps the most powerful normative critic against the old poverty measures is that they fail to preserve the original calorie norms (Deaton and Dreze 2008). Yet, the all-India urban headcount ratio of 25.7 per cent is noted. Thus, the urban poverty level in the new methodology is indirectly attached to the old calorie norm.

Second, the consumer expenditure figures are based on the NSS data with Mixed reference period (MRP), against earlier 30- days uniform reference period (URP). To derive the new urban all-India poverty line, Tendulkar committee used the MRP-equivalent of the old URP poverty line. Third, the reference poverty line is disaggregated to the state-level in both sectors with a new set of price indices, calculated from expenditure data. Many opined that the old price system often led to unlikely price and poverty outcomes, particularly in comparisons between the rural and the urban sector. It may be noted that the price level differences between the two sectors did not originate from actual price comparison, but instead from the different calorie needs and consumption patterns observed in two sectors.

Fourth, the new poverty lines are calculated for all Indian states, separately for the rural and the urban areas, against the old approach which calculated poverty lines for 23 large states. Hence, the calculated poverty lines have a broader coverage.

The magnitude of poverty at any given point of time depends on the criteria of norms used to define poverty and determine the poverty line. There are two criteria or norms usually employed to define the poverty line.

- Norms based on the concept of a nutritionally adequate diet
- Norms based on the concept of minimum level of living

A number of research scholars have attempted to estimate the cost of providing a nutritionally adequate diet. For example, Dandker and Rath (1971), on the basis of an average calorie intake of 2250 per capita per day, estimated the poverty line to correspond to a consumer expenditure of ₹ 15 per capita per month for rural households and ₹ 22.50 for urban households at 1960-61 prices.

As far as the second norm based on the concept of minimum level of living is concerned, a distinguished Working Group constituted by the planning commission, Government of India, in July 1962, deliberated on the question of what should be regarded as the nationally desirable minimum level of consumer expenditure. The study group recommended that a per capita monthly expenditure at 1960-61 prices of ₹ 20 for rural areas and ₹ 25 for urban areas should be deemed to be the national minimum. This does not include expenditure on health and education, which are expected to be borne by the state.

The official poverty estimates are based on the methodology recommended by the Expert Group (EG). The methodology suggested by the EG is summarised as follows (Radhakrishnan and Ray 2005). The poverty lines were anchored to a fixed commodity basket corresponding to the task force recommended poverty line (₹ 49.09 per person per month at 1973-74 prices for rural areas and ₹ 56.64 for urban areas). The rural commodity basket suggested by the EG contained 2400 kcal per capita per day in rural areas while the urban food basket had 2100 kcal per capita per day in 1973-74. The use of calorie norm was taken as an approximation to what may be considered as an acceptable minimum needs. The consumption basket was common to all states. In order to factor in changing tastes and preferences, the EG recommended that the consumption basket be revised every five years. This was to take into account minimum needs as derived from the chosen nutrition attributes as revealed by the behaviour pattern of consumers.

4.15 Human Poverty Index (HPI)

The Human Development Report 1997 (UNDP) presents an HPI and ranks 78 poor countries using it. The report asserts that poverty is multidimensional and poverty measures based on the income criterion do not capture deprivation of many kinds.

The HPI is based on the following three different types of deprivation (UNDP 1997a).

- Deprivation in survival, as measured by the percentage of people not expected to survive up to age of 40 years (P1).

- Deprivation in education and knowledge, as measured by the adult literacy rate (P2)
- Deprivation in economic provisioning (P3), which is computed as the mean of three variables: population without access to safe water (P31), population without access to health services (P32) and underweight children under the age of five years (P33) – all three expressed in percentages.

The HPI is then obtained as the cube root of the average of the cubes of the three components of deprivation. This is a power mean of the order three. The power mean of the order one is the simple mean, the average of the values. Out of the 78 developing countries, India's HPI was 36.7 and its rank was 47 (Singh 2009).

Notwithstanding the variations in measurement in 2004-05, as many as 302 million persons (27.5) per cent were living below the poverty line in India. According to Human Development Report (HDR) 2003 of the UNDP (2003), India has largest number of poor in the world and is home to one fourth of the poor in the world. A large number of poor are scheduled castes, scheduled tribes, Muslim minorities and people residing in remote and hilly locations (Singh 2009).

4.16 Issues of New Methods of Poverty Estimates

The planning commission recently released poverty estimates across states for rural and urban areas of India for 2009-10 (Government of India 2012). A matter of concern raised in the media was low poverty lines leading to a social experiment wherein the spending threshold was ₹ 32 per day for an adult.[16] It was also debated in academic circle.[17]

The study by Pathak and Mishra (2011), had identified five issues with regard to the new method of measuring poverty: doing away with calories norm, which was

---

[16] See http://www.ndtv.com/article/india/not-poor-if-you-earn-rs-32-a-day-planning-commission-135118

[17] A number of papers debating the pros and cons of the new method got published on a special issue of the Indian Journal of Human Development (2010). (See Alagh 2010), Berman 2010; Datta 2010, Kanan 2010, Raveendran 2010, Shah 2010 and Swaminathan 2010. Also see Planning Commission 2011, Rao 2010, Subramanian 2010 and Suryanarayana 2011. Independence of Poverty line debates also see a discussion on the right not to be poor from a political perspective by Chandhoke (2012).

how poverty estimates were being cited in India till 2004-05; the use of median expenditure on health and education; difficulty in reproducing the estimates; and the political economy of changing poverty shares.

4.17 Expert Group Considerations

The expert group had three important considerations. First the calorie norm pegged at 1973-74 may not be appropriate because of changes in age, gender and occasional patterns. And that one should go beyond calories to have a deeper understanding of nutritional requirements. In any case, the subsequent updating of poverty lines does not adhere to the calorie norm.

Second the earlier consumption of poverty lines was based on the assumption that education, health and sanitation requirements would be provided by the state, which is no more appropriate.

Third the consumption expenditure collected through a uniform recall period does not appropriately represent low frequency items like clothing, footwear, consumer durables, education and institutional health.

The 61st round recall of the NSS in 2004-05 collected expenditure data for such items with recall of both 30 days and 365 days. The expert group used the adjusted values of the latter to make them comparable with 30 days recall of the other items.

With regard to calorie requirement, the expert group implicitly conceded the need for nuanced nutritional basis. However in the absence of any norm they kept those concerns aside and delinked poverty measures from any calorie norm. One hopes that the new technical committee will deliberate on such issues. In 2009-10, updating of poverty line has been done for rural and urban areas of each state separately.

4.18 Recent Estimates of Poverty

The poverty estimates have been based on the recommendations made by experts periodically. In 2005 Planning Commission constituted an expert group under the chairmanship of Prof. Suresh Tendulkar to review the methodology for estimating poverty. The Tendulkar Committee submitted its report in December 2009 and computed poverty lines and poverty ratios for 2004-05. The committee also computed poverty lines and poverty ratios for 1993-94 with identical methodology. The methodology and estimations were accepted by Planning Commission.

In 1993-94, 40.24 crore were poor and of them 81.5 per cent were in rural areas. The number of the poor increased to 40.72 crore person in 2004-5. This was largely on account of an increase in the urban poor whose share increased from18.5 to 20 per cent. This trend in urban India was reinforced in 2009-10 with a continuing decline in rural areas the total number of poor decreased to 35.47 crore persons of which 78.4 per cent were in rural areas.

The change in the number of poor as also the changes in the shares of the poor across states could be linked to allocation and transfer of funds through centrally sponsored schemes for alleviation of poverty (Rao 2010). Any whittling down could be counterproductive because some of the reductions were due to existing schemes. Keeping this in the background, we compare the share of the poor for 2009-10 with that for 2004-05 with regard to the incidence of poverty.

The poverty risk in 2009 -10 was greater than that in 2004-05 for both rural and urban sectors with regard to incidence, depth and severity in Chhattisgarh, Assam, Bihar, Madhya Pradesh, Odisha, Uttar Pradesh and Jharkhand referred to as the CABMOUJ, pronounced as *kab mouj states* (Pathak et.al 2013). However, Odisha and Madhya Pradesh are performing better compared to other CABMOUJ states.

The rates of poverty estimated by Planning Commission and Tendulkar Committee have placed the figures at 27.5 per cent and 37.2 per cent respectively in 2009 (Planning Commission 2011). There are few studies to indicate how much increase in the rate of growth of GDP would reduce poverty and discrimination among the SC, STs, women and religious minorities. It is very interesting to find out that the government's social justice programme include schemes like Social Welfare Scholarship, fund for National Scheduled Castes Fund Development Corporation (NSCFDC), rehabilitation centres for physically challenged and 15-point programmes for religious minorities. But the implementation of such measures at the grassroots level and their impact in reducing social exclusion are yet to be studied. Probably, government's approach to economic growth takes care of only the electoral outcomes but not issues of social justice. It is in this context that the writing of Amartya Sen (Sen 2009) and John Rawls (Rawls 1999) seems to be useful.

Section II

Poverty is an important social, economic challenge in Central Asia, at present. Central Asia had constituted one of the least developed regions in former Soviet Union, the people living on margins. Jane Falkingham (1999b) viewed that poverty was not all together absent but was not the major concern during pre-independence period in Central Asian states. In 1991, collapse of Soviet Union and the withdrawal of the Soviet government brought sudden changes in the political and economic environment, referred to as transition. It was shift from a planned socialist economy to a market economy, and had great consequences on the social and economic aspects of people's lives. The sharp increase in poverty in the first decade of independence and deterioration in the standard of living made it obligatory to deal with the social-economic problem of poverty. Transition economy did not cause poverty directly but the situation of nearly 20 million poor worsened and they slipped to absolute poverty, according to an estimation in 2005 (United Nations 2010a).

Poverty in Central Asia is strongly related to well being along with income poverty. As all Central Asian states belong to either medium or high development group, their living standard as life expectancy, literacy are competent to region of Europe and Russia. The perspective on poverty is still in developing stage as these states have not developed stable polity affecting governance ultimately implementation and also collection of data for research and policy making. The increasing underemployment and unemployment, partly caused due to structural inequalities of the labour market are major reason of poverty in the region. Education sector is another crucial determinant of poverty in the region. The people living in rural and non capital towns are facing the problem of poverty. Poverty in Central Asia has spatial and structural dimension. There is urban rural divide in poverty in both material and access of resources and services, urban region being better off. Besides rural poverty, child poverty is major concern, the major trend being lack of accessibilities even to basic facilities as food and nutrition. The other trend being lack of child care due to long time absence of parents, migrating to other regions or states for employment.

World Bank defines poverty as 'pronounced deprivation of well being' which is attached to the command of resources (Haughton et al. 2009). Raghbendra Jha and Tu Dang (2009) note three important reasons analyzing poverty and vulnerability in Central Asia. It is based on the increasing focus on central Asia's economy and unexplored natural resources. The reformation policies from socialist to market economy caused the increase in incidence of poverty and the strategic location of Central Asia between Europe and Asia its accessibility. The present understanding of human development is largely seen through the lens of poverty. Human poverty is multidimensional phenomenon; it is a process rather than condition (UNDP 2013). With this background, the discussion on measurement of poverty describes the major approaches to determine poverty in Central Asian states.

Absolute poverty in pre-independence Central Asian states was non-existent because under soviet regime the states were better off. The countries were receiving financial support the central budget of soviet regime. However the poverty scenario changed after independence. While the poverty situation improved across the world, the situation worsened in Central Asia. As the states in Central Asia were moving from socialist economy to market economy, these states were undergoing various economic and political changes leading to decline in previously assured standard of living. The fall in economic output indicated in the decreasing Gross Domestic Product (GDP) and fall in real wages in the region were among the major causes of increasing poverty in the region (Falkingham 1999a). Under the soviet regime the society has centrally planned economy, ensured income through employment while in market economy the public and private redistribution of wealth led to unequal growth among various sections of society. During the transition in 1992 Atkinson and Micklewright () had calculated poverty line for comparing poverty in pre transition and post transition period which was 75 rubbles. Later by applying the poverty line of $ 4 PPP per person per day[18], Milanovic has calculated poverty line which was equivalent to 54 rubbles for the region. Kyrgyzstan has the highest incidence of poverty i.e., 84 per cent, while Uzbekistan has the highest population of poor of ten million.

The number of poor as people living below $ 1.25 a day in the region of Central Asia has increased from 45.9 per cent in 1990 to 95 per cent in 2005. Only Turkmenistan have shown relative decrease (Table 4.6) in poor population in contrast the other four states have shown increase in number of absolute poor population.

---

[18] The amount of $ 4 PPP is per capita per day is used by UNDP in the Human Development report 1997.

Table 4.6: Poor in Central Asia living on less than $1.25 a day

Region	1990	2005
Kazakhstan	0.5	1.2
Kyrgyzstan	4.8	21.8
Tajikistan	1.5	21.5
Turkmenistan	34.2	11.7
Uzbekistan	4.9	38.8
Total	45.9	95

Source: United Nations Report (2010a)

The number of people living in absolute poverty in Central Asia has increased more than 4 times, from 3.7 million in 1981 to 16.1 million in 2005 (United Nations 2010a). The World Bank defines 'poor' in Central Asia as subsisting on less than $2.50 a day, and vulnerable as below US $5 a day (World Health Organization 2010). In today's estimate, 40 million people in the Europe and Central Asia region are living below US $ 2.50 per day and less than 160 million below US $ 5 per day. World Bank suggests key determinants and correlates of poverty can be proved by characteristics at national, regional, community, household and individual levels (Haughton et. al 2009). In Central Asia conditions of sever contraction of GDP during early 1990s, high inflation, labour market and inequalities of wages and wealth distribution, education are major causes of poverty (Poverty in Central Asia 2004 and World Bank Reports).

Table 4.7: Absolute Poverty in Central Asia (2005- 2009) *(per cent)*

Country	Year	Total	Urban	Rural
Kazakhstan	2006	22	16	29
	2008	16	12	21
Kyrgyzstan	2005	43	30	51
	2008	32	23	37
Tajikistan	2007	54	49	55
	2009	47	42	49
Uzbekistan	2003	24	22	29
	2007	24	18	27

Source: Gassmann, F. (2011)

Absolute poverty line is widely accepted indicator to measure poverty. Moving towards the poverty in absolute number in Central Asia, the following table 4.7 gives the population living below absolute poverty line. Each state has different measures to calculate absolute poverty line. The entire Central Asian states show declining trend in poverty in recent time since 2007 (Gassmann 2011). All have higher concentration of poor in rural areas above national average while urban areas are relatively better off. Tajikistan has highest incidence of poverty 47 per cent (2009) while Kazakhstan has lowest 16 per cent in 2008. Kyrgyzstan has the highest gap between rural and urban poor is around 15 per cent in 2008 and Uzbekistan has lowest around 9 per cent in 2007. In the two most mountainous countries, Kyrgyzstan and Tajikistan, living in a high altitude area is also correlated with a significantly higher risk of poverty (World Bank 2007c).

4.19 Measurement of Poverty

Poverty is a socio-economic problem. Measurement of poverty includes development of poverty profile which helps to evaluate and assess the situation of poverty over a period of time. Poverty in Central Asia is multidimensional phenomenon hence it needs variety of approaches to measure poverty. Such approaches are absolute, relative, subjective, deprivation (UNDP 2013).

4.19.1 Absolute approach: The absolute measure of poverty is based on establishing minimum of basic need (subsistence minimum) and the quantity of resources essential satisfying those needs. It is thresholds defined on the grounds that this is the minimum needed for mere survival. It is most widely used approach based in income and expenditure of household. It is objective approach, unlike relative poverty. The incidence of poverty, expressed as a headcount ratio, is simply an estimate of the percentage of people with income below the subsistence minimum. The level of absolute poverty is much higher within Central Asian states in comparison to other former Soviet Russian states.

4.19.2 Relative approach: The relative poverty line defines poverty based on prevailing standard of living. The people are poor if they fall significantly below such living standard in the given society. Relative poverty uses wealth indicators for defining poverty and is related to the predominant level of material wealth in a given country. Unlike the absolute poverty which is in some way an objective standard people can move out of the line of poverty on the other hand the relative poverty exists all the time.

4.19.3 Deprivation approach: Deprivation poverty can be defined as failure to achieve certain standard of consumption, decided on the particular societal condition. Deprivation poverty does not just depend on minimum income and consumption level but also expect to follow certain minimum standard health, education and housing. In Kazakhstan, capabilities approach works similar manner as deprivation.

4.19.4 Subjective Approach: Subjective poverty approach is based on the people's assessment of their own living standards. The above four definition are not exclusive but are complementary to each other.

Measurement of poverty in case of material poverty is carried out with the help of defining absolute poverty lines. Such measurement of poverty is carried out on the basis of income and expenditure or consumption of household for given period. Capability poverty within a society can be measured directly by assessment of capability of population as literacy, health, reproduction, food and nutrition, education etc. Poverty measurement identifies poverty rate, share of population living below poverty line and the level of material insecurity. There is increasing recognition within scholars that there is need to consider other aspects like capability poverty in discussion of poverty and its reduction. McKinley (1997) through a system of complementary poverty measures had shown how the lack of access to resources, services and culture etc. leads to restricting the development of well being. While explaining the concept of McKinley, Falkingham writes, 'Capability poverty focuses on the capacity of individual to live healthy life, free of avoidable morbidity, having adequate nourishment, being informed and knowledgeable, being capable of reproduction, enjoying personal security and being freely able to actively participate in society.' The most significant feature of capability aspect of poverty is that it emphasis on active agency of people involved in the process as against the income or basic need approach which are passive criteria in nature (Falkingham, 1999a).

4.20 International Poverty Line

Poverty is problem prevalent in many states and the understanding of poverty is still evolving, as are the methods to understand it. Sharing knowledge and experiences on poverty has helped to understand it better. Until the 1990s, the data available was of national level and hence there were restrictions in comparing situations. To overcome this during the 1990s the World Bank developed the international poverty line, to compare poverty in different states and regions. The national poverty lines began to be measured with the help of purchasing power parity (PPP) adjusted to differences in domestic currencies. The PPP method was particularly useful to overcome limitations of currency exchange rate method. Since then the World Bank has revised the international poverty line from time to time. Initially it was US $ 1 (PPP) during the 1990s. It was revised in 2000 in order to take advantage of new PPP data covering large number of developing countries. The new international poverty line was set at $1.08 per day at (1993 PPP)[19]. At present the international poverty lines are $ 1.25 a day, $ 2.50 a day and $ 5 a day based on 2005 PPP.

4.21 Multidimensional Poverty Index (MPI)

Besides national and international poverty lines the other major indicator to measure poverty, MPI was introduced in 2010 (UNDP 2010). It is a composite and mathematical index, interconnected with deprivation. It identifies multiple deprivations the same households in terms of education, health, and standard of living. It helps to capture the failures in 'functioning.' Unlike income poverty it gives comprehensive picture of deprivation of basic capacities. It helps to identify poor people and their extent of deprivation within a state are based on two indicators, while the living standard is derived using six indicators. The deprivation index is then calculated based on data fetched from the same survey year. Justifying selection of these three indicators for MPI Sabina Alkire and Maria Santos (2010) writes that MPI uses same indicators as HDI because of their advantages as these are parsimonious and using only three dimensions simplifies comparisons with income poverty measures. As the HDI has been calculated for over period of twenty years there is consensus over this indicator while there could be some disagreement about working with other indicators such as work, empowerment, and physical safety in a poverty measure. Besides these have interpretability due to availability of substantial literature for these three indicators. The inclusivity of these three indicators of development human development appreciates both the intrinsic and the instrumental value (Alkire and Santos 2010). To get perspective about poverty and deprivation, the cut-off is decided at 33.3 per cent, equivalent to one third of weighted indicators; it is used to distinguish between poor and non poor in the region. If the score of deprivation is equivalent or greater than 33.3, then the household including all members is facing multidimensional poverty. If the score ranges between 20 and 33.3 per cent the household is are vulnerable to multidimensional poverty. All Central Asian states have scores 36 percent to

---

[19]   The year 1993 was taken as base year for calculating purchasing power parity.

40 percent, implying that they are facing multidimensional poverty. Tajikistan has the highest head-count of poor at 17.1, (Table 4.8) while Kazakhstan has the least at 0.6 (4.16).

Table 4.8: Multidimensional Poverty Index Figures in Central Asian Countries

Indicators	Kazakhstan	Kyrgyzstan	Tajikistan	Turkmenistan	Uzbekistan
Survey year	2006	2005/6	2005	NA	2006
MPI value	0.002	0.019	0.068	NA	0.008
Headcount (%)	0.6	4.9	17.1	NA	2.3
Intensity of deprivation (%)	36.9	38.8	40	NA	36.2
Vulnerable to poverty	5	9.2	23	NA	8.1
In sever poverty	0	0.9	3.1	NA	0.1
Below Income Poverty Line	0.1	6.2	6.6	NA	Na
Health	56.8	36.9	45	NA	55.7
Education	14.6	36.6	18.7	NA	23.2
Living Standard	28.7	26.4	36.3	NA	21.1

Source: All five countries Human Development Report (2013)
Notes: N.A: Not Available

4.22 Rural Poverty

During the transition because of regional disparities and lack of development avenues, rural inhabitants were poor (Grant, U. et al. 2004). All Central Asian republics have relatively higher concentration of poor in rural areas. In particular, rural areas that are experiencing a slow down in state- owned collective farming there has been a correspondingly high unemployment rate. Besides, due to deprivation of access to social -protection services, the rural population has suffered to a greater degree. Often such rural population has access to land resources, but low productivity has led to low standards of living. Cynthia Buckley (1998) argues that the historical legacy of soviet rule's development policies and differentials in demographic process resulted into disadvantaged position of rural inhabitants. She explains it through differentials in fertility and mortality rates and the phenomenon of ageing. Residents outside the capital were facing poverty in Kyrgyzstan and Uzbekistan, besides the residents of one company town where entire labour force were dependent on small group of enterprises were facing poverty due to closure of such enterprises (Falkingham 1999b).

4.23 Child Poverty

Child poverty is defined as children's experience of poverty. It is thought that the poverty determinant or causes can be similar but the experience of poverty differs for adults and children. It is an effort to recognise groups of population based on their age, due to which they shares some common experiences. Such recognition can help to understand the phenomenon better in order to tackle it. The concepts childhood poverty stresses the importance of childhood in life and the cycle of poverty being transferred from generation to generation so, the poor child grows into a poor adult, the poor adult becomes a parent and in turn passes on the poverty to their child, who eventually grows into a poor adult. The phenomenon has a long- term effect as the poor child who is deprived of basic food ,health and other facilities is most likely to become a poor parent in the future, at both material and physical levels (Marcus, R.et al. 2004). Child poverty in the region has increased in the last two decades. Poverty is closely related to the demographic characteristics of household. The child living in poverty may include children belonging to poor household as well as children who are deprived of many basic necessities of life, making such children poor population of society of particular age group. Kyrgyzstan, Tajikistan and to certain extent Uzbekistan shares the feature of child poverty (World Bank 2000b and 2003). The study of child poverty in Kyrgyzstan conducted by Yarkova and others (2004) suggest 'around 60 per cent of rural children less than 10 year live in poverty. Around 21 per cent of rural children and 12 per cent of urban children under 10 live in severe poverty. The most venerable group is children under one constitute around 65 per cent of rural children and 57 per cent of urban children living in poverty' (Yarkova et al. 2004). In Tajikistan children experience higher risk of poverty as compared with adults, the relative risk of poverty faced by children calculated by Tajikistan Living standards Surveys ranges in between 1.03 to 1.11. (World Bank 2000b) Single parents are also major groups affected due to lack of adequate income.

Causes for child poverty are considered as prevalence of poverty in community and household. Resulting into lack of access to basic facilities required for basic human development. Poor governance is one of the causes for child poverty. Since childhood is very important stage in human being's life, any lack in this has direct implications for human resource development and results into development of poor human resource (Marshall 2003). Such children are particularly vulnerable to exploitation and abuse due lack of social and legal protection. Children generally do actively contribute to household, community and even wider development from an early age.

4.24 Causes of Poverty in Central Asia

4.24.1 Unemployment and low income

Unemployment and low income were the main causes of poverty in Central Asia (UNDP 2001 and Falkingham 1999b). It is generally accepted understanding that all Central Asian states had and continue to have higher unemployment rate than officially claimed. During the transition, changes in the political and economic system led to an unprecedented increase in unemployment as direct a implication of closing down of numerous enterprises. Unemployment is considered to be one of the main causes of poverty during the transition-era. Tajikistan also shows similar trend of low official unemployment rate of three per cent TLSS data, 16 per cent by International Labour Organization standard while if hidden employment[20] is taken into account it is 20 per cent. If further involuntary part time workers added, it becomes 25 per cent and people who are unemployed but not looking for employment or discouraged workers makes it 31 per cent (World Bank 2000b).

4.24.2 Poverty Among Ethnic Groups and Minorities

The inequalities in well being are attributable to location (spatial poverty) and status (being child women, minority etc.). Although average poverty rates were declining from 2005, poverty has remained entrenched in rural areas and small towns. Such exclusion from economic life has resulted from inequalities in access to resources. Poverty has also remained prevalent among certain groups: youth, ethnic minorities, people living with disabilities and internally displaced peoples. The transition recession and the subsequent jobless growth in the region have also created a layer of discouraged workers, especially among women and the middle-aged. The major determinants of poverty in Central Asia are sudden contraction in gross domestic product (GDP), high inflation, labour market, education. Though there is no directly collected or available data about the situation of poverty among various ethnic groups. Some probable reason can be Central Asia focuses on demographic groups in their national surveys. But there is an evolving concern over the need to recognise ethnic groups also as a social group suffering from

---

[20] Hidden employment meaning the person is officially employed but effectively not working because of forced holidays.

poverty and deprivation. As Alexi Gugushvilli (2011) interpreting the study of Social Exclusion Survey 2009 for material deprivation in social class and for life course shows poverty and material deprivation in Kazakhstan is determined by occupational groups as social class and life course based on demographic stage. In his study, he develops a deprivation index according to which spatial dimension and level of economy are determining factors. Based on this, he identifies non- skilled manual, farmers, skilled manual, lower social class as deprived people. According to life course the children under five and single parents are groups suffering due to deprivation. Based on the ethnic composition of Kazakhstan it is observed that considerable sections of the country's inhabitants are materially deprived and poor. In Kyrgyzstan the study for vulnerability to poverty conducted by Raghbendra Jha and Tu Dang (2009) the distribution of poverty by ethnicity of household is highest among Uzbek constitutes 71 per cent and has poverty rate 65.3 per cent. Though Tajik ethnic group has poverty rate 68.8 per cent but population is only 0.4 per cent, where the poverty rate for Kyrgyzstan is 56.3 per cent. Similar study for Tajikistan gives distribution of poverty by ethnicity of household as Tajik 68.2 per cent, Uzbeks 28.5, Russians 1.2 per cent, and Kyrgyz 1.1 per cent. Poverty rate is observed highest among Kyrgyz (100 per cent), followed by Tajiks (95.5 per cent), Uzbeks (94.6 per cent) (Jha and Dang 2009).

4.24.3 Per- Capita Income

It is a measure of income, an amount of money that is being earned per person in a certain area. Grossly, it is taken as an average pointer for the economic condition of society. It helps to describe the average economic situation and living standard within society. Despite the recent gains in income growth, per capita income remains low by international standards (Table 4.9).

Table 4.9: Per Capita income in Central Asian Countries *(Constant 2005 international US $)*

Year	Kazakhstan	Kyrgyzstan	Tajikistan	Turkmenistan	Uzbekistan
2005	7,880	1,660	1,450	4,430	2,000
2010	9,569	1,865	1,910	6,722	2,838
2012	10,451	2,009	2,119	7,782	3,201

Source: World Bank (2012)

After analysing the data, it is evident that per- capita income has increased in all Central Asian Countries. Kazakhstan and Uzbekistan have reported better per capita income. Over the two decades after independence due to lack of economic development in their own states many people migrated to neighbouring Russia and Kazakhstan for employment. Migration and remittance have become an economic life for Central Asia. All Central Asian states have shown increase in per capita income, the highest growth is in Turkmenistan growth.

4.24.4 Subsistence Living

All central Asian states evaluate the poverty or standard of living with reference to minimum subsistence standards of living. The term basic minimum necessities to survive, in the context of poverty, refer to the living wages or subsistence income that is necessary to satisfy basic needs. The collapse of Soviet Union resulted in a dramatic slowdown of economic development and a total disruption of the existing social safety net (Petroversky 2005). The initiation in the new system of market economy had a negative impact on many sections of society. In Central Asia subsistence income is pegged at $1.25 per day. Among all the five countries Uzbekistan has highest percentage (38.8 per cent) of people has persistence living followed by Kyrgyzstan and Tajikistan. Surprisingly the situation has worsened in the Uzbekistan. The possible reasons could be increase in working population in contrast with the lack of job opportunities during the initial period of transition. There was also low growth elasticity that is per-cent change in poverty rate in relation with change in growth. It was caused due to underdeveloped infrastructure; administrative barriers and the absence of an efficient market system were some of the main causes for deterioration of the social situation regarding poverty (World Bank 2007b).

4.24.5 Hunger

Food is one of the basic necessities of human beings. Any discussion on poverty or conditions of poor has direct and indirect references to food and hunger. Hunger is defined by International Food Policy Research Institute in terms of under nourishment and malnutrition (IFPRI 2012). Despite the improving performance of Central Asian economies in the recent period condition for food security shows marginal change. Alessandra Bravi and Nathan Solbrandt (2011) attributed this to low productivity in agriculture and large disparity in income distribution. Generally the share of household budget required for food consumption is considered to be an indicator of vulnerability to poverty. Bravi and Solbrandt with reference to World Bank information said that in Central Asian, Uzbekistan and Tajikistan spent almost 80 per cent household income to secure food while Kyrgyzstan's household spends around 58 per cent of their household income. In Kazakhstan it is 42 per cent where as the developed countries the figures vary between 15 to 30 per cent (Table 4.10).

Table 4.10: Hunger Index for Central Asia and India

Rank	Country	2001	2012
9	Kyrgyz Republic	9.0	5.8
11	Turkmenistan	8.9	6.9
11	Uzbekistan	10.8	6.9
41	Tajikistan	24.6	15.8
	Kazakhstan[21]	5.4	<5
65	India	24.2	22.9

Source: IFPRI (2012)

Global Hunger Index (GHI) is calculated on the basis of percentage of undernourished population, prevalence of malnutrition among children under five and mortality rate of children less than five years. The values obtained are ranked as low, moderate, serious and alarming.[22] In Central Asia though the situation has improved in comparison to 2001, except Kazakhstan and Tajikistan all other three republics are facing moderate hunger while Tajikistan has a high value 15.8 and serious condition of malnutrition and undernourishment. Kazakhstan has low hunger value indicating the better situation nutrition and food. While India shows only a slight improvement the value decreasing by 1.3 still the situation is alarming regarding nutrition and access to food.

4.25 Poverty in Kazakhstan

Poverty in Kazakhstan is calculated on the basis of basic necessities as food basket or minimum calories intake per day following World Health Organization

---

[21]   Note: Kazakhstan is not included in the ranking since the hunger index is minimal less than five.

[22]   The values less than 4.9 reflect "low hunger", values between 5 and 9.9 reflect "moderate hunger", values between 10 and 19.9 indicate a "serious", values between 20 and 29.9 are "alarming", and values exceeding 30 are "extremely alarming" hunger problem.

standards (World Bank 2004). The consumer's basket consists of a food basket, which includes foodstuff necessary to meet a certain nutritional intake expressed by calorie intake (2172 Kcals), and 30 per cent added (World Bank 2004) for essential non-food items (such as clothes, shoes, and housing)and services that comprise a minimum requirement. Poverty in Kazakhstan is measured along monetary and non monetary dimensions, and includes consumption and housing and education poverty. The major cause of poverty in Kazakhstan is unemployment and low income, the purchasing power of salaries in many sectors of the economy ranges from low to medium. It is only in the finance and mining sectors that the purchasing power is very high (Agency of Statistics Republic of Kazakhstan 2011). The significant increase in the number of self -employed persons has brought additional developmental challenges, such as low wages, they are also insufficiently covered by social security schemes. A survey for (UNDP 2004) highlighted unemployment (54.7 per cent), low salaries and pensions (25.7 per cent) are the reason for poverty. The lack of health sector reforms has also played an important role in poverty in Kazakhstan. In Kazakhstan migration and demographic factors are also significant in determining poverty. Migration of people from rural to urban areas aggravates urban poverty. Women forms a major section of the poor, due to their large population and persistent socioeconomic inequalities. The three most common characteristics of poor households are large household size, low educational qualification of the head of the household and lower probability of employment of household adults.

Poverty is largely concentrated in rural areas, at present 47 per cent (Smailov 2011) of the country's population live in rural areas. Poor populations are concentrated in five oblasts. These are south Kazakhstan, Karaganda, Kostanay, Zhambyl, and East Kazakhstan. Jha and Dang (2009) notes southern, western and eastern regions have a higher poverty rate (69.1 per cent, 38.4 per cent and 31.5 per cent respectively). The highest percentage of poverty is observed in remote rural districts and in small towns. In rural areas the percentage of poor was 38.5 per cent in 2001 and highest percentage (World Bank 2004) of poverty was reported in remote province (Mangistau oblast). Jha and Dang (2009) divide spatial poverty in Kazakhstan as urban, poselki (smaller town) and rural. Urban areas have 30.3 per cent poverty rate and 42.8 per cent poor population, while rural areas have 40.3 per cent poverty rate and 48.8 per cent poor population. The suburban region poselkis have 36.3 per cent poverty rate and 8.4 per cent poor population.

The housing-related poor are the largest group of poor, at an estimated 28 per cent of the population. The education poor (15 years and above), referring to those who have at most completed primary education, are above 11 per cent of the population (UNDP 2002). Jha and Dang (2009) distribution of poverty by education of household shows that 36.4 per cent of population, with household heads who have had no training, faces the highest poverty rate of 45.4 per cent while the national average poverty rate is 35 per cent. The lowest poverty rate of 24.3 per cent is observed among the household heads who have had education of university level.

The Human Poverty index is calculated by United Nations for different countries based on three levels of development. Since Kazakhstan is a developing country, its Human Poverty Index is calculated based on longevity, knowledge and decent living standards of the population. Longevity here measured as percentage of people not surviving to age of 60 years. Knowledge is percentage of 16-year olds not enrolled in education (drop outs). The decent standard of living is calculated based on percentage of people with incomes below the subsistence level and unemployment rate (UNDP 2009).

Poverty is largely confined to the southern (South Kazakhstan, Zhymbly, Kyzylorda, Almaty) and western (Mangistau and Akmola) regions. These provinces are far away from the centre of power and have been largely neglected by subsequent ruler. The concentration of Kazakhs in these regions is evident, thereby also implying that the Kazaks here have suffered poverty. The Kazakh community has a concentration of nearly 89 per cent (Table 4.11) in the Kyzylorda region, located in South Kazakhstan. Kazakh populations are mainly located in the southern and western parts of the country, whereas Russians are dominant in the northern and eastern parts. Perhaps the Russians were ruler's till the formation of independent states in 1991 and hence also enjoyed prosperity. The last two decades have witnessed the Kazakhs moving towards prosperity because power base has moved into their hands. The notion of minimum subsistence is an important instrument in creating social policy and fighting against poverty. Poverty is closely related to economic inequality and should be addressed in conjunction with welfare levels in all segments of society. Kazakhstan has so far focused on anti- poverty measures for those in absolute poverty. Now it must take action to prevent people from falling into absolute poverty.

Table 4.11: Ethnic Compositions by Regions

Region	Name of the state (Oblast)	Percentage of Kazak population	Percentage of Russian Population	Other
Eastern Region	Eastern Kazakhstan	38	60	2
Western Region	Akmola	N.A.	N. A.	N.A.
	Atyrau	79.5	15	5.5
	Mangistau	51	33	16
	Western Kazakhstan	54.8	34.4	4.5 Ukrainian
Central Kazakhstan	Karaganda	45	43	12
North Kazakhstan	Aktyubinsk	56	24	30
	Kostanay	43	17	15 Ukrainian
	Pavlorda	28	55	17
	North Kazakhstan	30	66	4
South Kazakhstan	Almaty	45	30	25
	Zhambyl	48.8	26.5	24.7
	Kyzylorda	88.4	7.8	1.08 Ukrainian
	South Kazakhstan	55.7	15.3	2.4 Germans

Source: Research Analyst 2000; Note: Figures are approximate calculations

Central Kazakhstan has highest poverty index 21.4 constitutes Karaganda region and 0.799 income index. It is followed by Western region which has four oblasts average poverty index 19.77 with moderate average income index 0.762. North Kazakhstan has average poverty index 19.45, it has four oblasts. South Kazakhstan has three oblasts and two cities, poverty index around 17.12 which is around national average of 15.86. Eastern region constitute of Eastern Kazakhstan has poverty index 19.6 (Table 4A.8)

4.26 Poverty in Kyrgyzstan

Kyrgyzstan follows the basic needs poverty line using household food and non-food consumption items. The expenditure to reach the 2,100 calories per day per person is considered as food poverty line (World Bank 2003). The estimate of poverty is calculated by Kyrgyz Integrated Household Survey later on changed to National Statistics Committee (World Bank 2007c). The surveys are conducted on quarterly on a rolling basis. This threshold line is then used to calculate the extreme poverty line. The share of non food item of consumption is calculated for the reference group that is just above the extreme poverty line. These two calculations are added to estimate total poverty line based on consumption. The National Statistical Commission in the light of price rise updates the poverty line in 2008, which serves as the major shift in the national poverty line.

The incidence of poverty is higher in Kyrgyzstan among the young between the ages (15 to 29 years). Jha and Dang (2009) calculated distribution of poverty by household head less than 20 years age had highest poverty rate of 87.5 while national average is 56.3. The large household size is another. Poor households more usually have five or more members, including many younger children, Kyrgyzstan faces problem of child poverty as well. The extremely poor households are often headed by women, (Jha and Dang 2009) give distribution of poverty by female household head had poverty rate of 63.3 per cent while male household head has 54.5 poverty rate where national average poverty rate is 56.3. Where as in the poor household, the head can be a man or a woman. The level of education and migration also played important role in determining the poverty. The lower level of educational attainment of the household head is more likely to end the household in the poor category. Migration is another important driver affecting poverty. The people who can migrate from rural to other better parts raised the chances for better life. But the reverse migration is also a trend leading to failure of improving real condition of people.

4.27 Poverty in Tajikistan

The decade of 1990 shows intrinsic poverty in Tajikistan. Tajikistan shows multidimensional understanding of poverty. The living standard surveys collect the data on demographics and housing, expenditure and consumption, food security and agriculture, education and health, employment and migration etc. The poverty measurement depends on the choice of absolute or relative approach, choice of poverty line, the selection of welfare indicators, the valuation of in-kind benefits and home reduction. The food poverty line is based on the costs of purchasing 2,250 kcal per person per day, food consumption accounts 64 per cent of absolute poverty line. The limitations of poverty measurement in Tajikistan are that it represented data collected one point in time and excluded homeless.

The major causes of poverty are high unemployment rate, lack of access to quality education and degradation of land resources and lack of access to basic services as water, sanitation and electricity. The official unemployment rate is around two per cent while expert suggest the unemployment is around nine per cent. If the migrants are included the unemployment rate is high around 25-30 per cent. Jha and Dang (2009) give distribution of poverty by household size suggests that household with 6 and more members has poverty rate 96.6 per cent and contribute to 74.9 per cent of poor population. Only one third of population has access to chlorinated tap water and around 29 per cent uses water from centralized source remaining population uses water from watercourses or irrigation ditches (UNDP 2013).

4.28 Poverty in Turkmenistan

The country has abundant reserves of natural gas. Despite its gas wealth, much of Turkmenistan's population is still impoverished. The situation has slightly improved from 2007 after ascendance of new president Berdymukhamedov. The country's economy has remained underdeveloped (BTI Turkmenistan 2012).

4.29 Poverty in Uzbekistan

During transition period around 1993-94 based on $ 4 Poverty line for per day per capita at purchasing power parity Uzbekistan has around Uzbekistan has 29 per cent population living below poverty line (UNDP 1997b). This has reduced marginally to 27.5 per cent in 2003. Uzbekistan has around 6.8 million people unable to meet basic consumption needs (World Bank 2007b). In Uzbekistan poverty is determined by location as rural urban, employment status, attainment of education are also important determinant. Rural population is 35 per cent more likely to be poor and 58 per cent more likely to be extremely poor (World Bank 2003). Approximately 4.5 million people or 70 per cent of Uzbekistan's poor live in rural areas. The lack of agricultural policies to generate higher incomes in rural areas has a significant impact on poverty reduction. In Uzbekistan there exist differences between different nationalities or ethnic groups and labour market outcomes which are unexplainable (World Bank 2003). In Uzbekistan Russians ethnic group has an advantage of wage premiums of around 23 and 17 per cent in Public and private sector that cannot be explained by differential educational attainment, sector of work and location of residence. For individuals of non-Russian and non-Uzbek nationalities, the outcomes are very different depending on whether they work in the public or private sector.

Uzbekistan counts absolute poverty line based on fixed basket food and non-food consumption goods. It is because in the context of wage arrears, income is inconsistent while consumption is more helpful while calculating poverty line. Probably the informal economy and underreporting of income could be significant reasons. The food poverty line is decided on the cost of consumption of 2100 calories per day per person (World Bank 2007b). Thus, the consumption basket is based on actual consumption patterns of the poor population and is converted into *soums* using the prices faced by the poorer population. The extreme poverty line was calculated, for the caloric intake of 1500 calories per person per day (World Bank 2007b). It is justified on the grounds that such a low caloric intake is not life threatening in the short run; it is not sustainable in the medium or long term.

Annexure - 1

Table 4A.1: Average MPCE (₹) and Proportions Spent on Food by Social Groups, 2004-05

Social Group	Rural India		Urban India	
	Average MPCE	Per Capita Spent on Food	Average MPCE	Per Capita Spent on Food
Scheduled Castes	475	57.3	758	48.0
Scheduled Tribes	426	58.9	857	46.6
Other Backward Classes	557	54.9	871	45.9
Others	685	53.0	1306	39.4
All Social Groups	559	55.1	1052	42.5

Source: NSS Report No. 514; Note: MPCE Based on URP

Table 4A.2: Average MPCE by Social Groups, 2007-8 (₹)

Social Group	Rural	Urban
Scheduled Castes	652	1100
Scheduled Tribes	617	1221
Other Backward Classes	765	1231
Others	964	1817
All Social Groups	772	1472

Source: Calculated from NSS Database, 64th Round Consumer Expenditure Survey. *Note*: MPCE based on MRP.

Table 4A.3: Ratio of Average MPCE for SCs, STs, OBCs as compared to 'Others', 2007–8

Social Group	Rural	Urban
Scheduled Castes	0.7	0.6
Scheduled Tribes	0.6	0.7
Other Backward Classes	0.8	0.7

Source: Calculated from, 64th Round Consumer Expenditure Survey.
Note: MPCE based on MRP. 'Others' refers to the upper-castes, otherwise also referred to Forward Castes.

Table 4A.4: Incidence of Poverty (URP) by Social Groups, 1993-94 and 2004-05 (percent)

	Rural			Urban		
Year	SC	ST	All	SC	ST	All
1993-94*	48.3	52.0	37.3	48.8	40.1	32.4
2004-05#	36.8	47.7	28.3	39.8	33.9	25.7

Source: *calculated from NSS Report, 50th Round; #11th Five Year Plan, Planning Commission, Government of India.

Table 4A.5: Proportions of Poverty among SCs/STs in India 1993-94 to 2004-05

Year	Rural				Urban			
	SC	ST	Others	All	SC	ST	Others	All
Sundaram and Tendulkar								
1993-94	45.7	48.8	28.3	34.2	42.9	33.6	23.4	26.4
1999-2000	38.4	48.0	23.2	28.9	37.8	35.2	20.0	23.1
Planning Commission								
1977-78	64.6	72.5	NA	53.1	54.3	52.6	NA	45.2
1983	53.1	58.4	NA	45.7	40.4	39.9	NA	40.8
1987-88	55.2	59.9	NA	39.1	NA	NA	NA	38.2
1993-94	48.1	51.9	NA	37.1	49.8	41.1	NA	32.4
1999-00	36.3	45.9	NA	27.1	38.5	34.8	NA	23.6
2004-05	36.8	47.3	-	28.3	39.9	33.3	-	25.7

Source: R.R Birdar, 2008. "Multiple Facts of Social Exclusion in Rural India: Emerging Evidence", South India Journal of Social Sciences II (2): 30.
Note: OBC figures are included in "Others" category.

Table 4A.6: Incidence of Poverty by Religious Community, (MRP) 2007- 08 (Per cent)

Religious Community	Rural	Urban
Hindus	14.3	13.0
Muslims	13.3	23.7

Source: Calculated from NSS Database, 64th Round Consumer Expenditure Survey.
Note: Poverty based on Mixed Recall Period.

Table 4A.7: Poor living in Central Asia-1993-1994
(Poverty line =$ PPP 120 per capita per month at 1990 prices)

Name of Country	Per cent of population in poverty	Total number of poor in million
Kazakhstan	50	8.5
Kyrgyzstan	84	3.8
Turkmenistan	47	2.2
Uzbekistan	43	10.0

Source: Falkingham 1999b (Based on Milanovic poverty line 1998)

Table 4A.8: Poverty and Income Index by Region in Kazakhstan (2008)

Region	Name of the state (Oblast)	Poverty Index	Income Index
Eastern Region	Eastern Kazakhstan	19.6	0.784
Western Region	Akmola	21.2	0.779
	Atyrau	17.1	0.754
	Mangistau	23.3	0.763
	Western Kazakhstan	17.5	0.754
Central Kazakhstan	Karaganda	21.4	0.799
North Kazakhstan	Aktyubinsk	16.9	0.792
	Kostanay	21.0	0.774
	Pavlorda	18.4	0.793
	North Kazakhstan	21.4	0.771
South Kazakhstan	Almaty	15.4	0.824
	Zhambyl	17.5	0.734
	Kyzylorda	19.36	0.719
	South Kazakhstan	16.0	0.725
Kazakhstan		17.8	0.778

Source: UNDP Kazakhstan (2009)

Table 4A.9: Areas of Poverty in Tajikistan in per cent
(based on US $ 2.15 per day)

	1999	2009
Total	83.0	39.6
Urban	73.0	30.3
Rural	84.0	43.3

Source: UNDP (2013)

Chapter 5

Rights and Entitlements

Section I: Situation in India

Every citizen of the country has basic rights to food, shelter, education, employment, asset ownership, basic health facilities, and basis infrastructure support. Indian society has historically been stratified into different social groups and there are certain groups (SCs and STs) which have primarily remained outside the mainstream of society. The analysis of social groups SCs, STs and OBCs and Muslims deserves special mention in the context of a country where they constitute nearly 85 per cent of the population. In fact, the largest religious minority group, the Muslims, comprises 12.9 per cent of the country's population (NSSO 64th Round). These sections of Indian society suffer from multiple deprivations, and hence fail to enjoy the benefits of development. In recent years many studies (Planning Commission 2011 and Government of India 2006) have highlighted the exclusion of Scheduled Castes, Scheduled Tribes and Muslims. The following section is an attempt to highlight the exclusion of social excluded groups.

This chapter focuses especially on the question of whether the social indicators of excluded groups are converging or diverging with the rest of the population. The analysis provides interesting insights on the following points.

- Are various socio-religious groups such as SCs, STs and Muslims excluded in the development process?
- Is the economic growth of the country inclusive?

Among different dimensions of deprivation, the specific issues such as employment opportunities, ownership of assets, nutritional status, health care, educational attainments, drinking water and sanitation are discussed. This chapter attempts to determine whether high enrolment growth rate has really percolated to the deprived sections of society in terms of higher employment opportunities and improvement in their material conditions.

5.1 Employment Situation

Employment enhances human ability. It ensures economic security and supports general participation in society. This dimension deals with the key issues of labour force and workforce participation rates, unemployment rates, wages and skills of the workforce.

Labour Force Participation Rate across Social Groups

Labour Force Participation Rate (LFPR) for both SCs and STs was higher than for All Groups. This is not surprising since they tend to be poorer, and hence must work in order to live. In fact, LFPR was higher for STs than for SCs, suggesting their more vulnerable status. In both rural and urban India, the LFPR declined in 2009–10 as compared to 1993–4 in the case of both SCs and STs (Table 5A.1).[23] It is probably happening because access to education in both rural and urban areas has been improving over this period. However, the more interesting fact is that the urban LFPR for All Groups, including SCs and STs, is much lower than for rural areas—which is probably again explained by the easier access to education in urban, in contrast to rural areas. High LFPR is marked among STs particularly in rural areas due to poor access to education. While comparing the figures of table 5A.1, it is quite evident, and the labour force participation is gradually declining among SCs and STs. This positively indicates, that they have options other than participating in labour activities at an early age.

5.1.1 LFPR across Religious Communities

Across religious communities, LFPR the poor access of Muslims to all levels of education, including higher education, has adversely affected employment opportunities for women. Clearly, the low level of participation in the labour market, and lower educational attainment are significant indicators of gender

---

[23]   In the 1993–4 survey, the social group, Other Backward Classes (OBCs), was not considered as a separate category and was included as part of the 'Other' social group. Only SCs and STs were considered along with all social groups.

discrimination in the course of a woman's life. Thus it can be inferred that rural Muslim participation in education and labour force are inversely correlated. The labour force participation rate remained almost unchanged between 1993–4 and 2004–5 in both rural and urban India but declined by 2009–10 (Table 5A.2). Further, as was observed in the case of social groups, here also, LFPR in rural India was higher than that in urban India.

Among Muslims, the literacy rate and attendance at higher levels of education was much lower in rural areas as compared to urban areas. The much lower LFPR for Muslims, as against all other religious communities, is explained not merely by lower levels of education prevailing among them, but also by the fact that Muslim women do not access schooling on the same scale as the other communities do.

5.1.2 Worker Population Ratio across Social Groups

Worker Population Ratio (WPR) among SCs/STs declined while their access to education improved slightly across social groups in both rural and urban India. There was a decline in WPR for both the STs and SCs in 2004–05. This was true across social groups in both rural and urban India. What is most remarkable is the fact that, as compared to the entire population ('All Groups'), the WPR is much higher for both SCs and STs, which is hardly surprising, since the latter are poorer and must work in order to survive.

Across social groups in both rural and urban India, WPR was the highest in the case of STs (Table 5A.3). There was a decline in WPR for both the STs and SCs in 2004–5. This was true across social groups in both rural and urban India. One reason for the decline in WPR for SCs and STs could well be the greater participation in education of young SCs and STs. In fact, there has been an improvement in the literacy rates among SCs and STs between 1999–2000 and 2007–8 in both rural and urban areas. The improvement in literacy rate was greater in rural areas as compared to urban areas. It was found WPR among SCs/STs declined while their access to education improved slightly.

5.1.3 WPR among Muslims

While comparing WPR between Hindus and Muslims, it was found to be lower in the case of Muslims (Table 5A.4). The Sachar Committee (Government of India 2006) pointed out that the lower workforce participation rate (WFPR) among Muslims was essentially due to the lower participation of women in economic activities. For the prime age group of 15–64 years (rural and urban together), rural WFPR for Muslim women was only 25 per cent, which was much lower than the WPR for Hindu women (70 per cent) (Government of India 2006). The Sachar Committee further noted that a higher dependency rate among Muslims due to a higher share of younger population was one of the reasons for lower WFPR among Muslim women.

5.1.4 Unemployment Rate across Social Groups

The unemployment rate across social groups was higher for SCs in rural India and STs in urban India (by current daily status). Between 1993–4 and 2004–5, the unemployment rate (by usual principal and subsidiary status) increased for SCs in both rural and urban India (Table 5A.5).

As per current daily status for the country as a whole, there was a decline in the unemployment rate between 2004–5 (8.3 per cent) and 2007–8 (8.1 per cent). However, rural and urban India showed opposite trends. While urban India experienced a decline in unemployment rate, rural India experienced a marginal increase (Table 5.1).

Table 5.1: Percentage of Social Groups Unemployment Rate (CDS)

Social Group	Rural			Urban		
	2004-05	2007-08	2009-10	2004-05	2007-08	2009-10
SCs	12.0	11.9	9.4	11.4	10.1	7.0
STs	6.5	7.5	6.3	7.5	10.0	7.8
OBCs	7.7	7.9	6.5	8.5	7.7	6.2
Others	6.6	6.4	5.3	7.1	6.0	4.6
All	8.2	8.4	6.8	8.3	7.4	5.8

Source: Calculated form NSS database, 61st and 64th round

Across social groups, the unemployment rate by current daily status was the highest for SCs in both rural (12 per cent) and urban (7 per cent) India. As against this, the unemployment rates for 'Others' in rural and urban India were 5.3 per cent and 4.6 per cent, respectively. Further, the unemployment rate for STs increased in both rural and urban India (Table 5.1). In fact, in urban India, the unemployment rate increased only for STs. However, for all other social groups it declined, thereby causing an overall decline in unemployment rate in urban India during this period.

Since urban areas are the heart of economic activities, unemployment rate is increasing for STs at the urban areas. This indicates that economic growth is not inclusive enough. At the policy level, capacity building of Tribals is needed.

5.1.5 Unemployment Rate among Religious Groups

In rural India, the unemployment rate (by usual principal and subsidiary status) increased for all major religious communities in 2004–5 as compared to 1993–4. In urban India, the unemployment rate increased only in the case of Muslims (before falling) while for all other religious communities there was a marginal decline (Table 5A.6). It is noticed that open unemployment rate is increasing for Muslims.

The unemployment rate according to the current daily status, a far more sensitive indicator of the state of the labour market in India than the usual principal status indicator, increased for the two largest religious communities (Hindus and Muslims) in rural India in 2007–8 as compared to 2004–5, before falling. In urban India, however, the decline in unemployment rate was observed even in the case of Hindus and Muslims (Table 5.2).

Table 5.2: Percentage Unemployment Rate of Religious Communities (CDS)

Religious Community	Rural			Urban		
	2004-05	2007-08	2009-10	2004-05	2007-08	2009-10
Hindus	8.0	8.3	6.8	8.1	7.3	7.0
Muslims	8.4	8.8	6.4	8.1	7.3	7.8

Source: Calculated from NSS database 61st and 64th Round Report

5.2. Asset Ownership

Assets are the most important indicators of a household's material well-being, particularly in rural areas. In addition to their productive potential, assets also have collateral value and can be sold in the market. Thus, ownership of assets also provides a certain degree of security against adverse economic shocks. In other words, assets act as a cushion against income vulnerability, and households can fall back on them in times of income shortfalls, either by selling them or by using them as collateral to obtain credit. Asset ownership is critical to both resilience and escaping poverty (Shepherd 2010).

Chittaranjan Senapati

5.2.1 Asset Ownership across Social Groups

In this section, the ownership of assets across social groups is analysed only for the 59[24] round of AIDIS[24] (2002–3)[25]. In the 48th round of AIDIS (1991–2), OBCs were clubbed together with 'Other' social groups and were not considered as a separate entity. Hence, comparison between the 48th and 59th rounds of AIDIS is not possible for all the social groups. In both rural and urban India, SC households were the most disadvantaged in terms of ownership of assets. The average value of assets owned by the SC households was the lowest, both in rural and urban India (Table 5A.7). The average value of assets was the highest for the 'Others' social group, with a value more than thrice that of SC households, in both rural and urban India. It marked lower value of Access Index for SCs and STs.

The lack of ownership of assets among SC and ST households was reflected in the values of their Access Indices. Among all the social groups in rural and urban India, the value of the Access Index[26] was the lowest for SCs households followed by ST households (Table 5.3).

Table 5.3: Distribution of Households and Assets, by Social Groups, 2002-3

Sector	Social Group	Households (%)	Assets Owned (%)	Access Index
Rural	Scheduled Castes	22.0	10.4	0.47
	Scheduled Tribes	10.2	5.2	0.51
	Other Backward Classes	41.0	41.1	1.00
	Others	26.7	43.1	1.60
Urban	Scheduled Castes	14.6	6.4	0.44
	Scheduled Tribes	2.9	1.7	0.57
	Other Backward Classes	34.7	27.8	0.80
	Others	47.7	64.1	1.34

Source: Planning Commission 2011

---

[24] AIDIS – All India Debt and Investment Survey

[25] According to AIDIS (All India Debt and Investment Survey), household assets represented everything that was owned by the household and had money value. Assets were broadly categorized as land, buildings, livestock, agricultural machinery and hand implements, non-farm business equipment, transport equipment, durable household goods, and financial assets (shares, dues receivable, deposits, and the like). Assets were valued at the current market prices in their existing conditions prevailing in the locality.

[26] Access Index = Per cent of assets owned *(divided by)* Per cent of households.

5.2.2 Assets Ownership across Religious Communities

In 2002-3, Hindus were by far the largest religious group in the country constituting 83.6 per cent of all households. Muslims came second (11 per cent of households). It was found that Muslims were the most disadvantaged among all (Table 5A.8).

When households were classified simultaneously into religious communities and social groups, it was observed that the value of the Access Index varied considerably across social groups within Hindus. Within Hindus, the value of Access Index was the lowest for ST households (0.43 (per cent) followed by SC households (0.45 per cent). The value of access indices for Hindus and Muslims was less than 1 i.e. 0.9 and 0.7 per cent respectively (Planning Commission 2011).

The relative deprivation of SCs, STs, and Muslims was evident in their ownership of assets as well. The Access Index of Asset Ownership[27] across social groups was the lowest for SCs, while across religious communities it was the lowest among Muslims in 2002-3 (Planning Commission 2011).

5.3. Right to Food and Nutrition

The right to food is a human right. The right to food is to ensure availability of food for all with human dignity. The present central government has guaranteed right to food for 75 per cent (50 per cent rural and 25 per cent urban) population. Addressing the problems of hunger, food insecurity, and malnutrition has far-reaching implications for enhancing individual capabilities. Despite so much economic growth, nearly half of India's children under three years of age are malnourished (Planning Commission 2011). As per the World Bank's estimates, approximately 60 million children are underweight in India (World Bank 2005). Given its impact on health, education and productivity, persistent under nutrition is a major obstacle to human development and economic growth in the country, especially among the poor and the vulnerable, where the prevalence of malnutrition is highest.

In some states, the status of hunger and malnutrition is troublesome. In 12 of 17 major states the condition is 'alarming' (IFPRI 2010). A higher percentage of rural

---

[27] Access Index of Asset Ownership is defined as the share of assets owned by the community divided by the community's share of population.

children suffered from malnutrition as compared to those residing in urban areas. A primary reason for the high incidence of malnutrition amongst the rural poor is lower food intake; a majority of the socially marginalised (SC and ST) groups live in rural areas.

The findings of the Nutrition Report (2009) of the National Family and Health Survey 3 with respect to social groups are as under:

- SCs and STs have a higher percentage of women with BMI<18.5[28]
- SCs and STs are diverging from the national average in terms of female malnutrition
- Among the industrial states, Gujarat has a very high incidence of malnutrition among SC and ST women;
- More than 50 per cent of ST children are underweight and stunted;
- More than 75 per cent of ST children have anaemia; and
- There is an increasing trend of anaemia among women for all caste groups.

The NFHS reports 2 (1998-99) and 3 (2005-6) reveal that the percentage of women with BMI less than 18.5 is acute among STs (46.0 per cent and 46.6. per cent respectively) followed by SCs 42.1 per cent and 41.2 per cent respectively) and OBCs (35.8 per cent and 35.7 per cent respectively). The data confirms, malnutrition has not decreased much in between the two time periods.

According to NFHS 3 report, female malnutrition among the SCs and STs is higher than the national average; it is worse amongst both these groups in the low per capita income states (Bihar and Orissa). Further, female malnutrition among SCs and STs has been steadily increasing. The maximum underweight and stunted children are recorded for STs (54.5 per cent and 53.9 per cent respectively) followed by SCs (47.9 per cent and 53.9 per cent respectively). Children belonging to STs had the highest percentage suffering from anaemia in 2005–6, followed by SCs.

The incidence of female malnutrition and children suffering from anaemia and stunting is above the national average among Muslims. Next, while female

---

[28]   BMI (Body Mass Index) is defined as weight in kilograms divided by height in metres squared and reflects the nutritional status of adults. A cut-off point of 18.5 is used to define thinness or under nutrition. The percentage of persons with BMI below 18.5 kg/m² indicates the severity of malnutrition among adults.

malnutrition has been reducing over time, it is increasing for Muslims (data between 1998–9 and 2005–6). The percentage of women suffering from anaemia, has increased in all communities, including Muslims, in this period. Women malnutrition among Muslim community is 34.1 per cent (NFHS 2) and 35.2 per cent (NFHS 3). Their situation is better than their Hindu counterparts. Inclusive growth, which has been a goal of the Twelfth Five Year Plan (2012–17), is unachievable without hunger and malnutrition declining significantly.

5.3.1 Child Malnutrition

Highest percentage of underweight and stunted children is recorded among the STs. Across social groups, the highest percentage of underweight and stunted children were recorded among STs at more than 50 per cent. Among SCs and OBCs the percentage is closer to the national average, though the percentage of underweight and stunted SC children is more than that of OBCs. It can be seen that the general category has the lowest percentage of children in all the three anthropometric indicators). This suggests that socially marginalized groups are in a disadvantageous position, and this is a hindrance to India's inclusive growth strategy (Table 5.4).

Table 5.4: Children with Anthropometric Indicators by Social Groups, 2005-6 (per cent)

Anthropometric Indicators	SC	ST	OBCs	Others
Underweight (Weight for age)	47.9	54.5	43.2	33.7
Stunning (Height for age)	53.9	53.9	48.8	40.7
Wasting (Weight for age)	21	27.6	20	16.3

Source: NFHS 3

Unlike other indicators, the share of underweight and wasted children is higher among Hindus. Hindus recorded the highest percentage of chronically underweight children followed by Muslims, and both of them are close to the national average (Table 5A.9).

5.3.2 Anaemia Cases

Iron deficiency anaemia (IDA) is the most widespread micronutrient deficiency in the world, and is associated with increased infections, reduction in work capacity and poor concentration. In India, anaemia is rampant among women in the reproductive age group, children, and low socio-economic strata of the population. IDA reduces the capacity to learn and work, resulting in lower productivity and loss of wages, thereby limiting economic and social development. Anaemia in pregnant women leads to adverse pregnancy outcomes such as high maternal and neonatal mortality, low birth weight, increased risk of obstetric complications, and increased morbidity; it also seriously impairs the physical and mental development of the child. Anaemia remains one of the major indirect causes of maternal mortality in India (Planning Commission 2008).

5.3.3 Anaemia among Social Groups

Anaemia among women has increased for all caste groups over the years. While ST women are the worst off with regard to anaemia, the percentage of women suffering from anaemia increased for all caste groups during the period 1998–9 to 2005–6. Across caste groups, the highest percentage of anaemic women is amongst STs in NFHS 2 and 3 reports. It is closer to the national average for SCs and OBCs in 2005–6. It is found that, the percentage of women with anaemia has increased for SCs and STs. Both the NFH surveys reveal that anaemia among ST women is highest (64.9 per cent and 68.5 per cent respectively) followed by SC (56.0 per cent and 58.3 per cent respectively) and OBCs (50.7 per cent and 54.4 per cent respectively).

5.3.4 Anaemia among Religious Communities

No difference has been found between Hindus and Muslims with respect to anaemia among women across all religious communities. However, there is an increase in the incidence of women suffering from anaemia between 1998–9 and 2005–6. The increase was observed to be the highest for Muslim women with about six percentage points. The prevalence of anaemia among Hindus and Muslims is closer to the overall national average. The figure for Hindu women was greater than Muslim women in 1998–9; however, the trend was reversed in 2005–6. According to NFHS 2 and 3 reports, anaemia among Muslims is 49.6 per cent and 54.7 per cent respectively. Their situation is marginally better than their Hindu counterparts (52.4 per cent and 55.9 per cent respectively). Economic prosperity alone cannot address the problem of malnutrition among women since they have been historically discriminated against.

Among major religious communities it has been observed that there is no difference between Hindus and Muslims in terms of women's malnutrition. Hindus recorded the highest percentage of underweight and stunted children. Further, there is no difference between anaemia among Hindu and Muslim women.

5.3.5 Anaemia among Children

The prevalence of anaemia was a serious problem among SC and ST children. STs had the highest percentage (77 per cent) of children suffering from anaemia in 2005–6, followed by SCs (72 per cent). Children in the OBC had a prevalence rate similar to the national average of 70 per cent. Further, it has been observed that amongst SCs and STs a very high percentage of children suffering from anaemia belong to the states with low per capita incomes. The states with a high concentration of Muslims in the population have a higher percentage of children suffering from anaemia. Both Hindus (69.8 per cent) and Muslims (69.7 per cent) have same level of anaemia among children.

The prevalence of anaemia is very high among adolescent girls and severe anaemia among pre-school children. Educational or economic status does not seem to make much difference. This may be due to the cultural and historical gender discrimination against girls.

5.4 Health and Demography

Health is regarded as a vital component in the growth and development of any country. There are mainly three forms of inequities that persist in India's health sector (Baru *et al.*2010). Historical inequalities are rooted in the policies and practices of pre-independence India. Socio-economic inequities and inequities pertaining to availability, utilization, and affordability of healthcare are rampant in India. Of these, the latter two pose serious issues. The situation is worse in the case of the poor, particularly those belonging to SC and ST communities and living in the less developed states, because they are prone to multiple deprivations. Improving health outcomes is crucial to pro-poor growth.

The mother's health status affects not just the child's nutritional status but also the child's survival prospects. Thus, indicators like IMR, U5MR, and life expectancy at birth are also linked to the mother's health status. In India, neonatal mortality (death within 28 days of birth) accounts for 60 per cent of infant mortality, partly due to delivery without medical supervision.

5.4.1 Child Mortality

Infant Mortality Rate refers to the number of deaths in the first year of life per 1000 live births. It reflects the probability of a child dying before attaining age one year due to poor health of either the child or mother, or poor healthcare.

Across social groups, SCs (83.0 per cent in 1998-99 and 66.4 per cent in 2005-06) have high incidence of IMR followed by STs (84.2 per cent in 1998-99 and 62.1 per cent in 2005-06) and OBCs (76.0 per cent in 1998 -99 and 56.6 per cent in 2005-06).

IMR among Muslims is less than that among SCs and STs. There is a decline in the all India average for 2005–06 over 1998–99 for almost all major religious communities. Hindus have the highest IMR at both points of time (77.1 per cent in 1998–99 and 58.8 per cent in 2005–06); followed by Muslims (58.8 in 1998-99 and 52.4 in 2005-06). The data also suggests that IMR for Hindus shows the highest decline; Muslims have shown marginal improvements (58.8 per cent in 1998-99 and 52.4 in 2005-06).

5.4.2 Under five Mortality Rate

Under Five Mortality Rate (U5MR) indicates the level of child health. U5MR refers to the probability of children born in a specific period dying before reaching the age of five years and is expressed as number of deaths per 1,000 live births.

The U5MR was higher than the national average for these social groups in 2005–6 and was the highest for the STs (95.7). It declined for the three social groups (SCs, STs and OBCs) during the period 1998 to 2006 by over 30 per thousand during two NFH survey periods. Despite huge improvement, U5MR among SCs (88.1 per cent), STs (95.7 per cent) and OBCs (72.8 per cent) are greater than Muslims (70.0 per cent), NFHS 3 revealed.

The U5MR declined for both Hindus and Muslims in 2005–6 compared to 1998–9. Hindus performed the worst among the major religious communities. For Muslims U5MR fell from 83 in 1998–9 to 70 in 2005–6. In the case of both IMR and in U5MR the gap between Hindus and Muslims is decreasing. This seems to be due to the slower improvement among the Muslim population and a faster improvement among the Hindu population, as was also evident in the discussion on IMR. U5MR is highest for Hindus but Hindu–Muslim gap is decreasing.

5.4.3 Total Fertility Rate (TFR)

The TFR is defined as the number of live births a woman would expect to deliver if she were to live through her reproductive years (age 15–49 years) and to bear children at each age in accordance with the prevailing age specific fertility rates. On the TFR indicator, there is some good news. There has been an appreciable decline in the total fertility rate over the decade in major states reaching the replacement level of 2.1. However, while SCs and Muslims are converging with the national average, STs are seen to be diverging with respect to TFR.

All the major social groups have TFRs above the replacement level, the highest being for STs at 3.12. Between NFH 2 and 3 surveys there was a fall in TFR for all groups except for the STs. The OBCs had a lower fertility rate in comparison to SCs and STs in both the periods -. The average TFR in India is 2.6 and the TFR of the poorest groups (STs, SCs, and Muslims) is higher. However, for SCs and Muslims it is converging towards the national average over time. TFR among SCs and Muslims is approaching the national average. In the year 2005-6, TFR is 2.92 per cent, 3.12 per cent and 3.09 per cent for SC, ST and Muslims respectively (NFHS 3).

ST women have the highest TFR among all social and religious groups. High TFR is essentially the outcome of poverty and lack of education/awareness about contraception. The poor consider every child to be a source of income. Thus, STs and Muslims have high TFRs not because of their socio-religious status but due their to economic condition.

While on religious groups, the highest fertility rate was observed among Muslims at 3.09 per cent with an accompanying high population growth rate of 2.9 per cent per annum, again the highest among the religious communities. This is due to the relatively high proportion of Muslim women in the reproductive age group, and also their lower use of contraception compared to other religious communities. Between 1998–9 and 2005–6 there was a decline in TFR for all major religious communities, the maximum fall being found among Muslims. Hindus also have fertility rates above the replacement level (NFHS 2 and 3).

5.4.4 Sex-Ratio

The sex-ratio is indicative of the composition of the population. It is defined as the number of females per 1,000 males. What is striking is that India has had a female deficit for a long period of time. Gender discrimination, as indicated in an adverse sex ratio, is serious and more marked in the case of non-SC/ST and Hindu households, compared to Muslims, SCs and STs.

5.4.5 Sex Ratio among Social Groups

The SCs and STs have higher sex ratio than non-SC/ST households. Muslims have higher sex-ratio compared to Hindus. Interestingly, ST households have a sex-ratio at birth above the national average of 933. Not only this, STs have a greater sex-ratio than SCs as well as non-SC/ST households, in both rural and urban India. The sex-ratio is the lowest for non-SC/ST households, at well below the national average (Table 5.5).

Table 5.5: Sex Ratio at Birth by Social and Religious Groups

Place of Residence	SC	STs	Non-SC/ST	Hindus	Muslims
Rural	921	940	896	903	930
Urban	917	934	901	897	934
Combined	920	940	897	901	931

Source: Calculated from Census of India (2001)

5.4.6 Reproductive Child Health

The performance of the health outcome indicators like child mortality (IMR, U5MR), maternal mortality (MMR), and death rate crucially depends on the efficiency of the RCH programme. The place of delivery is crucial in determining the maternal health status and is a good indicator for assessing the demand for the public health system.

Among the social groups, a significant proportion of deliveries took place at home during both the time periods. This reflects their backward status. In the case of STs, the percentage was as high as 82 in 2005–6. Moreover, there was no change in this proportion over time. The reason is that most of the STs live in rural areas. The OBCs were relatively better placed (Table 5.6).

Table 5.6: Percentage Distribution of Live Births by Social Groups

Place of Delivery	SC		ST		OBCs		Others	
	1998-99	2005-06	1998-99	2005-06	1998-99	2005-06	1998-99	2005-06
Institutional	26.8	33	17.1	17.7	36.1	37.8	40.1	52.6
Home	72.1	66.8	81.8	82	62.8	61.9	59	47.3

Source: NFHS 3

Across religious communities, there were significant inter-religious disparities in the place of delivery. In 2005–6, only a third of the deliveries among Muslims were institutional it was below the national average of 39 per cent. Hindus performed slightly better. To sum up, one-third of Muslim and Scheduled Caste women had institutional deliveries, while Scheduled Tribes even fewer (Table 5A.10).

A major factor determining the occurrence of institutional deliveries is education. It can be seen that as the number of years of education increases, more and more women choose institutional deliveries. This is because educated women are aware of the importance of hygiene during delivery, quality postnatal care, and maternal and child care.

5.4.7 Prevalence of Contraception

Family planning and reduced family size are important processes in shaping the health outcomes of a household. Spacing of children helps improve the health status of the mother and the child, which has positive implications for improving life expectancy. In addition, a smaller family size also improves the chances of a poor family being able to afford food, nutrition, and education for all the children.

The prevalence of contraception increased among all social groups over time. Except for STs, the prevalence of contraception was above 50 per cent in 2005–6 (Table 5A.11). However, despite improvements, SCs and OBCs are at the level that 'Others' were in 1998–9. The prevalence of contraception increases with a rise in the household wealth status. This is to say that with a better standard of living, people are more aware of the benefits of contraception and thus the usage. CPR (Contraception Prevalence Rates) among SCs, STs, and Muslims are converging with the all India average, and it is at the highest pace for SCs.

The prevalence of contraception increased for all major religious communities in 2005-6 as compared to 1998-9. Muslims had the lowest CPR in 1998-9 However, during this period there was a commendable increase in CPR among Muslims, in fact, it was the highest percentage improvement for any religious community. It is this increase in the CPR which has led to a fall in the TFR among Muslims. However, the CPR among Muslim households in 2005-6 was still below that for ST households (Table 5A.11). Overall, the maximum fall in TFR was observed among Muslims along with a sharp rise in CPR.

5.4.8 Antenatal Care (ANC)

Women in India suffer when they do not avail healthcare services during pregnancy. In 2005–6, while more than 70 per cent had at least one ANC visit, the proportion of pregnant women who had three or more antenatal visits was much lower (Planning Commission 2011).

Among SCs, STs, and OBCs the percentage of women who had at least one ANC visit or three or more ANC visits was below the national average. The OBC women, however, were relatively better placed than SC and ST women. The ST women suffer the most on this account and this can partly be attributed to the fact that they are concentrated in rural areas (Table 5A.12). It is reported not even 50 per cent Muslim, SC and ST women receive three or more ANC visits.

In 2005–6, among the religious communities, Muslims had the lowest percentage of pregnant women receiving ANC services. More specifically, less than half of the Muslim women received three or more ANC visits (Table 5A.12).

5.4.9 Immunisation

To assess the percentage of children receiving vaccination, the section has focused primarily on the best case and the worst case scenarios. The percentage of children receiving all vaccinations reflects the best-case scenario, and the percentage of children receiving no vaccinations the worst case scenario.[29]

The percentage of children receiving all vaccinations increased for STs in 2005–6 as compared to 1998–9, but decreased in the case of SC and OBC children. The percentage of children receiving no vaccinations declined for all social groups in 2005–6 compared with 1998–9 (NFHS 2 and 3). In the year 2005-6, SC, ST and OBC children receiving all vaccinations were 39.7 per cent, 31.3 per cent and 40.7 per cent respectively (NFHS 3). A lower percentage of SC children received no vaccination compared to ST and Muslim children.

Between 1998–9 and 2005–6 all major religious communities experienced a fall in the percentage of children receiving no vaccination. The fall was steep amongst Muslims. In the year 2005-06, Hindus receiving no vaccination were merely 4.3 per cent, while the same was 7.6 per cent for Muslim children (NFHS 3).

5.5 Sanitation Facilities

Sanitation coverage, which ought to be a way of life to safeguard health, is inadequate in India. Access to sanitation facilities is still a challenge—almost 50 per cent of households have no toilets. Furthermore, the practice of Open Defection (OD) in India remains a major challenge for achieving the MDGs.

The proportion of households without toilets is much above the national average of 49 per cent for SCs, STs, and OBCs. However, OBC households are relatively better placed compared to SCs and STs around 54 per cent of OBC households are without toilet facilities as against 69 per cent ST households and 65 per cent SC households.

Across social groups, there has been an increase in the proportion of households with improved sanitation facilities that is, septic tanks/flush toilets and pit toilets, during the period 2002 (NSS 58th round) to 2008–9 (NSS 65th round). In 2008–9, OBC households had the highest proportion of households with access to improved sanitation at 43.2 per cent. ST households were the worst off with only 28 per cent households in urban areas using improved sanitation facilities. The situation was worse in the case of their rural counterparts, with only 22 per cent of rural ST

---

[29]   All vaccinations include BCG, measles, and three doses each of DPT and polio vaccine (excluding polio vaccine given at birth)

households having access to improved sanitation facilities. Not even one-fourth of rural ST households had access to improved sanitation facilities. Septic tanks and pit latrines have together been classified as improved sanitation by the NSS (2008–9).

Among major religious communities, Hindus were the worst off as 50 per cent of households lacked toilet facilities, compared to 36 per cent for Muslims (Table 5.7). The relatively higher access to toilet facilities among Muslims is probably explained by the fact that a higher proportion of Muslims (than Hindus) live in urban areas. One-third Muslim households and around two-thirds of SC and ST households lack toilets.

Table 5.7: Distribution of Households by Type of Toilet Facility by Social and Religious Groups

Social and Religious Groups	Pit		Septic Tank/Flush		No Latrine	
	2002	2008-9	2002	2008-09	2002	2008-09
Scheduled Castes	0.3	10.2	2.7	22.4	74.9	65.0
Scheduled Tribes	0.3	11.0	1.5	16.5	78.0	69.1
Other Backward Classes	0.2	10.3	2.3	32.9	65.9	54.2
Others	0.4	16.6	4.1	53.2	38.8	26.2
Hindus	NA	10.3	NA	34.7	NA	52.5
Muslims	NA	21.9	NA	35.4	NA	35.8

Source: NSS 58th and 65th rounds

5.5.1 Drinking Water

Safe drinking water is essential for healthy living. Taps and tube-wells were the two major sources of drinking water. In addition to these, protected wells and harvested rainwater are considered to be improved sources of drinking water.

Over time, all social groups have experienced a rise in the proportion of households using taps and tube wells/hand pumps with a corresponding fall in the proportion using wells, which are not considered to be safe sources of drinking water. Across social groups, OBCs have a greater proportion of households using taps compared to SCs and STs who used tube wells/hand pumps as major sources of drinking water (Table 5.8).

While on religious communities, 36 per cent Muslims households are dependent on tap water. Over half the Muslim households are dependent on tube wells/hand pumps. On their part, nearly 44 per cent Hindu households are dependent on tap water.

Table 5.8: Distribution of Households by Sources of Drinking Water by Social and Religious Groups.

Social and Religious Groups	Tap		Tube Well/ Hand Pump		Well	
	2002	2008-9	2002	2008-09	2002	2008-09
Scheduled Castes	35.4	38.4	49.9	51.4	12.9	7.1
Scheduled Tribes	20.9	24.0	47.7	52.2	23.8	17.9
Other Backward Classes	39.4	43.3	42.1	42.5	16.1	10.5
Others	49.6	51.6	36.9	37.7	10.8	6.4
Hindus	NA	43.7	NA	43.6	NA	8.9
Muslims	NA	35.8	NA	51.8	NA	9.2

Source: NSS 58th and 65th rounds

5.6. Right to Education

Education has a positive impact on all types of human development outcomes. The economic motive is not the only reason why education is vital for the individual's well-being. Education is important in other ways as well—such as improving self esteem, enhancing social status, and gaining confidence. Among all the parameters of educational attainment, literacy is the most fundamental one as it paves the way for further learning and training in the formal sector.

5.6.1 Literacy

Literacy adds value to a person's life and plays a crucial role in his/her overall development. It also adds tremendous value to society at the macro level. There is a strong correlation between lack of literacy and poverty, both in the economic sense and in the broader sense of deprivation of capabilities (UNESCO 2006).

In recent years, the overall literacy rate in India has increased to 74 per cent in 2011 (Census 2011). The female literacy rate has improved considerably by 50 per cent from 224 million in 2001 to 334 million in 2011. Overall, female literacy rate in India was 65 per cent and male literacy rate was 82 per cent in the year 2011.

5.6.2 Literacy across Social Groups

Across social groups, STs had the lowest literacy rate in rural India, while SCs had the lowest literacy rate in urban India in 2007–8. Compared to rural India, the status of literacy in urban India was much better across all social groups, and also across genders within any particular social group. The rural–urban gap was much greater in female literacy than that in male literacy (Table 5.9). More than half of the SC and ST females in rural India were Illiterate.

Table 5.9: Percentage of Literacy Rate by Social-Religious Groups (Rural)

Social and Religious Groups	Males		Females		Persons	
	1999-2000	2007-08	1999-2000	2007-08	1999-2000	2007-08
Scheduled Castes	58.8	70.6	33.6	49.9	46.6	60.5
Scheduled Tribes	53.8	69.3	30.1	47.8	42.2	58.8
OBCs	67.8	77.7	41.1	55.4	54.8	66.7
Others	78.1	84.6	56.7	68.8	67.7	76.9
All Social Groups	*67.8*	*77.0*	*43.4*	*56.7*	*56.0*	*67.0*
Hindus	68.2	77.4	42.5	56.2	55.7	67.0
Muslims	61.4	71.7	42.1	55.0	52.1	63.5

Source: Calculated from NSS 55th and 64th Round, *Note*: For population 7 years and above.

5.6.3 Literacy across Religious Communities: Across religious communities the literacy rate was the lowest among Muslims, both in rural and urban India in 2007–8. In rural India only 55 per cent of Muslim females were literate (Table 5.10). The female–male differentials in literacy were the greatest for Hindus and Muslims. All leaders, especially religious leaders among Hindus and Muslims, can perhaps play a greater role in exhorting their communities to acquire basic literacy and numeracy skills. Despite improvement Muslims have the lowest literacy rate

Table 5.10: Literacy Rate by Social and Religious Groups (Urban) in Percentage

Social and Religious Groups	Males		Females		Persons	
	1999-2000	2007-08	1999-2000	2007-08	1999-2000	2007-08
Scheduled Castes	76.0	83.1	55.7	66.1	66.2	74.9

Scheduled Tribes	78.1	86.0	61.2	69.0	70.0	78.0
OBCs	83.5	88.3	66.4	74.6	75.3	81.7
Others	91.4	93.8	81.0	85.5	86.5	89.9
All Social Groups	*86.5*	*89.9*	*72.3*	*78.0*	*79.8*	*94.3*
Hindus	88.0	91.6	73.4	79.3	81.1	85.8
Muslims	76.7	80.9	62.2	68,8	69.8	75.1

Source: NSS 55th Round, Report No. 473 (1999–2000) and NSS 64th Round (for 2007–8).
Note: For population 7 years and above.

Over the years the literacy rates for SCs, STs, and Muslims are approaching the national average. As compared to 1999–2000, there has been an improvement in the ratio of literacy rates for SCs, STs, and Muslims with respect to the national average in both rural and urban India (Table 5A.13). This convergence was most pronounced among STs in rural India. Among SCs, STs and Muslims, the three most capability-deprived groups in India, SCs are doing slightly better than STs, but are worse off than Muslims, in terms of literacy.

5.6.4 Gross Enrolment Ratio

Between 2004–5 and 2007–8, GER improved at all levels of education. However, it was observed that GER subsequently declined at higher levels of education, from primary to upper primary to secondary/higher secondary (Table 5.11). This was true for SCs and STs as well. For the country as a whole, GER declined from 114.6 per cent at the primary level to 45.5 per cent at the secondary/higher secondary level in 2007–8.

Table 5.11: Gross Enrolment Ratio
for School Education by Social Groups

Social Groups	Primary		Upper Primary		Secondary /Higher Secondary	
	2004-5	2007-8	2004-5	2007-8	2004-5	2007-8
Scheduled Castes	115.3	124.9	70.2	76.3	34.7	39.0
Scheduled Tribes	121.9	129.3	67.0	74.4	27.7	30.8
All Social Groups	107.8	114.6	69.9	77.5	39.9	45.5

Source: Annual Reports, Ministry of Human Resource Development, Government of India.

5.6.5 Net Enrolment Ratio

Despite attaining internationally comparable levels of gender parity index (GPI), enrolment among girls belonging to Muslims and OBCs remains a major concern. For the country as a whole, the enrolment of girls belonging to Muslim and OBC communities at the primary and upper primary levels is less than 50 per cent (Table 5A.14). Considerable improvement of NER is reported at the primary level.

5.6.6 Net Attendance Ratio (NAR)

As per the NSS, 'current attendance' refers to whether a person is currently attending any educational institution or not. Enrolment is necessary for attending any educational institution, while the reverse is not true. It means, though enrolled but not attending the institution currently. Information on attendance captures the true educational opportunity of students better than information on enrolment. Accordingly, the net attendance ratio (NAR) is considered to be a measure of current attendance status.[30] A sharp decline of NAR is reported at upper-primary level despite narrowing the gender gap.

5.6.7 NAR across Social Groups

According to NSSO, NAR is defined as the ratio of number of persons in the official age group attending a particular standard of education to the total number of persons in that age group. Among the social groups, NAR is lower for SCs and STs at both primary and upper primary levels. There is a decline in NAR at the upper primary level as compared to the primary level, and this is observed for all social groups in both rural and urban India. The decline is much sharper in rural India as compared to urban India, particularly for rural females, for whom NAR has come down from 80 per cent at the primary level to 58 per cent at the upper primary level (Table 5A.15). A sharp decline in NAR for rural females from primary level to upper primary level is quite evident.

---

[30] As per NSSO, net attendance ratio is defined as the ratio of the number of persons in the official age group attending a particular standard of education to the total number of persons in the age group.

NAR was lower among SCs and STs as compared to other social groups in the case of secondary and higher secondary education as well. In rural India, across social groups, NAR was the lowest for STs, at both secondary and higher secondary levels *(Tables 5A.17 and 5A.18)*. In urban India, NAR for SCs was the lowest among social groups.

Overall, for all social groups, NAR was biased against females at all levels of education. This gender disparity was much more pronounced in rural areas. Further, NAR for SCs and STs was lower than other social groups, and the disparity across social groups intensified at higher levels of education. In other words, the declining trend in NAR at higher levels of education was sharper in the case of SCs and STs.

5.6.8 NAR across Religious Communities

Among all religious communities, Muslims had the lowest NAR at all levels of education, in both rural and urban India (Table 5A.15, 5A.16, 5A.17, 5A.18). In fact, in rural India, low NAR among STs was comparable with that of the Muslims at the secondary and higher secondary levels. In urban India, NAR for Muslims was even lower than that for SCs and STs at all levels except at the higher secondary level, where they were similar.

In the case of Muslims, the sharpest decline in NAR was observed from the primary level to the upper primary level in rural areas. The decline was as high as 30 percentage points for both males and females in rural India. In urban India, this decline was in the range of 20–25 percentage points. This sharp decline at the upper primary level was, in fact, the starting point of the disparity in the NAR between Muslims and other religious communities.

5.6.9 Out of School Children

One of the important drawbacks of the school education system is the existence of a very large number of out of school children in the country.[31] If we consider the age group 6–17 years, close to one-fifth of the children have either never

---

[31] The estimate of out of school children is derived from the survey on 'Participation and Expenditure in Education' (NSS 64th Round). It is derived by adding up the number of children who have never attended an educational institution and the number of children who have attended an educational institution in the past but are currently not attending.

attended school or attended school in the past but are currently not attending.[32] In simple terms, these children can be considered to be out of school. Though the proportion of out of school children has come down from 29 per cent in 1999–2000 to one-fifth in 2007–8, it poses a serious challenge to the success of SSA, which has universalization of elementary education as an important objective. One-fifth of the children in the age group 6–17 years are out of school.

Across social groups, the incidence of out of school children was the highest among STs especially among females (Table 5.12). Across religious communities, the problem of out of school children was most pronounced among Muslims (Table 5.13). Remarkably, the proportion of out of school children among Muslims was much higher in 2007–8 than SC, ST or OBC children—for girls as well as boys. Unless this grim situation is corrected very quickly, the prospects for greater upward mobility of Muslims remain bleak. It is already noted that the incidence of poverty among Muslims was one-third, which was much higher than for India as a whole (about 26 per cent). A critical explanatory factor is the high proportion of Muslim children who are out of school.

Table 5.12: Out of School Children by Social and Religious (6 to 17 years), 2007–8 (%)

Social Groups	Males	Females	Persons
Scheduled Castes	21.0	25.0	22.8
Scheduled Tribes	21.7	28.4	24.8
Other Backward Classes	16.6	22.2	19.2
Others	12.7	16.3	14.3
All Social Groups	16.9	21.8	19.2
Religious Community			
Hindus	15.5	20.2	17.7
Muslims	26.4	31.5	28.8

Source: Calculated from NSS database 64th round

Across religious communities, it has already been pointed out that Muslims have the highest proportion of out of school children in the country. One-third of

---

[32]   In the calculation of NAR, the NSS 64th Round considered six years of age to correspond to grade one, and 17 years of age to correspond to grade 12.

Muslim females in the age group 6–17 years are identified as out of school children (Table 5.13) who suggest that even the next generation of young Muslim women will remain severely deprived educationally? Policymakers in these states urgently need to address this situation.

Among the various reasons for discontinuation or dropping out, the three most important reasons identified in the survey (NSS 64th Round) are lack of interest by parents, lack of interest by children, and financial constraints. These three factors together accounted for half of the cases of dropouts across all social groups and also among Hindus and Muslims in the case of religious communities (Table 5.13). By and large, financial constraint was the most important factor for discontinuation/dropping out for all other social groups and religious communities.

Table 5.13: Major Reasons for Discontinuation/Drop Out 2007-8 (per cent)

Social and Religious Groups	Parents not Interested in Studies	Financial Constraints	Child not interested in Studies
Scheduled Castes	21.0	25.0	22.8
Scheduled Tribes	21.7	28.4	24.8
OBCs	16.6	22.2	19.2
Others	12.7	16.3	14.3
All Social Groups	*16.9*	*21.8*	*19.2*
Hindus	15.5	20.2	17.7
Muslims	26.4	31.5	28.8

Source: Calculated from NSS database 64th round

5.6.10 Mean Years of Schooling[33]

It has already been pointed out that in India close to one-fifth of the children in the age group 6-17 years were out of school in 2007–8. The incidence of out of school children was particularly high among STs, SCs, and Muslims. The high incidence of poverty, malnutrition, and lack of effective childhood care have

---

[33] Mean years of schooling is derived from information on educational levels collected by NSSO through the employment and unemployment survey (1999–2000) and expenditure on education survey (for the year 2007–8). 'Educational level' here refers to the highest level successfully completed. So, for instance, if the educational level for an individual was reported to be primary, it was assumed that the individual had completed five years of schooling.

all resulted in high dropout rates. Hence, the average years of schooling for the population have remained very low.

Across social groups, SCs and STs had lower mean years of schooling in both rural and urban India. Among major religious communities, Muslims had the lowest value for mean years of schooling in both rural and urban India (Table 5.14). This was not at all surprising given the fact that SCs, STs, and Muslims lagged behind the rest of the population in terms of several socio-economic indicators.

Table 5.14: Mean Years of Schooling by Social and Religious Groups 2007-8

Social and Religious Group	Rural	Urban	Combined	Ratio of Mean Years of Schooling[34]
Scheduled Castes	2.9	4.6	3.2	0.76
Scheduled Tribes	2.6	5.2	2.8	0.67
Other Backward Classes	3.5	5.6	3.9	0.92
Others	4.6	7.3	5.7	1.35
All Social Groups	*3.5*	*6.2*	*4.2*	*N. A.*
Hindus	3.6	6.5	4.3	1.02
Muslims	2.8	4.3	3.3	0.78

Source: Calculated from NSS 55th and 64th Rounds
Note: For population in the age group of 7 years and above, N. A. Not Applicable

5.7 Representation of School Teachers by Social Groups

Not only was the proportion of male teachers higher than that of female teachers, the highest proportion of teachers belonged to the 'Others' social group (44.6 per cent). At the all India level, the proportion of teachers belonging to SC, ST, and OBC social groups were 12, 9, and 33 per cent, respectively. The proportion of teachers belonging to SCs and OBCs was lower than their share in the total population. It may be recalled that the share of SCs in the total population was 20 per cent and that of OBCs was 42.3 per cent (NSS 64th Round). In other words, it appears from the available data that these social groups are under-represented among the teachers of the country. However, in case of the STs, the share of teachers is not very different from the share of STs (8.6 per cent) in the total

---

[34] Ratio Calculation: Combined figures of all social groups divided by figure of particular social group. Same rule is applied for religious community.

population. Under-representation of SC teachers adversely affected participation of SC students in the education system.

Due to their poor economic condition, SC/ST students mostly attended government schools where the teachers are mostly from higher castes. The under-representation of teachers belonging to SCs and STs, created a social distance between teachers and students. The Public Report on Basic Education (PROBE), 1999 survey noted that the social distance was one of the reasons why many teachers had limited commitment towards the educational advancement of their students.

5.7.1 Out-of-Pocket Expenditure on Education

Out-of-pocket expenditure on education includes expenditure on different kinds of fees, purchase of stationery and books, expenses on conveyance, private coaching, and the like. The 64th Round of NSS (Participation and Expenditure on Education in India, 2007–08) collected information on private expenditure on education for persons in the age group 5–29 years who are currently attending educational institutions.

For the country as a whole, during 2007–08, (NSS 64th round) the average annual expenditure on general education for currently attending students in the age group 5–29 years was Rs 2,461. Across social groups private expenditure on general education per student was the lowest for STs—one-third that of 'Others' in 2007–08. Across religious communities, average annual private expenditure per student in general education was the lowest for Muslims.

5.7.2 Out-of-Pocket Expenditure on Higher Education

Higher education requires greater public investment for ensuring greater participation from among the economically deprived socio-religious communities. For the present purpose, higher education is considered to be all diploma and certificate courses at the graduate level and above. The private unaided institutions are the most expensive, while government institutions are the least expensive. The average annual expenditure per student in higher education in private unaided institutions was more than thrice that in government institutions (Planning Commission 2011)

This variation in average annual out-of-pocket expenditure was considerable for all social groups and religious communities. In the case of social groups, the average annual expenditure per student in higher education was the lowest in the case of SCs and STs, while across religious communities Muslims had the lowest average annual expenditure per student in higher education (Table 5.15)

Table 5.15 Out-of-Pocket Expenditure per Student (5-29Years) in Higher Education, by Social and Religious Groups, 2007–8 (₹)

Social Religious Group	Government	Local Body	Private Aided	Private Un-aided	All Types of Institution
Scheduled Castes	5376	2468	11264	19390	8988
Scheduled Tribes	6744	1496	6406	24953	9896
OBCs	7668	5118	15521	20964	13148
Others	10526	14785	16832	36091	17898
All Social Groups	*8650*	*9378*	*15247*	*28322*	*14710*
Hindus	8531	9148	15600	27875	14561
Muslims	7131	5237	11673	20598	11277

Source: Calculated from NSS database 64th round

It may be noted that the majority of SC and ST students were enrolled in government institutions, which was one of the reasons for the lower average annual expenditure per student in higher education (Table 5.16).

Table 5.16: Distribution of Students (5–29 years) by Social and Religious Groups, 2007–8 (per cent)

Social and Religious Group	Government	Local Body	Private Aided	Private Un-aided
Scheduled Castes	53.4	0.9	33.0	12.7
Scheduled Tribes	58.4	1.1	22.5	17.9
OBCs	43.4	1.3	32.2	23.1
Others	48.6	1.2	28.6	21.6
All Social Groups	47.7	1.2	30.3	20.8
Hindus	48.1	1.3	30.3	20.3
Muslims	48.4	0.5	29.8	21.3

Source: Calculated from NSS database 64th Round

The high cost associated with higher education was an important deterrent to participation in higher education. This was particularly true for SCs, STs, and Muslims, who were characterized by high incidence of poverty. The participation of STs in higher education was the lowest among all social groups followed by SCs, while Muslims had the least participation among major religious communities (Table 5A.19).

As compared to the 'Others' social group, the participation of SCs, STs, and OBCs in higher education was less than half, one-fourth, and half respectively. In the case of Muslims, the participation in higher education was only 60 per cent that of Hindus (calculated from (Table 5A.19) Clearly, lower participation in higher education in the case of SCs, STs, and Muslims adversely affected their employability in terms of quality of jobs. Economic vulnerability, measured in terms of the higher incidence of poverty among SCs, STs, and Muslims, was therefore higher than other social groups. High incidence of poverty and low participation in higher education feed on each other. This vicious cycle can only be broken by establishing public funded institutions of higher education which can ensure greater participation from among the economically disadvantaged communities.

5.8. Supporting Human Development: Housing, Electricity, Telephony and Roads

Poverty alleviation and human well-being are important goals in themselves, and should not be merely by-products of economic growth. But neither human well-being nor economic growth is possible only through the provision of economic infrastructure. It is social infrastructure—health and education—along with support infrastructure such as shelter, sanitation, power, telephony, and road connectivity that can give economic growth a human face. By improving the quality of human resources and enhancing capability, these indicators act as stimulants to growth.

5.8.1 Housing

Shelter and quality of housing are important inputs for human development. Investments in shelter and housing not only expand and improve the stock of housing units, but also enhance the working and living environments.

Over time, all the social groups registered an increase in the percentage of households living in pucca houses. The rural areas too saw an improvement in the housing conditions. In fact, STs experienced a sharp increase in the percentage of households residing in pucca houses. Overall, OBCs are better placed than SCs and STs in terms of housing conditions (Table 5.17).

Table 5.17: Distribution of Households by Pucca andKutcha Houses by Social and Religious Groups (per cent)

Social and Religious Group	Pucca Houses		Kutcha Houses	
	2002	2008-09	2002	2008-09
Scheduled Castes	22.9	38.3	23.2	16.4
Scheduled Tribes	39.5	57.9	22.2	18.8
OBCs	44.7	66.6	17	12.4
Others	61.3	77.9	10	7.7
Hindus	NA	65.4	NA	12.7
Muslims	NA	63.8	NA	14.7

Source: Computed from NSS 58th and 65th round

When looked at in absolute terms, as far as housing conditions are concerned, SC and ST households are below the national average for both points of time– 2002 and 2008–9 (Planning Commission, 2011). In addition, in terms of the percentage of households residing in pucca houses, this gap is widening with respect to the national average.

Among major religious communities, Muslims had the lowest proportion of households residing in pucca houses groups. Hindus are better off than Muslims by a small margin (Table 5.17). As expected, all religious groups had better living conditions in urban areas than in rural areas. SCs and STs are diverging from the national average for households residing in pucca houses. A greater proportion of Muslims live in pucca houses than SCs and STs.

The housing policies of the government lays special emphasis on vulnerable sections of society such as the SCs, STs, OBCs, minorities and the urban poor and seeks to promote development of rural and urban areas.

5.8.2 Electricity

Electrification holds the key to increased productivity in agriculture and labour, improvement in the delivery of health and education, access to communications, improved lighting after sunset, effective use of all sorts of machines and appliances to reduce drudgery, and increased public safety through outdoor lighting. In order to meet the aspirations of the rural population, therefore, it is essential to provide viable and reliable electricity services.

There has been an increase in the proportion of households that have electricity for domestic use across all social groups. OBC households have relatively better access to electricity as compared to SCs and STs at the all India level (Table 5A.20). In 2008-09 OBCs were relatively better placed with 75 per cent households having electricity, while only 66 per cent of SC households and 61 per cent ST households had electricity for domestic use. In terms of electricity for domestic use, SC and ST households are converging with the all-India average

Among socio-religious groups, it is found that OBC households are better placed in terms of quality of housing and access to electricity as compared to SCs and STs, Hindu households fare the best among major religious communities. Muslim households, though relatively better off as compared to SCs and STs, were the worst off amongst the major religious groups in terms of quality of housing and access to electricity.

5.9 Child Labour

A large proportion of the world's child labourers lives in India. The incidence of working children among SCs and STs is higher than the average for all social groups which is again a reflection of the government school system is absorbing them. According to NSSO (2004–05 and 2007–08), children from STs are twice as likely to work as child labour than the children from the upper castes (Table 5.18). However, it is important to note that the fall in child labour was faster among SCs and STs compared to OBCs and 'Other' castes for the first half of the decade. After that, the decline in child labour became stagnant for SCs and STs, and a very marginal dip was observed for OBCs and 'Other' social groups. The STs largely live in forests, and in remote and hilly areas, from where it takes longer than the average time to reach schools.

Among the major religious groups, Muslims have the highest child workforce participation rate (Table 5.18). Among Muslims, the child workforce participation rate (3 per cent) was higher than the national average (2.4 per cent) in 2007–08. Child labour among the Hindus declined from 4.2 per cent in 1999–2000 to 2.3 per cent in 2007–08, whereas child labour among Muslims declined from four per cent to only three per cent during the same period (Table 5.18).

Table 5.18: Child Workforce Participation Rate by Social and Religious Groups

Social* and Religious# Groups	1999-2000	2004-2005	2007-2008
Scheduled Castes	4.5	2.8	2.8
Scheduled Tribes	7.7	3.8	3.8
OBCs	4.1	2.9	2.3
Others	2.7	2.0	1.7
All	*4.1*	*2.7*	*2.4*
Hindus	4.2	2.5	2.3
Muslims	4.0	3.5	3.0

Source: *Derived from NSS Unit level data of 61st Round and 64th Round; # NSS 55th, 61st, and 64th Round.

This is a reflection of the slower improvement in the literacy rate and net attendance rate in schools among Muslims for the same time period. Figures from 'Education' section of the present chapter clearly bring out the low literacy rate, the high percentage of 'out -of school children' and the very low net attendance rate, particularly for Muslim girls. The net attendance rate among Muslim girls declines very sharply after the primary level and dips to as low as 24 per cent at the secondary level for rural areas. The trend is similar for Muslim boys, which has resulted in stagnation in the proportion of child labour among Muslims.

5.10 Entrepreneurship

The issue of Dalit entrepreneurship has been in debate for some time. Despite micro level studies on Dalit entrepreneurship, the all-India data do not portray a shift to self-employment. SC men are, less likely to own enterprises, but self-employment is rare among most men in India, and the hurdles for small enterprises are well documented Kishwar (2002) and, Nilekani (2008). Self-employment is more relevant in urban areas than in rural areas, where farming is still the major basis for employment.

It seems that, in rural areas, SC and ST men have a huge disadvantage in self-employment. This may be because most rural self-employment is ancillary to agriculture and SC and STs typically do not own land. Alternatively, rural SC/ST men have fewer social networks and less access to credit, markets, and raw materials relative to their urban counterparts. SCs and STs are in an disadvantaged because they are traditionally typecaste into caste-based occupations.

Table 5.19: Enterprise Ownership by Social Group (1999-2005, in Per cent)

Years	Population share			Share of Enterprise Ownership			Share of Employment		
	Non SC/ST	SC	ST	Non SC/ST	SC	ST	Non SC/ST	SC	ST
1990	75.8	16.6	7.6	87.5	9.9	2.6	90.6	7.4	2
1998	75.8	16.5	7.7	87.3	8.5	4.2	89.4	6.9	3.8
2005	75.9	16.4	7.7	86.4	9.8	3.7	88.5	8.1	3.4

Source: Teltumbde, Anand (2013)

Average employment per enterprise for 2005 was 2.3 indicating that a vast majority of firms were single-person Enterprises. The incidence of such enterprises was far higher in the SC and ST categories. As (shown in Table 5.19), during the globalisation period the share of Dalit ownership of enterprises more or less remained the same, refuting the claim that globalisation had boosted Dalit enterprise.

5.10.1 Energy Use

Energy use, particularly, electrification holds the key to increased productivity in agriculture and labour, improvement in the delivery of health and education, and access to communications. Access to electricity is a major challenge that the country is facing. As per Census 2001 estimates, there has been a rise in the percentage of households that have electricity connections. Lack of access to electricity is a more serious problem for the rural households.[35] In the absence of electricity, people resort to use of other resources such as kerosene, gas and candle Table 5.20 highlights NSS Report findings on energy use in India by various social groups. The table shows that material used for cooking of different social

---

[35] In 2001, about 44 per cent of rural households and 88 per cent of urban households had access to electricity.

groups depends on the availability of resources according to their traditional uses and availability.

Table 5.20: Primary Source of Energy for Cooking by Social Group per 1000 Households

Source of Energy	ST		SC		OBC		Other		All		Estimated number of Households (Hundreds)		Sample Households	
	R	U	R	U	R	U	R	U	R	U	R	U	R	U
Coke coal	4	44	9	41	7	18	13	21	8	23	13627	15956	461	921
Firewood and Chips	888	267	810	308	763	228	662	79	763	175	1240743	119512	41534	8989
LPG gas	43	524	62	484	117	602	193	743	115	645	187464	439750	11971	27011
Gobar/cow dung	0	0	1	0	1	0	4	0	2	0	2476	95	128	5
Dung cake	11	3	75	15	71	18	63	8	63	13	102684	8697	2945	507
Charcoal	0	4	0	0	0	1	1	1	0	1	492	586	19	97
Kerosene	4	61	8	94	8	63	9	58	8	65	13103	44153	567	2159
Electricity	0	7	0	3	0	2	1	3	1	3	852	1766	54	162
Others	9	5	27	11	21	4	33	15	24	10	38929	6710	1022	277
No Cooking Arrangement	40	84	7	45	12	64	21	72	16	65	25988	44508	387	1562
All	1000	1000	1000	1000	1000	1000	1000	1000	1000	1000	1626461	681770	59097	41697

Source: NSS Report No 542 (66th Round): Energy Sources of Indian Households for Cooking and Lighting
Note: R-Rural; U- Urban

Conclusion

From the empirical evidence, it becomes clear that SC, ST, Muslims continue to suffer lower human development, higher deprivation and poverty. The continuing exclusion-induced deprivation of disadvantaged groups indicates that social exclusion can be addressed by poverty reduction measures.

In this context, the inclusion of excluded groups is different from the social inclusion of materially deprived people. Fighting discrimination therefore calls for additional policies complementing anti-poverty and economic development programmes. But there is also considerable overlap, and therefore the need to combine and complement programmes against poverty and economic deprivation and policies for equal rights and social inclusion of disadvantaged groups.

Recognising the discrimination and social exclusion, several countries (Malaysia, Indonesia) have formulated equal opportunity policies to compensate the excluded groups Equal opportunity policy is the subject of discussion in the next chapter.

Section II: Entitlements in Central Asia

Entitlements are legal, political, and economic provisions and not just moral philosophy imposing duties on governments to deliver. J. Swinnen et.al (2011) defines entitlements as a set of commodities based on which a person can exercise his or her access to resources that are necessary for living. Such access to resource needs command over legal, political, economic and social arrangements of society in which they live. It forms one of the essential aspects of modern governance system. As the Central Asian states are at the early stage of statehood, government plays significant role in three key areas – (a) employment, (b) education, (c) health and nutrition. In Central Asia, social benefits systems were severely hit by the global financial crisis. Unemployment increased and unemployment benefits expired.

Today, the region faces various challenges in the field of social exclusion as one third of population is marginalised due to various reasons. Women are often excluded in the developmental process. Thus entitlements and rights have been affected notably. On a positive note, countries have moved towards democratic governance, which has facilitated functioning of public institutions. Labour force participation is consistent and employment situation is relatively better. The following is an attempt to analyse attainment of entitlements in each country of the region.

5.11 Employment

Work and employment ensures present and future material needs, self-respect and dignity of individual within society. Participation in economic activities ensures income and help to secure material wellbeing. Employment ratio persistently decreased in all five countries after independence. Withdrawal of soviet government from labour market can be major reason for fall in output of economy. Recently, ILO expressed concern over deteriorating employment situation since the introduction of fiscal consolidation policies. Unequal wage distribution is driving inequality among people. The increase in inequality is marked in the structure of employability.

Kazakhstan registered a steady decline in labour force in the 1990s (UNDP 1995). The situation improved somewhat in the last decade. The employment of labour resources varied across regions primarily due to distribution of industrial facilities. The highest rate of employment was registered in Northern and Western Kazakhstan dominated by Russians and Kazakhs signifying high employment of these two communities.

Kazakhs constitute 38 per cent of total workers. This is significantly lower than their total percentage in population. Nearly 50 per cent Kazakhs are engaged in forestry, health care, social insurance, agriculture, administrative bodies, education, culture and art. Similarly, 35 per cent representation is marked in industry, construction, data processing science and research. The disparity in the wages is related to ethnic origin of labourers and historical factors of employment structure. Kazakhs are mostly engaged in low wage sectors such as, agriculture and education.

5.11.1 Vocational Education

In comparison to other ethnic groups, Kazakhs and Russian have better employment conditions. Earlier, Russians were mostly employed in high skill sector jobs such as oil, natural gas and industry. After independence, situation is changing and Kazakhs are entering into these sectors.

In Kyrgyzstan, agriculture accommodates maximum (38 per cent) labour force followed by trade and allied services (17 per cent). While in rural employment, 65 per cent of working population is engaged in agriculture. Similar to India, agricultural jobs are seasonal and low paid. The remaining 35 per cent jobs are in urban areas. Private sector dominates in urban area jobs such as trade and other services (UNDP 2010).

In Tajikistan, agriculture provides employment to nearly two third of population. The industrial sector experienced decrease in employment during economic recovery period of 2000 to 2010. The employees of IT sector, credit, construction and public insurance sector have benefitted from higher wages.

Since 2000, Uzbekistan's labour force experienced new job opportunities in service sector and lesser dependence on agriculture. The country is concerned for external labour migration and out flow of trained manpower for better opportunities. Nearly, five per cent of labour force migrates annually for seasonal jobs (UNDP 2007-2008).

Across the region, the employment situation has rather worsened in last two decades. But Kazakhstan has shown significant and Kyrgyzstan marginal improvement in last decade. Contrarily, Tajikistan showed a negative trend (Table 5.21).

Table 5.21: Percentage of Employment in Central Asia (Age 15-59) *(in per cent)*

Countries	1990	2000	2010
Kazakhstan	81.4	67.9	75.6
Kyrgyzstan	73.2	63.2	65.1
Tajikistan	72.3	54.0	49.5
Turkmenistan	74.1	82*	N.A.
Uzbekistan	73.9	65.3	N.A.

Source: UNICEF 2012 Trans Mon EE, * The data is for the year 2001.

Employment by sector shows Central Asia has mixed trend where agriculture and service sector accommodates major labour force. Industry as employer contributes highest share in Turkmenistan (63.6 per cent) and Uzbekistan (63.9 per cent). The share of employed in agriculture is lowest in Kazakhstan (26.5 per cent) and highest in Tajikistan (53 per cent). Industry including construction recruits around 21 per cent in Kyrgyzstan followed by Kazakhstan and Uzbekistan each 19 per cent. The service sector has highest labour force accommodation in Kazakhstan (54.6 per cent) followed by 47.7 per cent in Kyrgyzstan, 42.1 per cent Uzbekistan and 31.5 per cent Tajikistan. Data for Turkmenistan is unavailable. Barring Tajikistan (Turkmenistan excluded) all other state have largest share of employment in service sector, followed by agriculture and industrial production (Table 5.22).

Table 5.22: Employment by Sector in Central Asia for 2011*(percent)*

Country	Year	Agriculture	Industry including construction	Service
Kazakhstan	2011	26.5	19.0	54.6
Kyrgyzstan	2010	31.2	21.1	47.7
Tajikistan	2009	52.9	15.6	31.5

Turkmenistan	N.A.	N.A.	63.6	N.A.
Uzbekistan	2009	38.5	63.9	42.1

Source: European Training Foundation 2013; Notes: NA Not Available

5.11.2 Women Employment

The situation of women in employment was not much promising in last two decades. The inequality of opportunities made it difficult for women to participate in new areas of employment. Women were mostly confined to traditional sectors like health, education, social services and taking up unpaid work at home. In many Central Asian countries, women are paid two times lower wages than men. Women also face exploitation and uncomfortable working conditions at workplace. Men's migration for employment also has negative implications for women. Often such women are left behind in vulnerable conditions, and many times the in-laws deny taking responsibilities. The vulnerability of such women is aggravated due to unfavourable inheritance and property rights (Bassiuoni 2011).

5.11.3 Unemployment in Central Asia

All Central Asian states face the challenges of underemployment. Barring Uzbekistan, unemployment rate is on higher side in all the Central Asian countries. The highest unemployment is marked in Tajikistan and lowest in Uzbekistan. Disguised unemployment or underemployment is quite high in the region.

5.11.4 Labour Force Participation Rate (LFPR)

Table 5.23: Labour Force Participation Rate of Population
(age 15 Years and Above)

Name of Country	1990	2000	2010
Kazakhstan	69.8	70.1	71.3
Kyrgyzstan	66	64.9	66.4
Tajikistan	66.7	66.7	65.7
Turkmenistan	60.2	60.5	60.6
Uzbekistan	59.3	59.6	60.8

Source: World Bank (2013)

LFPR is the proportion of population with 15 years and above engaged in economic system. LFPR is varying between 60 to 70 per cent (Table 5.23). Increase in LFPR in the region is around 0.8 in last two decades. On an average Kazakhstan has the highest participation rate (70 per cent) followed by Tajikistan (66 per cent) and Kyrgyzstan (65 per cent), while the lowest (59 per cent) is marked in Uzbekistan. Uzbekistan has relatively small industrial base as against large trained human resource (UNDP 1999) contributing to low participation. There is need for a mindset change in society at large in order to improve the employability of the labour force through improved vocational education and active labour market policies. The small-scale private sector including the social economy can play helpful role (UNDP 2011).

5.12 Education

Off late, all Central Asian states have recognized the importance of education as a key area for betterment of society and are taking efforts to improve education scenario. All Central Asian states have recognized the right to education in their respective constitutions and have provisions for compulsory free education. The education system advocates regular education till 17 years. It has pre-school, secondary vocational and high school level of education. All countries are committed to education for all irrespective of income, place of residence, physical ability and ethnic identity.

The place of residence, income, ethnicity, gender factors often determine the access to education in Central Asia. Children from specific groups, conflict zones, economically disadvantaged families continue to be excluded from school in Central Asia (UNICEF 2011). Many reports (UNDP 2004b, UNDP 2010, Government of Republic of Tajikistan 2012 and UNDP 2007-08) suggest that urban areas get privileged in receiving the resources, facilities and finance in education. Rural children are deprived of education and better opportunities.

5.12.1 Literacy

Central Asia has high adult literacy rates. Almost the whole population of 15 years and above is considered to be literate in all five Central Asian countries. Over all the literacy rate and access to education is relatively better off with some intra and inter-country variations. Both Kazakhstan and Tajikistan have achieved cent per cent literacy (Table 5.24).

Table 5.24: Adult Literacy Rate

Country	Male		Female	
	1985-94	2005-11	1985-94	2005-11
Kazakhstan	99	100	96	100
Kyrgyz Republic	N.A.	100	N.A.	99
Tajikistan	99	100	97	100
Turkmenistan	N.A.	100	N.A.	99
Uzbekistan	N.A.	100	N.A.	99

Source: World Bank 2013

5.12.2 Pre-Primary Education

Pre-primary education is imparted between three to six years in Central Asia. It plays a crucial role in developing the child's capabilities and socialisation process. During the Soviet regime, the access to the pre-primary education was better. According to current statistics, Kazakhstan has 52.9 per cent children without pre-primary education followed by 17.2 in Kyrgyzstan (Table 5A.23). Children without attending pre-primary education face difficulties in education leading to poor performance of these children. In Kazakhstan, the increased cost of pre-schooling has made it unaffordable for some. The Republic of Kazakhstan is the only country among Central Asia that has granted right of the child to pre-schooling in the law. In Tajikistan around 90 per cent children attended primary schools have not attended pre-school making them difficult to cope up with the primary education. Uzbekistan also faces inadequacy of Pre-school education. Hike in pre-school fees deters parents to send children to pre-school.

Rural urban differences are hugely marked in pre–primary education. UNESCO study (2000a) in Uzbekistan reveals around 80 per cent children are deprived of preschool education in urban areas while in rural areas the extent of deprivation is more. In 2006 pre-primary attendance rates were merely 3 per cent children from poor household while 45 per cent children were from rich families (UNESCO 2009).

5.12.3 General Secondary Education

In Central Asia, the education system is markedly different from that in India. It emphasises both general education and vocational education (Table 5.A24).

The world development indicator shows that access to knowledge Central Asian Republics is measured by the mean year of schooling. This has improved after an initial decline immediately after independence. Kazakhstan has shown better performance in mean year of schooling for adults (increase of 2.7 years) followed by Kyrgyzstan 1.2 years and Tajikistan 0.8 years. Turkmenistan shows the constant performance of 9.9 years of schooling for adult since 2000 (Table 5A.25). At present Uzbekistan and Kazakhstan have the highest year of schooling of 10 years in the region (World Bank 2013).

The Central Asian countries have maintained better enrolment ratio. However, achievement of universal education and reduce dropout of children in schools are two major challenges. Kyrgyzstan faces the challenge of declining Net Enrolment Ratio (NER). Roughly around 4 per cent of children entering the lower secondary are still out of purview of education. The major reasons are out of pocket expenses, distance of school and labour market demand. In case of girls' education, social, cultural and economic circumstances are major hurdles to achieve universal education

Kazakhstan follows Dakar Framework of Action[36] to achieve education for all. It plans to achieve it through ensuring access to girls, children from problem families and ethnic minorities. Kazakhstan introduced various programmes to address the issues of accessibility and quality of education (UNESCO 2000b).

Kyrgyzstan inherited the soviet system of education but lack of resources led to problem of accessibility and quality of education. Previously, the education system was strongly linked to the labour market ensuring high employment rate. Kyrgyzstan gradually diversified the education system. It imparted education in different mediums such as Kyrgyz, Russian, Uzbek and Tajik. The programme of access to education (*Jetkincheck in Kyrgyz language*) addressed the issues of accessibility and quality of education (UNESCO 2000c). After independence the enrolment rate further reduced at all levels of education barring the tertiary level. In fact Kyrgyzstan has achieved greater gender parity in education in comparison to other Central Asian states (UNESCO 2000c). The UNESCO study observed that 7.8 per cent of children in primary school (1- 4 classes) 3.2 per cent students at lower secondary (5-9 classes) are not attending the classes. The report suggests that around 4.11 per cent children aged 5-17 years are not attending schools.

---

[36] Dakar Framework of Action of 2000 is to achieve millennium development goal of education.

Of the total drop outs, boys (63.3 per cent) significantly outnumbered the girls (36.7 per cent). Very often students seek for vocational training on the basis of incomplete education and significant number enters into labour market as unskilled force. The other major reasons of drop out are poverty, high cost of education, corruption, bribery in the education institutions, poor quality of teaching and learning environment.

Tajikistan has dismal educational scenario. The enrolment rates are high at primary but low at secondary level. The gender gap in enrolment rate is sharply marked. Nearly 74 per cent girls are enrolled at secondary level as against 87 per cent for boys. This gender gap has widened in recent years. The research carried out by international organizations like UNICEF and UNESCO shows that not just poverty but post-Soviet stereotype culture characterized by strong gender based roles led to deprivation of girls from education. Significant number of girls could not even finish compulsory education till 9th grade. Poverty is also significant barrier to girl's education. Tajikistan has high prevalence of child poverty (66 per cent). The poor infrastructure at school, poor quality teaching and irrelevance of education in labour market are common reasons of low enrolment. Under-qualified teacher is a major concern of the country.

Table 5.25: Primary Education Completion Rate (*Per cent of relevant age group*)

Country	Total		Male		Female	
	1999	2011	1999	2011	1999	2011
Kazakhstan	93	116	92	116	93	116
Kyrgyz Republic	94	96	94	96	93	95
Tajikistan	92	104	NA	106	NA	102
Turkmenistan	NA	NA	NA	NA	NA	NA
Uzbekistan	96	93	101	94	100	92

Source: World Bank Development Indicators

Among those employed Kazakh and Russian constitute maximum population with higher education degrees, whereas Uzbeks constitute the lowest? Similarly, maximum number of Russians and Ukrainians has vocational education (Table 5.25).

5.12.4 Vocational Education

The vocational education in Central Asia is imparted at primary and secondary level. Such vocational training included initial training, re-training and continuous education courses for workers and specialists. The region of Central Asia has Gross Enrolment Ratio of 12 per cent in vocational education. Girl's enrolment in the programme is around 39 per cent. Vocational education acts as bridge between education and employment. Many students in the region view it as safety net.

Vocational education is beset with numerous problems such as lack of qualified teachers, shortage of industrial training specialists, lack of educational and methodical literature and equipment especially lack of modern textbooks, visual and learning aids especially in state language. Uzbekistan has started the process of restructuring vocational-technical education with due emphasis in the rural areas.

5.12.5 Higher Education

Kazakhstan has well developed higher education system. It has both public and private higher education institutes. Over 70 ethnic groups are represented in Kazakh higher education institutes. The majority are Kazakh (69.6 per cent) and Russian students (21.5 per cent). Other ethnic groups include Ukrainians (1.6 per cent), Uzbeks (1.4 per cent), Tatars (1.2 per cent) and Germans (1.15 per cent). The medium of teaching in higher education institutes are mainly Russian and Kazakh (World Bank 2007d).

Kazakhstan's education policy promotes equal opportunities for higher education. The country provides reservations for rural people (30 per cent), people with Kazakh ethnicity (2 per cent) non Kazakh citizens (0.5 per cent) and disabled people (1 per cent). Government provides financial support in terms of fellowship and educational loan to poor students.

Kyrgyzstan has managed to survive the transition from command education to market based education system with strong negative impact of poverty and unemployment on the education sector. Its higher education system is based on two principles, achieving and maintaining past successes and innovative reforms to allow national educational institutions to integrate into the international educational community. As expected, Kyrgyz students are the highest in number (69.5 per cent) followed by Russian (11.7 per cent); Uzbek (9.4 per cent) and

Kazakh (2.9 per cent). Majority students receive education in Russian (67 per cent), Kyrgyz (29.9 per cent) and Uzbek (1.29 per cent) languages (World Bank 2007d).

Tajikistan during the past five years, higher education in Tajikistan has got significant boost. The number of higher education institutions increased by ten per cent in last decade. Girl's education is a matter of concern in Tajikistan. The country provides presidential quota reservation for girls.

Access for low income groups to tertiary education is difficult in Uzbekistan. The major hurdles are affordability due to high tuition fees, and distance of higher education institute, which makes it difficult for rural students to access the same.

In Central Asia, the decline in quality of education is a matter of concern. The teacher quality, class size and equipment have worsened in recent years. The traditional trend in most schools is to give emphasis on university rather than vocational education. University education does not meet the skill requirement for industrial workers. It has led to a mismatch between the knowledge attained and the skills that the labour market demands. The main challenge in an inherited education system is inflexibility and the inability to adopt changes. Overall, the challenges that remain to be tackled are financing of education, inadequate quality of learning and outcomes, and inadequate links to labour market.

5.13 Health

In Central Asia the health-care system is in transition from a command and control model to a decentralised and pluralistic model. The major limitations and challenges have been inherited from the Soviet regime. During the transition, Central Asia has had to incur a high human cost reflected in its declining health indicators like low life expectancy, high morbidity and inaccessible health services. The newly independent states have undertaken several reforms. The major challenges are lack of institutional capacity and insufficient trained man power due to outmigration of existing skilled personnel. Most of them were Russians and other European origin. The governments have arranged for increasing financial resources through various measures such as health insurance and public revenues. However, these efforts were limited. Only Kyrgyzstan has successfully implemented health insurance programmes. Kazakhstan has introduced mandatory health insurance in 1996 but had to withdraw later on. Now health services are carried out at government expenditure. Tajikistan health system is publicly funded from state taxes. Uzbekistan continued to finance health care system from government taxes and state enterprises (Falkingham, J. et al. 2002).

After independence, Kazakhstan had the biggest challenge of establishing health care system on a financial viable basis. Consequently people had to pay for all the health expenses. People of rural areas, particularly the Kazak nationals were the biggest sufferers in the process. Kyrgyzstan has implemented comparatively better health sector reforms. The major concern for Kyrgyzstan is ensuring equal access to essential health services for poor sections of society.

Owing to civil war from 1992 to 1997 in Tajikistan, the country could not give adequate attention to health sector reforms. So far it has focused on strengthening primary health care and training human resource. The out of pocket expenditure was as high as 60-70 per cent in Tajikistan (UNICEF 2011).

Turkmenistan, while reworking the inherited health care system, has focused rationalizing hospital services and strengthening primary health care. In primary health care training human resource and developing appropriate infrastructure were major focuses.

During implementing reforms, Uzbekistan have focused child and maternal care, promoting privatization, improving health care services, minimizing optimum cost, decentralization of health service management. The low health expenditure is major concern in the region. The out of pocket expenditure in the region was around 50 per cent (UNICEF 2011). All the countries of Central Asia had strived to improve various components of health care. The following is an attempt to analyze each component of health care.

5.13.1 Life Expectancy at Birth

Life expectancy at birth is one of the important health indicators. It gives broad sense of the health situation in the society. In the case of Central Asia, under the Soviet the regime the life expectancy was similar that in Russia except Turkmenistan. After independence, the sudden change in political, economic and social situation has resulted in decline of life expectancy for the region. The differences in life expectancy by gender offer some important insights into determinant of diseases. Life expectancy for males in central Asia used to be better than it was in Russia, while for females it was worse. After independence the trend changed and female life expectancy improved (Falkingham 2002). Republic of

Tajikistan was undergoing civil war[37] and communal violence has seen dramatic decline in life expectancy.

Table 5.26: Life Expectancy at Birth in CARs *(in years)*

Country	1990	2000	2012
Kazakhstan	66.7	63.5	67.4
Kyrgyzstan	66.3	66.2	68.0
Tajikistan	62.9	63.6	67.8
Turkmenistan	62.8	63.9	65.2
Uzbekistan	66.8	67.0	68.6

Source: UNDP (2013)

All Central Asian states show improvement in life expectancy during late 1990s to 2012. The highest increase in life expectancy is seen in Tajikistan (4.9 years). Probably, end of civil war in 1997 and achievement of relative peace can be the major reasons along with improvement in governance and health facilities. Turkmenistan also reported high life expectancy, followed by Uzbekistan and Kyrgyzstan (Table 5.26). Though at present, Uzbekistan (68.6 years) and Kazakhstan (67.4 years) have the highest life expectancy and Turkmenistan has the lowest (65.2 years) and improvement in life expectancy is marked in Central Asia, major health services are inaccessible for rural folks.

5.13.2 Child Mortality

Child mortality measured as sum of infant and under five mortality. Often the access to medical services is dependent on the socio-economic background. In Central Asia the overall access to health services is better. Overall infant mortality has gone down except Kazakhstan where, it has slight increase of 1.3 per thousand. The infant mortality rate is the highest in Tajikistan (34). Ethnicity is a crucial factor affecting child mortality. According to a survey (USAID 2003), rural areas have higher infant mortality rate than urban areas. The rural-urban difference is higher in Kazakhstan followed by Turkmenistan and Kyrgyzstan (Table 5.27). In Central Asia male mortality rates are greater than female mortality. This is

---

[37] A civil war continued for five years (1992-1997) in Tajikistan. Garmis and Pamiris were most affected ethnic minorities in the war. Under representation of ethnic minorities was the cause of discontent.

evident in all the surveys (USAID 2003). This unusual finding needs further investigation.

Table 5.27: Rural/Urban/Gender Differences in Infant Mortality Rate *Per 1000 live births*

Country	Year	Gender		Rural-Urban		
		Male	Female	Rural	Urban	Difference Rural Vs Urban
Kazakhstan	1999	62.0	47.3	63.8	43.7	20.1
Kyrgyzstan	1997	71.9	60.2	70.4	54.3	16.1
Turkmenistan	2000	83.0	59.7	79.9	60.1	19.8
Uzbekistan	1996	50.2	36.7	43.8	42.9	0.9

Source: (USAID 2003)

5.13.3 Maternal Mortality Rate

Maternal mortality is considered to be one of the significant indicators of women's health in society. Central Asian states have maternal mortality rate ranging from 13 to 17 per cent. The only exception is Uzbekistan having MMR 2.4 per cent which shows better maternal health care and practices. Low MMR is recorded in most of the Central Asian countries.[38] Tajikistan has high percentage of under five mortality followed by Kyrgyzstan (Table 5A.28).

5.13.4 Care of Pregnant Women

Though overall life expectancy rate at birth for women is averagely 70 years in Central Asia; maternal mortality still remains a major concern. It has still one of the important causes of untimely death of women. Tajikistan has poor condition

---

[38] Low MMR is recorded in most of the central Asia countries because of the variations in data collections. The most significant being central Asian states do not record the deaths caused due to use of abortion as alternative to contraception, often carried out illegally. The predominance of causes like gestational toxicities and obstetric hemorrhages in maternal mortality reflects the lack of adequate access to medical services for pregnant women, poor qualification among primary care and prenatal care workers, problem with early diagnosis of complications and lack of training among gynecologist, the most important the poor health among mothers, rural areas record high maternal mortality rates (UNDP 2010).

with around 77 per cent of women could access the prenatal care, followed by Kyrgyzstan with the 97 per cent (Table 5A.29).

5.13.5 Total Fertility Rate (TFR)

Fertility, understood in terms of child bearing, is dependent on many factual and societal circumstances, such as cultural traditions, education and development of the society and community. The most commonly used measure of fertility is the total fertility rate[39] (TFR). Total Fertility rate in Central Asia is steady over a period of time from 2005 to 2010. Tajikistan has highest fertility rate of 3.6 (Table 5.28).

Table 5.28: Total Fertility Rate in Central Asia

Country	2005	2006	2007	2008	2009	2010
Kazakhstan	2.3	2.4	2.5	2.7	2.6	2.6
Kyrgyzstan	2.5	2.7	2.8	2.8	2.9	3.1
Tajikistan	3.3	3.6	3.6	3.6	3.6	3.6
Turkmenistan	2.6	2.6	-	-	-	-
Uzbekistan	2.4	2.4	2.6	2.6	2.5	-

Source: UNICEF 2012 TransMONEE

Ethnicity as Factor in Total Fertility

The majority ethnic groups such as Kazakhs, Kyrgyz, Turkmen, and Uzbeks have high fertility rate. On the other hand, minorities including women of European origin, primarily Russian but also Ukrainian, Tatar, German, etc. have low fertility rates. The total fertility rates for European ethnicity in the region ranges between 1.1 and 1.5 births per woman (Table 5A.30) and it is lower than that of the major ethnic groups in each republic (between 2.5 and 3.6 births per woman). The differences in fertility range from 1.1 births per woman in Kazakhstan to 2.4 births per woman in Uzbekistan. Factors like education, residence and age have affected the level of fertility among different sections within the society.

---

[39] Total Fertility rate is defined as a number of children that a woman would have over her childbearing years.

5.13.6 Prevalence of Contraception

Availability of contraceptives allows women and men to have control over child birth and prevent unintended pregnancies. More than fifty per cent women use contraceptives to prevent unintended pregnancies (Table 5.29).

Table 5.29 Contraceptive Prevalence (*per cent*)

Country	Year	Any Method	Modern Methods
Kazakhstan	2006	51	49
Kyrgyzstan	2005/2006	48	46
Tajikistan	2007	37	32
Turkmenistan	2000	62	45
Uzbekistan	2006	65	59

Source: United Nations, Department of Economic and Social Affairs, Population Division (2011)

5.13.7 Immunization

Many states have observed re-occurrence of vaccine preventable diseases. Though the immunization coverage rates are high, the inequality exists in coverage varying by wealth possession, settlement, mother's education and gender.

Over all Central Asia has better immunization incidence, where all states had above 95 per cent children covered under immunization for DPT and measles (Table 5.30). The immunization data indicates that Tajikistan has made significant improvement in the immunization with around 10 per cent increase.

Table 5.30 Immunization for DTP and Measles (*in Per cent*)

	Kazakhstan		Kyrgyzstan		Tajikistan		Turkmenistan		Uzbekistan	
Year	2001	2011	2001	2011	2001	2011	2001	2011	2001	2011
DPT	95	99	99	96	85	96	95	97	99	99
Measles	95	99	99	97	88	98	98	99	99	99

Source: World Bank Development Indicators

5.14 Food and Nutrition

Food is one of the basic necessities to lead healthy and nourished life. Tajikistan has the highest 30 per cent followed by Uzbekistan 11 per cent (Table 5A.31)

Kazakhstan and Uzbekistan has high percentage of overweight children under-five among five countries. Tajikistan has the highest percentage of low weight babies (Table 5.31).

Table 5.31: Food and Nutrition in Central Asia (2005-2006) (in percent)

Indicator	Kazakhstan	Kyrgyzstan	Tajikistan*	Turkmenistan*	Uzbekistan
Malnutrition prevalence, height for age (per cent of children under five)	17.5	18.1	33.1	NA	19.6
Malnutrition prevalence, weight for age (per cent of children under five)	4.9	2.7	14.9	NA	4.4
Prevalence of anaemia among pregnant women	NA	NA	44.6	30	NA
Low-birth weight babies	5.8	5.3	9.7	NA	4.8
Prevalence of wasting (per cent of children under five)	3.7	3.4	8.7	NA	4.5
Prevalence of overweight (per cent of children under five)	14.8	10.7	6.7	NA	12.8

Source: World Bank Development Indicators; * The data is for the year 2005.

5.14.1 Anaemia

Inadequate volume of red blood cells and low concentration of haemoglobin causes anaemia. It is generally outcome of nutritional deficiency. Anaemia is highly prevalent in Central Asia republics. Iron deficiency is main cause found with poor eating habits like large intake of inhibitors, insufficient consumption of vegetables and food, chronic illnesses such as intestinal parasites and decline in purchasing power are some of the major causes of prevalence of anaemia in Central Asia (Table 5.32).

Table 5.32: Prevalence of Anaemia in Central Asia: 2004 (*per cent*)

Country	Anaemia in Children under 5 year	Anaemia in women age 15-49
Kazakhstan	49	36
Kyrgyzstan	42	31
Tajikistan	45	42
Turkmenistan	36	46
Uzbekistan	33	63

Source: McKee, M. et al. (2007)

5.15 Drinking Water

Water is vital resource for human survival. The access to drinking water in Central Asia is relatively better. It can be inferred that only around 4-11 per cent of population in the region could not get access to drinking water. Tajikistan's people have poor access to drinking water. Further the rural areas face worsening conditions In Kazakhstan and Uzbekistan 30 per cent of rural population is deprived of such access to drinking water (Table 5.33).

Table 5.33: Access to Drinking Water in Households (In Per cent)

Country	Year	Proportion of households within 15 minutes from a source of drinking water[40]	
		Urban	Rural
Kazakhstan	2006	93	70
Kyrgyzstan	2005/06	95	72
Tajikistan	2005	89	60
Turkmenistan	2000	96	89
Uzbekistan	2006	94	70

Source: United Nations (2010b)

---

[40] Households, whose members need less than 15 minutes to go to the main source of drinking water, get water and come back.

The access to water in Kazakhstan households has declined since independence (Table 5.33) Availability of services varies greatly by oblasts (regions). As the services are better in urban and deficient in rural areas, Kazakh and Uzbek ethnic groups have suffered most. Russians mainly reside in urban areas and have availed of better amenities.

5.16 Housing

As shown by the 2009 Census of Kazakhstan and Kyrgyzstan different kinds of houses are used for residential purposes in Central Asia. These are individual houses, shared houses, residential apartments, common apartments, dormitories, dachas, hotels and other residential premises (huts, yurts, tents). Besides, other non-residential premises (garages, kiosks, rooms in institutions) are used for habitation. 'Adequate housing' in Central Asia includes access to water, housing amenities, and energy. The Kyrgyz poor in rural areas reside in individual residential houses. The ethnic minorities such as Uzbeks and Russians were mostly residing in urban areas. Individual residential houses or separate residential apartments were the houses of Kyrgyz, Uzbeks and Russians (Table 5A.34).

Sanitation Situation

Central Asian states have relatively better access to basic sanitation facilities, which is 100 per cent in Uzbekistan. When, 98 per cent sanitation is claimed by Turkmenistan which is second highest among central Asian countries followed by Kazakhstan. Whereas rural sanitation is better in Kazakhstan, urban sanitation is better in Turkmenistan (Table 5A.35).

5.17 Energy Sources

Some poor households use cooking wood, straw, shrubs, grass, crop residue, animal dung, coal, lignite or charcoal for cooking purposes. These types of fuels are associated with increased indoor air pollution.

Table 5.34: Access to Solid Fuel in Central Asia

Proportion of Households Using solid fuels for cooking (%)			
Country	Year	Urban	Rural
Kazakhstan	2006	7	41
Kyrgyzstan	2005/06	12	56
Tajikistan	2005	8	48
Turkmenistan	2000	*	1
Uzbekistan	2006	1	25

Source: United Nations (2010b)

In Central Asia LPG natural gas is used for cooking, followed by biogas, electricity and other solid fuels. LPG constitutes around 95-97 per cent of use (Ministry of Health and Medical Industry, Turkmenistan 2001).

Annexure - 2

Table 5A.1: Labour Force Participation Rate in UPSS by Social Groups (Per cent)

Sector	SCs			STs			All Groups	
	1993-94	2004-05	2009-10	1993-94	2004-05	2009-10	1993-94	2009-10
Rural	71.8	69.8	62.4	81.9	79.8	69.9	68.6	60.4
Urban	59.4	57.1	53.5	59.3	56.7	51.5	53.3	48.8

Source: NSS report Numbers 425 and 516
Note: For population aged 15 years and above.

Table 5A.2: Percentage of Religious Communities Labour Force Participation Rate (UPSS)

Sector	Hindus			Muslims		
	1993-94	2004-05	2009-10	1993-94	2004-05	2009-10
Rural	69.8	68.9	61.4	58.0	57.1	52.8
Urban	53.5	53.3	49.0	52.8	51.6	47.4

Source: Calculated from NSS database, 50th and 61st rounds
Note: For population aged 15 years and above.

Table 5A.3: Percentage of Worker Population Ratio by Social Groups (UPSS)

Sector	SCs		STs		All Groups	
	1993-94	2009-10	1993-94	2009-10	1993-94	2009-10
Rural	71.1	61.4	81.4	68.9	67.8	59.5
Urban	56.8	51.8	57.0	49.2	50.9	47.2

Source: NSS report Numbers 425 and 516
Note: For population aged 15 years and above.

Table 5A.4: Percentage of Religious Groups' Worker Population Ratio by UPSS.

Sector	Hindus			Muslims		
	1993-94	2004-05	2009-10	1993-94	2004-05	2009-10
Rural	69.0	67.9	60.5	56.8	55.7	52.8
Urban	51,0	0.9	47.4	50.9	49.5	45.9

Source: Calculated from NSS database, 50th and 61st rounds
Note: For population aged 15 years and above.

Table 5A.5: Percentage of Unemployment Rate of Social Groups (UPSS)

Sector	SCs		STs		All Groups	
	1993-94	2009-10	1993-94	2009-10	1993-94	2009-10
Rural	71.1	61.4	81.4	68.9	67.8	59.5
Urban	56.8	51.8	57.0	49.2	50.9	47.2

Source: NSS report numbers 425 and 516
Note: For population aged 15 years and above.

Table 5A.6: Percentage of Major Religious Communities Unemployment Rate by (UPSS)

Sector	Hindus			Muslims		
	1993-94	2004-05	2009-10	1993-94	2004-05	2009-10
Rural	1.1	1.5	1.5	2.1	2.3	1.9
Urban	4.7	4.4	3.4	3.6	4.0	3.1

Source: Calculated from NSS database, 50th and 61st rounds
Note: For population aged 15 years and above.

Table 5A.7: Average Value of Assets by Social Groups, 2002-03
(Rs in Thousands)

Social Group	Rural	Urban
Scheduled Castes	126	182.3
Scheduled Tribes	136.6	240.3
Other Backward Classes	266	334.2
Others	429.6	560.5
All Social Groups	265.6	417.2

Source: Planning Commission 2011

Table 5A.8: Distribution of Households and Assets,
by Major Religious Communities, 2002-3

Religious Community	Households (%)	Assets Owned (%)	Access Owned
Hindus	83.6	81.3	0.9
Muslims	11.0	8.2	0.7

Source: Planning Commission 2011

Table 5A.9: Children with Anthropometric Indicators
by Religious Groups, 2005-6(per cent)

Anthropometric Indicators	Hindus	Muslims
Underweight (Weight for age)	43.2	41.8
Stunning (Height for age)	48.0	50.3
Wasting (Weight for age)	20.3	18.4

Source: NFHS 3

Table 5A.10: Percentage Distribution of Live Births by Religious Community

Place of Delivery	Hindus		Muslims	
	1998-99	2005-06	1998-99	2005-06
Institutional	32.9	39.1	31.5	33
Home	66	60.6	67.5	66.8

Source: NFHS 3

Table 5A.11: Prevalence of contraception by Social Groups and Religious Community

Year	Social Groups				Religious Community	
	SC	ST	OBC	Others	Hindus	Muslims
1998-99	44.6	39.1	46.8	53.5	49.2	37
2005-06	55	47.9	54.2	61.9	57.8	45.7

Source: NFHS 2 and 3

Table 5A.12: Health Services Received by Pregnant Women across Social and Religious Groups (Per cent)

Services	Social Groups				Religious Community	
	SC	ST	OBC	Others	Hindus	Muslims
At least one ANC visit	73.5	69.2	74.1	83.9	77.1	72.2
3 or more ANC visits	45.7	40.1	49.9	63.5	52.5	45.7

Source: NFHS 3

Table 5A.13: Ratio of Literacy Rates for SCs, STs, and Muslims to National Average

Social Group/ Religious Community	Rural		Urban	
	1999-2000	2007-2008	1999-2000	2007-08
SCs	0.83	0.9	0.83	0.89
STs	0.75	0.88	0.87	0.92
Muslims	0.93	0.95	0.87	0.89

Source: Ratio calculated[41] from above tables (5.22 Rural and 5.23 Urban)

---

[41] Ratio was calculated by dividing scheduled caste person in year 1999-2000 (table 5.10) with all social groups in the same year 1999-2000. Same formula was applied for other ratio calculations in the table 5.24

156

Table 5A.14: Enrolment of Girls at Primary and Upper Primary Levels, 2007–8 (*per cent*)

Religious/Social Groups	Primary	Upper Primary
Muslims	48.7	49.4
OBC	48.4	46.7

Source: District Information System for Education (2010)

Table 5A.15: Net Attendance Ratio at Primary Level, by Social and Religious Groups 2007-8 (Per cent)

Social and Religious Groups	Rural		Urban	
	Males	Females	Males	Females
Scheduled Castes	81.5	77.4	80.1	80.9
Scheduled Tribes	82.4	78.7	82.3	82.8
Other Backward Classes	83.3	81.0	81.4	79.4
Others	85.6	83.8	84.0	80.9
All Social Groups	*83.3*	*80.5*	*82.2*	*80.4*
Hindus	84.2	81.5	83.3	83.2
Muslims	78.7	74.9	77.6	70.6

Source: Calculated from NSS database 64th Round

Table 5A.16: Net Attendance Ratio at Upper Primary Level, by Social and Religious Groups and 2007–8 (Per cent)

By Social and Religious Groups	Rural		Urban	
	Males	Females	Males	Females
Scheduled Castes	60.7	55.4	66.0	60.3
Scheduled Tribes	58.8	54.9	73.1	72.5
Other Backward Classes	62.0	55.7	68.0	63.3
Others	67.2	67.1	72.1	72.3
All Social Groups	*62.5*	*58.1*	*69.6*	*66.6*
Hindus	64.5	60.0	73.6	70.7
Muslims	48.7	45.3	49.1	50.8

Source: Calculated from NSS database 64th Round

Table 5A.17: Net Attendance Ratio at Secondary Level, by Social and Religious Groups 2007-8 (per cent)

Social and Religious Group	Rural		Urban	
	Males	Females	Males	Females
Scheduled Castes	33.3	30.0	41.7	45.4
Scheduled Tribes	25.5	25.9	54.0	38.8
Other Backward Classes	42.8	35.7	50.3	49.9
Others	47.1	43.4	57.7	54.3
All Social Groups	*40.0*	*35.0*	*52.0*	*51.0*
Hindus	41.7	36.9	55.9	56.3
Muslims	26.0	23.5	31.8	32.1

Source: Calculated from NSS database 64th Round

Table 5A.18: Net Attendance Ratio at Higher Secondary Level by Social and Religious Group, 2007-8 (percent)

Social and Religious Group	Rural		Urban	
	Males	Females	Males	Females
Scheduled Castes	20.6	16.4	23.8	24.5
Scheduled Tribes	12.7	8.5	39.3	35.5
Other Backward Classes	26.4	19.9	38.8	36.5
Others	29.4	24.3	42.7	44.9
All Social Groups	*25.0*	*20.0*	*40.0*	*39.0*
Hindus	26.2	19.9	40.8	42.0
Muslims	10.9	11.3	24.4	25.8

Source: Planning Commission 2011, Chapter: Education

Table 5A.19: Participation in Higher Education by Social and Religious Groups,2007–8 (%)

Social and Religious Group	Per cent of Students
Scheduled Castes	3.9
Scheduled Tribes	2.4
Other Backward Classes	4.7
Others	8.9
All Social Groups	5.6

Social and Religious Group	Per cent of Students
Hindus	5.8
Muslims	3.5

Source: Calculated from NSS database 64th round

Table 5A.20: Distribution of Households With Electricity for Domestic Use by Social and Religious Groups (per cent)

Social and Religious Groups	2002	2008-09
Scheduled Castes	47	61.2
Scheduled Tribes	52.2	66.4
OBCs	66.4	62.7
Others	75.3	76.7
Hindus	NA	75.2
Muslims	NA	67.5

Source: Computed from NSS 58th and 65th Rounds

Table 5A.21: Primary Source of Energy Used for Lighting by Social Group per 1000 Households

Sources of Energy	Per 1000 Households (Rural)					Per 1000 Households (Urban)				
	ST	SC	OBC	Others	All	ST	SC	OBC	Others	All
Kerosene	391	409	317	268	334	72	92	56	23	47
Gas	0	2	1	1	1	1	2	1	1	1
Candle	1	2	1	2	1	5	4	2	2	2
Electricity	589	583	675	726	657	892	896	935	963	940
Others #	8	3	4	2	3	21	4	4	8	6
All*	1000	1000	1000	1000	1000	1000	1000	1000	1000	1000

Notes: * includes NR (not reported), #includes other oil
Source: NSS Report No 542 (66th Round): Energy Sources of Indian Households for Cooking and Lighting

Table 5A.22: Unemployment in Central Asia *(In Per cent)*

Country	Year	15-64 years
Kazakhstan	2011	5.4
Kyrgyzstan	2010	8.7
Tajikistan	2009	11.6
Turkmenistan	N.A.	N.A.
Uzbekistan	2008	0.4

Source: European Training Foundation 2013

Table 5A.23: Pre-Primary Enrolments: Age 3-6 years *(In per cent)*

Country	1990	2000	2005	2010
Kazakhstan	53.7	25.6	37.9	52.9
Kyrgyzstan	30.3	8.0	12.2	17.2
Tajikistan	15.2	5.6	7.1	7.1
Turkmenistan	33.0	20.1	22.7	N.A.
Uzbekistan	39.2	19.1	21.3	N.A.

Source: UNICEF (2012) TransMONEE

Table 5A.24: General Education Pattern in Central Asia

Standard of Education	Class
Primary Education	class 1- 4
Basic Education	Class 5- 9
General Secondary Education	Class 10-11
Vocational Secondary Education	Class 10-11*

Source: Author's compilation
Notes: *Major Thrust on Vocational Learning

Table 5A.25: Mean Year of Schooling in Central Asia

Indicators	Years	Mean Year of Schooling (years)	Increase in Mean Year of Schooling [2012 — 1990]
Kazakhstan	1990	7.7	
	2000	9.9	2.7
	2012	10.4	
Kyrgyzstan	1990	8.1	
	2000	9.2	1.2
	2012	9.3	
Tajikistan	1990	9	
	2000	9.6	0.8
	2012	9.8	
Turkmenistan	1990	Na	
	2000	9.9	N A
	2012	9.9	
Uzbekistan	1990	Na	
	2000	Na	N.A
	2012	10	

Source: UNDP 2013

Table 5A.26: Ethnic Composition and Level of Education of Employed Population in Kazakhstan (per cent)

Ethnic Group	Higher Education	Secondary Vocational Education
Kazakhs	30.2	25.9
Russian	24.4	39.3
Uzbeks	15.4	18.0
Ukrainians	19.7	39.3
Uyghur	17.1	22.4
Total employed	27.2	29.7

Source: Smailov A. A. (2011)

Chittaranjan Senapati

Table 5A.27: Infant Mortality in Central Asia *Per 1000 live births*

Country	2005	2010
Kazakhstan	15.2	16.5
Kyrgyzstan	29.7	22.8
Tajikistan	65.1	34
Turkmenistan	12.1	N.A.
Uzbekistan	14.9	10.9

Source: UNICEF/TransMONEE 2012

Table 5A.28: Under Five Child and Maternal Mortality Rate in Central Asia 2005-2010

Country				Under Five mortality rate (%)	Maternal Mortality Rate (%)
Kazakhstan				15	14
Kyrgyzstan				17	15
Tajikistan				13	17
Turkmenistan				2.4	13
Uzbekistan				116	2.4

Source: United Nations 2010

Table 5A.29: Care of Pregnant Women (*per cent)*

Country	Pregnant women who received prenatal care 2000-2008	Deliveries attended by skilled attendants 2000-2007
Kazakhstan	100	100
Kyrgyzstan	97	98
Tajikistan	77	83
Turkmenistan	99	100
Uzbekistan	99	100
Central Asia	94	96

Source: United Nations (2010b)

Table 5A.30: Total Fertility Rates per Women (Ethnic Groups)
Age group 15–44 years

Country	Year	Women by majority ethnic group (Dominant national group of the country)	Women by European Ethnicity (Russians, Ukrainian, Tatar, German),
Kazakhstan	1997-1999	2.5	1.4
Kyrgyzstan	1995-1997	3.6	1.5
Turkmenistan	1998-2000	3.0	1.5
Uzbekistan	1994-1996	3.5	1.1

Source: U.S. Department of Health and Human Services for CDC (2003)

Table 5A.31: Undernourishment in Central Asia (In Per cent)

Country	1990-1992	2005-2007
Kazakhstan	<5	<5
Kyrgyzstan	17	10
Tajikistan	34	30
Turkmenistan	9	6
Uzbekistan	5	11

Source: Food and Agriculture Organization 2011

Table 5A.32: Stunting and Wasting in CARs

Stunting[42] *(Low Height for Age)*				Wasting *(Low Weight for Height)*		
Country	Year	All	Urban	Rural	All	Urban	Rural
Kazakhstan	1999	9.7	5.8	12.3	1.8	1.5	2.4
Kyrgyzstan	1997	24.8	14.8	27.7	3.4	4.3	3.2
Tajikistan	2003	36.2	..	..	4.7	..	..
Turkmenistan	2000	22.3	19.5	24.1	5.7	6.6	5.2
Uzbekistan	2002	21.1	16.3	23.8	7.1	7.9	6.7

Source: McKee, M. et al. (2007)

---

[42] Long term chronic malnutrition and reflected over a period of time causes stunting.

163

Table 5A.33: Households with Water Supply System in Kazakhstan *(per cent)*

Households with Water Supply System	Total Nation Wide	Urban Areas	Rural Areas
1999	67	86.8	22
2003	54.1	81	8.3

Source: Statistics Agency of Kazakhstan and UNDP 2004b

Table 5A.34: Residence by Type of Houses (in Per cent)

Type of House	Urban	Rural
Individual residential houses	48.5 (Uzbeks)	94.5 (Kyrgyz)
Separate residential apartments	44.0(Russians)	4.3
Individual residential houses	2.0	0.4
Common (communal) apartments	1.6	0.2,
Dormitory -	3.3	0.1

Source: Census (2009)

Table 5A.35: Sanitation Situation in Central Asia 2008 *(per cent)*

Improved Sanitation Coverage	Total	Urban	Rural
Kazakhstan	97	97	98
Kyrgyzstan	93	94	93
Tajikistan	94	95	94
Turkmenistan	98	99	97
Uzbekistan	100	100	100

Source: United Nations Data

Chapter 6

Inclusive Policies in India and Central Asia Policies of Equal Opportunities

Section I:

6.1 Social Inclusion in India

Development of social inclusion policies requires information on the forms, nature and mechanism of exclusion in social, political and economic spheres and their consequences on human development. The studies on exclusion in political and economic spheres have received much less attention. There is need to bring more insights on the forms and nature of economic discrimination particularly the market discrimination in private domain. This will enable the understanding of economic and political processes of exclusions and help to develop policies of economic and political inclusion. These are characterised by a high degree of exclusion based inequalities, deprivations and poverty of vast section of their population. This will also help to bring out the issue of group based, exclusion-linked deprivation and poverty.

The term 'social inclusion' originated in French social policy in the 1970s. It gained relevance in the 1980s economic crisis (Benn 2000) when republican tradition of solidarity was in trend (Bhalla and Lapeyre 1997). By the year 1990 the term was theorised by scholars like Bourdieu and Luhmann (Sonwal 2008). Luhmann (1990) defined the concept in the following terms.

Inclusion means the encompassing of the entire population in the performances of the individual function systems. On the one hand, this concerns access to these benefits and, on the other, dependence of individual modes of living on them. To the extent that inclusion is achieved, groups disappear that do not or only marginally participate in social living.

Sen (2001) says that an inclusive society is "characterised by a widely shared social experience and active participation, by equality of opportunities and life chances for individuals and by achievement of a basic level of well-being for all citizens". Social inclusion is conceptualised in terms of the processes (policies and conditions) that contribute to justice.

Social inclusion requires respect for and recognition of the identities and contributions of all social groups and individuals regardless of their backgrounds, and providing equal opportunities for all. Social inclusion is a positive driver of social transformation and change. Social inclusion should be not only a mechanism for integration into existing norms and structures, but also an opportunity for greater diversity and well-being which ultimately enriches social and economic life and leads to a more equitable society.

Planning has traditionally focused on the need to provide special support to historically disadvantaged groups. The SCs and STs have a special status under the Constitution. Other disadvantaged groups needing special support are OBCs and minorities. The Eleventh Five Year Plan (2007–12) adopted a three pronged strategy for social inclusion:

1) Social empowerment—removing existing inequalities besides providing easy access to basic services with a top priority to education.
2) Economic empowerment—promoting regular employment and income generating activities with an objective of making them economically independent; and
3) Social justice—striving to eliminate discrimination with the strength of legislature, affirmative action, awareness generation and change in knowledge, attitude and practices of the people.

6.2 Paradigms of Inclusive Growth

Understanding of inclusive growth is essential to identify social sectors where an inclusive growth strategy is deployed to yield results. The following are covered in the inclusive growth paradigm for bringing about equalities and development in society (Malhotra 2010).

(1) Food – The right to food is a human right. Right to food means that governments must not take actions that result in increasing levels of hunger, food insecurity, and malnutrition. Addressing the problems of hunger, food insecurity, and malnutrition has far-reaching implications for enhancing individual capabilities. Inadequate food intake by children often leaves them 'wasted', 'stunted', or 'underweight'. The recent Food Security Bill has the potential to reduce poverty and usher overall growth.

(2) Education – Education is the key to ensuring greater inclusivity. Within the social sector, the influence of education is the most widespread, and education impacts all types of human development outcomes. Education (especially of the girl child) influences other development indicators like health, nutritional status, income, and family planning. Education is one of the most prominent determinants of movements out of chronic poverty.

(3) Health – Health is vital for growth and development. Healthy children are said to have better learning and better earning capacity in the latter life. In contrast, ill health causes capability deprivation, poverty, and loss of financial and human resources. Poverty induced by poor health reinforces ill health. Poverty leads to nutritional deficiencies, denial of basic amenities like sanitation and clean drinking water cause infections. Improved health has direct impact on labour productivity and individuals' earning capacities.

(4) Social security – It is necessary to ensure a wider provision of social security and welfare for unorganised workers. Promoting social inclusion also requires the government to provide social safety nets (labour employment protection policies, minimum wage, and social insurance) to mitigate the effects of natural disasters, macroeconomic transitions, social upheavals etc. The aged, the poor and the landless are vulnerable to vagaries of the market. They need to be provided social security. Lack of social safety breeds 'exclusion'.

(5) Financial inclusion – Financial inclusion is the delivery of financial services, to marginalised and lower income groups. Affordability and accessibly to public goods and services are the requirements of an efficient society. Financial services are considered to be for the public good. The availability of banking services to all without discrimination is the prime objective of financial inclusion.

(6) Housing – Housing or shelter is a basic need to sustain human life. For the shelter less, possessing a house provides a sense of identity, security, and safety. For a majority of the rural poor and urban slum dwellers, housing is their foremost necessity. Many studies have found a positive relationship between the level of economic development and the quality of housing and access to basic amenities like electricity, safe drinking water, and toilets (Kundu 2009).

(7) Employment – In most developing countries there is a large informal economy where most jobs and job creation are concentrated. According to an NSS report (2005) 93 per cent of India's total labour force and 82 per cent of non-agricultural labour force is engaged in informal sectors. Informal workers produce legal goods and services, but engage in operations that are unregistered and not regulated by, labour laws. They construct buildings, manufacture household goods and machine parts and weave clothes. Inclusive growth expands the employment coverage by bringing more labour force into its ambit.

(8) Political participation – Political participation has important effects on policy choices. Political participation provides direct utility to an individual. Historically, India has witnessed a political participation based on discrimination. Though present political participation, as mandated by the Constitution is based on equality, a lot needs to be done to bring people within the participatory framework.

(9) Poverty eradication – It implies creation of employment opportunities and making them accessible to poor. Inclusive growth makes poverty reduction measures more effective and sustainable. The role of the government in establishing the entitlement of the poor has acquired a greater urgency, since many of the functions of government are being rolled back. The past experience has shown that democratic institutions, affirmative action, and decentralization are necessary but not sufficient to create an even playing field. Investment in human resources development is essential to enabling the poor to realize their entitlements and to develop their capabilities to take advantage of the opportunities offered by globalization. In India, the poverty headcount ratio should come down to 18.6 per cent by the year 2015 (Planning Commission 2011).

Recognising the consequences of discrimination and social exclusion, several countries have formulated equal opportunity policies both to compensate the excluded groups for the denial of rights and equal opportunities and developed legal and other safeguards against it.

6.3 Techniques of Social Inclusion

6.3.1 Decentralisation

Decentralisation of governance plays a very important role in an inclusive growth strategy. Decentralisation is employed to achieve social inclusion by ensuring maximum participation of people in the decision making process. It is known that per-capita income of a country has correlation with quality of government and decentralised governance (Fisman and Gatti 2002). Development is accompanied by decentralization. India introduced a system of local governance and decentralization with the 73rd and 74th Amendments to Constitution of India 1993.

The 1993 constitutional amendment made three levels of elected government, *zilla parishad* at district level; *block panchayat* at block level and *gram panchayat* at village level (municipalities in towns and cities). One-third of all seats at each level of local government were reserved for women candidates. This has brought the marginalised groups such as SC, ST, Muslims and women into the political decision making process.

Twenty-nine subjects[43] in the State List of the Indian Constitution ought to be transferred to the Panchyati Raj Institutions (PRIs), although, many states have transferred the powers, funds and the officials responsible for performing those functions have not been transferred. In other words, the accountability of officials for those subjects still remains to their vertical line ministry in the State capital, rather than to their local clients. PRIs account for merely four per cent of total government expenditure of all levels of government combined. It may be suggested that decentralisation adds to the inclusive growth strategy in India.

6.3.2 Financial Inclusion

Financial inclusion is the process of ensuring access to appropriate financial products and services needed by vulnerable groups such as weaker-sections and low- income groups at an affordable cost in a fair and transparent manner (Government of India 2008b). There is a need to develop a range of pro-poor services, such as Mortgage-free credit services, access to risk- mitigation measures such as health, weather, asset and life insurance, access to vulnerability-reducing

---

[43]　Schedule XI –Article 243G of the Constitution of India.

services like storage or warehouse facilities, and access to financial services like credit, saving and remittances. Despite several initiatives by the government for financial inclusion, only 40 per cent of the population still has bank accounts in rural India. Financial inclusion measures promote social inclusion.

Technology such as mobile, telephone, and bio-metric cards can usher. States can bring legislations to ensure financial inclusion and make bank accounts mandatory. Although micro-finance institutions (MFIs) have changed the lives of millions of poor, their activities are constrained by regulatory mechanisms of the government. RBI's new initiative to allow for-profit MFIs to act as banks may usher infinancial inclusion.

In India, there are supply-side and demand-side factors driving inclusive growth. Banks and other financial institutions mitigate the supply-side processes which will enhance access to financial systems by disadvantaged social groups. Financial inclusion promotes credit and thrift activities among poor, which helps in access to small loans at the time of need. The Empirical evidence shows that countries with a large proportion of population excluded from the formal financial system also show higher poverty ratios and higher inequality (Government of India 2008b).

Good governance is based on inclusive growth. Growth is impossible without achieving financial inclusion. Thus, financial inclusion is a policy compulsion today. Banks and non-banking financial institutions are a key driver for inclusive growth.

Millions of Indians cannot access financial services because they are unable to produce identification documents. The Aadhaar or the unique identity card[44] may facilitate in attaining financial inclusion in India.

6.3.3 Nation-Building as a Model of Social Inclusion

The leadership of different South Asian societies visualised the model of 'nation-building' as solution for inclusive society. It provided a modern ideological basis for unification of their population into a national society and new states to acquire a national identity—an identity overriding all other identities in the society.

---

[44] Aadhar or unique identification card is 12 digits unique identify for every individual. This is randomly generated devoid of any classification based on caste, creed, religion or geography.

At a more general level, the model was seen as a paradigm of social transformation. Thus, the Indian ruling elites conceived nation-building as a state-driven process, through which it sought to bring about economic development, social transformation and cultural integration of the country as a whole.

Similarly, the problems of persistent social inequality and exclusion arising from divisions based on caste hierarchy and ethnic identifications were redefined by the state. This new discourse sustained by democratic politics had many outcomes:

(a) It prevented the emergent majority of the populous, subaltern communities from aggregating and acquiring majority political religious identity;

(b) It brought the caste and ethnic conflicts within the ambit of social policies of the state and;

(c) It encouraged and induced diverse and conflicting communities to process their social and cultural problems through the open, competitive politics of elections and parties.

The model, however, has not been able to address effectively to the issue of ensuring equal access to means of achieving social equality. The ruling elite did not connect affirmative action with other policies that were conceived by them as a part of the larger vision of inclusive nation-building. For example, the education policies, despite laudable recommendations of many commissions has all along favoured the urban, upper-caste English-educated sections of the population, enabling their social and physical mobility, but resulting in massive illiteracy for the members of the poor, lower status communities.

6.3.4 Market as an Instrument of Inclusion

It is argued that market has emerged as an important solution to several of our problems. The policy makers have adopted it as an instrument that brings inclusiveness. Market in the Indian context appears to be inclusive in its coverage and content. Market is entering into all spheres of life both in rural and urban areas and is capturing traditional and modern institutions. Market appears to have covered the non-monetised segment of agriculture sector in all its potency through the process of forward markets. Sen has even indicated (2009) that markets have helped to acquire property at the global level to push the boundaries of justice to grow larger. But the same institution is responsible in creating inequalities that have strengthened social exclusion of those who are weak and marginalised. Therefore Sen himself has advocated the establishment of new social and political institutions to protect the weak from the markets. The 12th Plan document adopted some of the policy prescriptions in its strategic initiatives for inclusive development.

6.3.5 Political Inclusion

Though Indian economy is riding high on the inclusive-growth mandate, it has a flip side. The voting percentage is around fifty per cent in national and state elections. The role of local self- government is crucial to political inclusion in India. Streamlining the three elements of Panchayati Raj Institutions - function, functionary and funds- is essential to create clear delegation between the state and PRIs, between PRIs and line agencies, and across the tiers of the PRIs (World Bank 2006). Thus streamlining Panchayati Raj institutions will go a long way in facilitating political inclusion.

6.3.6 Policies towards Political Inclusion

Political affirmative action consists in introducing structures that ensure that each group participates in political decision-making and power. In a democratic system, structures ensure that minorities participate in decision-making and power. Full participation and empowerment requires initiation and control over major decisions in each of the arms of government and at each relevant level. It implies an empowering role not only with respect to not only the political branches of government but also the military, police and civil service. The socially excluded are discriminated against politically in many different ways and appropriate policies therefore vary accordingly. For example, some groups are completely disenfranchised (immigrant groups). In other cases, majority democracy effectively weakens minority groups (Muslims in India, Hindus in Bangladesh). In practice, as one would expect, political affirmative action rarely achieves full empowerment, but pushes groups somewhat further towards this goal than would occur without it.

Reservation of seats in parliament (political reservation): This is very common, but the reservations are rarely sufficient to prevent ethnic domination, although they do extend representation to the socially excluded, as for example, in the case of India's backward classes. A strong and ethnically balanced judiciary combined with constitutional human rights, can limit the possible abuse by the central government towards any particular group. However, this is more likely to be an outcome of a successful inclusive society than a cause.

Political affirmative action is especially important in relation to conflict, since, as argued above, political exclusion can generate a leadership that mobilises those who are socially and economically excluded to take political action. Moreover, political affirmative action might also be expected to be both a necessary and sufficient condition for improving the economic position of deprived groups. Yet the evidence is less clear on this.

6.3.7 Social and Cultural Inclusion

Social and cultural inclusions are considered to be pillars of inclusive growth. In Indian perspective social exclusion has a historical significance[45] that is an obstacle in the growth of the country. The policies for inclusive growth should distinguish between two types of inequality. One is driven by unequal access to opportunity and circumstances beyond the control of individual - reflecting social exclusion. The other is driven by differences in effort and reflects the rewards and incentives that a market economy provides for citizens who work harder, look for opportunities and take risks in seizing them. Thus inclusive growth requires social inclusion to ensure that every individual has equal access to opportunity. This means investing in social sectors to bring in equality and establish a level-playing field for all.

Policies towards reducing social exclusion are a type of affirmative action. Affirmative action enhances allocation of political and economic entitlements to members of specific groups; in the Indian context, this action covers the public-sector activity.

6.4 Overcome Challenges of Social Exclusion

How to face the challenges of exclusion has been debated for long. There are two divergent viewpoints that have emerged from the debate. The theoretical stand predicts that in competitive markets, discrimination is - temporary phenomenon as employer will select employees who are profitable for the entity. This proposition

---

[45] Reference may be drawn from Constitution of India, which has proscribed untouchability (Article 17 of the Constitution of India) (a social exclusion system in ancient India) and contemplated equality for all (Article 14 of the Constitution of India).

sees the erosion of profits as a solution for eliminating discrimination. This view suggests the promotion of competitive markets to reduce economic and social discrimination. However, others argued for interventionist policy to overcome economic and social discrimination. This school of thought attributes the following reasons for social and economic discrimination.

Firstly, even if the markets are sufficiently competitive, exclusion and discrimination will continue to persist. The discrimination may persist if all the firms/producers practise discrimination, the possibility of which is quite high. The persistence of decades of labour market discrimination in high-income countries attests to the resilience of market discrimination. Secondly, not all markets are competitive. Indeed, in most of the under developed and developing countries, the markets are governed by monopolistic market situations, which empower the firms to discriminate.

Thus, discrimination is an inherent feature of the economic system. Competition is either too weak to offset the group dynamics of identity and interest, or it actually operates to sustain discrimination. Discrimination is due to the dynamics of group identification, competition and conflict rather than irrational, individual attitudes. Market mechanisms must be scrutinised to achieve the goal of equality of opportunity.

These two views have different policy implications for overcoming discrimination. The view, that predicts discrimination to be self-correcting, argues for strengthening competitive market mechanisms. The alternative view asserts that market discrimination will persist, despite the presence of competitive market forces. Therefore, interventionist policies will be necessary. In their view, correcting discrimination will require legal safeguards against discrimination and policies for facilitating a fair share in various spheres. It calls for state interventions, not only in land, labour and capital markets, but also in product and consumer markets, and for fulfilling social needs such as education, housing and health.

6.4.1 Equal Opportunity Policies

Equal opportunity polices believe that all people should be treated equally, without prejudices. Everybody should have "an equal chance to compete within the framework of goals and the structure of rules established." Reservation policies are equal opportunity policies in Indian context. Comparable procedures in other countries are "positive discrimination" in the United Kingdom, and "employment equity" in Canada. Reservation in India is intended to improve the well-being of backward castes and religious minorities.

Currently, the Indian government is faced with the problem of developing equal opportunity policies for communities suffering from social, educational and economic deprivations. This has emerged particularly in the context of the Government's initiative to extend reservation for SCs and STs to the private sector, for the OBCs in public education, for women in politics, and for Muslims in government jobs. Two sets of policies have emerged viz "social and economic empowerment" and "equal opportunity". We, therefore, discuss the relevance of these two policies.

The policy of social and economic empowerment is essentially directed towards improving the ownership of capital assets like agricultural land and business and the educational levels and skills of the discriminated groups. These measures are supposed to augment the capacities of the discriminated groups to undertake business and to enhance their employability by enhancing their education and skill levels. Generally, the policies of economic and social empowerment take the shape of pro-poor policies involving measures to increase access to capital assets including agricultural land, employment, education, housing and food. However, when it comes to equal opportunities in the private sector, the contention does not find similar favour. It is argued that labour, and other markets, generally work in a neutral manner and access to markets is determined by considerations of merit and efficiency. As such, there is no need for safeguards against possible market and non-market discrimination. Thus, while policies for the general education and economic empowerment of discriminated groups are favoured, those ensuring equal share and participation through reservations are marked with differences of opinion. Why is the need for equal opportunity policies for the discriminated groups? The theoretical literatures indicate that the problems of discriminated groups like the former untouchables, women and similar groups are different from those of other groups. The first problem they face is the lack of access to income-earning capital assets like agricultural land and non-farm businesses, quality employment and education due to the denial of these assets to the discriminated groups. The second problem is the continuation of discrimination in various markets and non-market transactions. Therefore, the problem of discriminated groups requires a dual solution—one set of remedies for improving the ownership of land and capital assets, quality employment, and augmenting their educational levels, as compensation for the denial of basic rights in the 'past' and another set of remedies to provide safeguards against discrimination in the 'present'. While the former is based on the principle of compensation for denial of rights in the past the latter is based on the assumption of providing safeguards against discrimination in the present.

These two sets of policies, namely 'economic empowerment' and 'equal opportunity policies' are complementary to each other. The policy of economic empowerment is expected to enhance the capacities of the discriminated groups to take advantage of the social and economic progress. Improved access to livelihood assets will improve the capacities of the discriminated groups. Educational and skill development are expected to increase employability and enable them to gain access to jobs in both private and public sectors. However, the policy of economic empowerment needs to be supplemented by equal opportunity policies. In the absence of equal opportunity policies in the form of reservation, the marginalised groups may face denial of opportunities. It is for this reason that reservation policies have been framed. The complementary nature of these two policies will help the discriminated groups to improve their capabilities and receive due share in the economic and social progress.

6.4.2 Rationale of the Reservation

The reservation policy entitles the SCs and STs to receive three types of benefit. (1) Political reservations: Seats in the Parliament, state-legislatures and Panchayati Raj Institutions, are reserved in proportion to their percentage in the population. (2) Job reservations: Seats are reserved for SCs and STs in all government and public sector jobs, in proportion to their percentage in the population. (3) Educational reservations: Seats are reserved in premier educational institutions.

Although affirmative action started in India in the first decade of the 20th century (Seth 2004) the present set of policies, including reservation, derive their legitimacy from the Indian Constitution. The package addresses three sets of policy goals:

1. Ending of social and religious disabilities suffered by certain specified groups by virtue of their social segregation and ritual exclusion (SCs) and spatial and cultural isolation (STs)
2. Facilitating and promoting equal participation of all socially disabled and disadvantaged groups (OBCs) by means of preferential treatment in education and government employment.

3. To protect, if necessary through legislative action, all these groups, generally identified as the backward classes from all forms of social injustice and exploitation.

In articulating these goals, the policy has widened its scope. Reservations have opened up in the pursuit of an equitable social policy. A series of laws (Untouchability Offences Act of 1955, Protection of Civil Rights Act of 1976, Prevention of Atrocities Act of 1989) have furthered the cause of social justice. Protective laws have been passed preventing alienation of land owned by a tribal to any one belonging to a non-tribal community. Besides, there are many other promotional schemes and programmes for backward classes concerning land allotments, housing, scholarships, subsidies and credits aimed at providing physical security as well as promoting occupational mobility of these groups.

6.4.3 Reservation in Services

The reservation in services is extended to SCs, STs, and OBCs. They constitute nearly 86 per cent of Indian population. Despite 27 per cent posts being reserved for OBCs since 1993, the overall representation of OBCs in government service is abysmally low, just 4.53 per cent. Only 3.9 per cent, 2.3per cent and 5.2 per cent, respectively of Group A, B, and C posts are occupied by OBC population (Table 6.1). This is indeed a matter of concern.

Table 6.1: Percentage of Various Groups Representation in Central Government Services

As on Jan 1, 2010

Social Group		A	B	C	D (Excluding Sweepers)	Total (Excluding Sweepers)
	Total	88896	173493	2070666	665739	2998788
SCs	Number	10315	26495	330167	123780	490727
	Per cent	11.6	15.3	15.9	18.6	16.36
STs	Number	3998	9923	153844	47702	215467
	Per cent	4.5	5.7	7.4	7.2	7.19
OBCs	Number	7505	10648	306176	101114	425443
	Per cent	8.4	6.1	14.8	15.2	14.19

Source: Annual Report, Department of Personnel and Training, GOI, 2011-12 p.38

6.5 Performance of Reservation Policy

Despite tardy implementation of the policy of reservations, it has worked reasonably well. It can, in fact, claim some significant achievements not only for the beneficiary groups of SCs, STs and OBCs, but for the whole nation. First, reservations have changed the nature and composition of the Indian middle-class, making it more inclusive. A sizeable section of India's middle-class consists of the second and third generation beneficiaries of reservations.

Second, about 60 years ago Dalits, Tribals and OBCs could aspire only to a limited degree of upward mobility and that too as collective groups functioning within the caste structure. Today, with reservations opening up avenues for the middle-class, not only the incidence of their upward mobility increased, their dependence on ritualistic modes sanctioned by the caste system, such as sanskritization has decreased. This changed pattern of social mobility—a larger number of individual members of 'lower castes' acquiring middle-class identity—has deeply shaken the economic and cultural roots of the caste system. Thus, consumerization rather than sanskritization has become a middle-class marker.

Third, working for over a period of 60 years reservations have made a cumulative and lasting impact on India's political system. With educational and occupational opportunities provided by reservations a new political leadership has emerged from among the SCs, STs and OBCs for example, the growth of Bahujan Samaj Party (BSP), or the formation of trade-union associations of *Dalits* and the backward-class government employees.

In short, reservations have contributed to changing the old balance of power in the society.

The need to continue and strengthen the policy of affirmative action is greater today than ever before. As the economy is freed from state control, the government has to see that the weaker and vulnerable sections in the society are protected from market practices. No economic reforms can work unless a vast majority of a country's population—who in India go by such names as SCs, STs and OBCs—acquire a stake in them. Liberalisation does not mean, not even in the most liberalised economies of the world, that governments cease to rule and surrender the fate of the country's poor and deprived to the 'market forces'.

6.5.1 New Policy Initiatives

In view of the above, there is a need to reinvent the affirmative action policies:

1. An exit policy from reservations for members of those beneficiary communities who may be found, after careful investigations, having ceased to be socially and educationally backward. This will enable those extremely backward communities who are technically entitled to reservation benefits but do not receive them in reality. A lion's share of such benefits goes to a small elite-minority that has emerged among them. The exit policy, however, should not apply to *dalits*, at least until their discrimination in public sphere totally ceases and incidence of 'atrocity' on them completely stops. Same will apply to a section of tribals still living in conditions of physical isolation.

2. Special developmental and promotional measures need to be thought of and implemented for reaching directly the poor and 'backward' households among the upper-caste communities. These developmental and promotional measures should *not be* confused or tied with the reservations made for the socially deprived under affirmative action policies, which are founded on an entirely different value premise and rationale.

3. The recruitment policy of the private sector needs to be modified and adapted to the principle of diversity. It is now being recognised that

having culturally diverse personnel working at any workplace is not just healthy management but, also beneficial to the company. The policy of diversity should particularly be conceived as special promotional measures for the routinely unrepresented cultural groups in business and the organised economy, but it should not be equated or confused with existing affirmative action policies, which aims at, among other things, inclusion of the traditionally and systematically excluded groups in the power-structure of the state and institutions.

6.5.2 Current Reservation Issues

Indian society has discriminatory characteristics. This discrimination has arisen due to caste, ethnicity and religion identities. Many countries have faced such discrimination among people. The government of the country has enacted laws and policies. Specifically, policies adopted by Malaysia and South Africa, as a way of correcting centuries of historical discrimination could also serve as pointers.

The government's initiative to bring the private sector within the ambit of reservation policy and to extend reservations to the OBCs in public educational institutions has led to a renewed discussion on reservation in the private sector. Many questions are cropping up such as: are separate policies necessary for the lower castes? If yes, what should be the nature of such policies? Some argue that reservations involve costs in terms of efficiency, merit and reverse discrimination.

6.6 International Experience

Given the evidence on inter-social group inequality and discrimination, a policy for overcoming the consequences of past discrimination and providing legal safeguards against present discrimination is inevitable. There are lessons to be drawn from international experiences, which have often been quoted for the issue of private sector reservation in India, particularly with respect to two aspects: (1) the type of economic sectors and (2) the methods used.

First, with regard to the economic sphere, most countries have developed legal and equal access policies through affirmative actions for the discriminated groups in multiple economic and social spheres.

Second, with regard to the method, at least three kinds of "procedures" are used. The first method incorporates protection against discrimination in the form of "anti-discrimination laws". The second method utilises equal access measures of various types known by different names such as affirmative action/reservation/ fair access policies and involves proactive measures to ensure fair access for the discriminated groups. In some countries, formal and informal quota systems are incorporated to achieve equity in access to resources. However, in both aspects, the population or labour force is used as an indicator to measure and ensure the fair share of representation.

The third method is known as "reparation or compensation". It is a fact that reservation programmes are intended to address the problems of present discrimination and address the issue of cumulative impact of historical discrimination. The instruments of "compensation", on the other hand, are specifically designed to compensate for the denial of property rights and education to the discriminated groups as a one-time settlement and through continuous efforts in compensatory modes.

6.7 Lessons Learnt

Adoption of these three-tier measures for the lower castes in India will largely depend on the nature deprivation faced by them. The residual impact of the caste system and continuing forms of discrimination in the present are not in question; but the question centres on the nature of interventions for securing equal rights to lower castes.

The strategy of "compensation" is possibly necessary to repay for the denial of property rights in agricultural land, business and education. Essentially, the "compensation" principle is justified on the basis of the need to repay the lower castes for the historical material losses suffered by them.

Policies for increasing the ownership of agricultural land for lower castes should be incorporated within the framework of "compensation" principles. Among other countries, the Malaysian programme to improve the ownership of agriculture land for the indigenous Malay community is an example under which large tracts of agricultural lands were acquired and distributed to the Malays as a one-time settlement. Similarly, the government in India too, should group together government land and land acquired under ceiling laws, as well as land free from legal problems and classify them together as a "pool of common land" and redistribute it to the low castes to compensate for the historical denial of land Rights in a onetime settlement.

Like in agriculture land, the lower castes, particularly the SCs were also debarred from undertaking any business activity on account of the notions of purity and pollution. It is important therefore, that the policies for improving business ownership by the lower castes be treated mainly in a compensatory mode – developing programmes to improve their ownership of businesses and their share in private capital. The measures for the promotion of such businesses may include reservations in government and private contracts of various types and reservations in the purchases of agricultural and other products by the government and private sector.

This is necessary to provide safeguards against the exclusion faced by the low castes in sale of goods and services. There is also a need to increase the ownership of corporate capital among the lower castes. In this respect, again there is a lot to be learnt from the Malaysian and the South African experience. The systematic redistribution of private capital ownership to a minority community was undertaken in Malaysia, whereby, the share of the Malay community rose from two per cent to thirty per cent over three decades. For this purpose, the Malaysian government fixed the quotas in the share capital of private companies and set up special institutions to finance the equity participation of the Malaya minority (Thorat 2004b). The Malaysian experience, therefore, could guide the efforts of the Indian government to ensure that the share of the lower caste in private capital of the lower castes increases. Coming to employment policy, the pattern of employment among lower castes is such that a majority of them are primarily casual wage labourers. As a vast majority of these casual labourers are adequately represented, there seems to be no need of developing a reservation policy, but legal safeguards against selective discrimination in hiring and wage payments in the form of anti-discrimination law is necessary. In the non-farm sector, the discrimination in employment is possibly of a high order in certain categories of jobs, if not all. Therefore, it is imperative that a strategy of legal safeguards along with reservations be developed for the non-farm sector.

Lastly, educational policies for lower castes should also be considered in the twin framework of compensation for the past denial of right to education and provision of equal opportunity against present discrimination. The lower castes need to be compensated by implementation of a comprehensive programme of education designed specifically for their empowerment.

It is necessary to recognise that the exceptionally high proportion of the higher-caste students in educational institutions is marked because education was artificially reserved for them by putting entry barriers to the vast section of lower castes till the beginning of the 20th century. Perceptibly, the present higher share of the high castes in education is the result of continuous privileges enjoyed by earlier generations which continues today as well. It is this social debt, which higher castes owe to the lower castes which needs to be repaid by compensatory policies.

How to develop inclusive policies so that the high-caste and the low-caste youth have an equal share in accessing education is an issue. An inclusive policy which benefits both the groups should be developed.

6.8 On Alternatives, Merit and Creamy Layer

A number of issues related to alternative policies, merits and creamy layer have figured in the discussion on reservation. The first issue relates to the suggestion of using general policies to improve employability and human resource capability of lower castes instead of reservation. It needs to be recognised that lower castes need both because their problem is two-fold – namely lack of access to fixed capital assets, employment and education due to denial in the "past", but also continuing discrimination in the "present". Therefore it requires a dual solution. Improving education and employability alone will not help the lower castes unless it is supplemented by strategies of equal access in the form of reservations to overcome discrimination. It is not coincidental that in several countries the policies of economic and educational empowerment for discriminated groups are supplemented by equal opportunity policies of affirmative action and reservation (Thorat 2004c).

Social and economic inequality: There is a need to distinguish between economic and social inequality. Social inequality is the result of discrimination perpetuated by society for centuries. This then leads to a deficit of what Velaskar (1986) calls "cultural capital". Cultural capital is the ability to use knowledge, gained from praxis and contemplation to both understand the world around us well as articulate a world view that defines our identity (Mohanty 2006). All communities therefore accumulate cultural capital. But in hierarchical societies, certain kinds of cultural capital are privileged over others because certain groups had access to society's knowledge. The denial of cultural capital and the lack of access to education prohibit ability to deal with knowledge. Therefore it is unfair to think of similar situation of a poor SC, ST and upper caste Hindu. Deshpande and Yadav (2006) view caste inequality and income inequality as two different paradigms.

The former involves historical institutions perpetuating discrimination while the latter is income disparity. Equating the two nullifies the point of caste-based reservations. So caste and income inequality must not be equated.

6.9 Reservation on Economic Criterion:

The second issue relates to suggestions that reservation should be based on economic criterion rather than caste or ethnicity. Insights from theory indicate that the basis of discrimination is group identity and not economic powerlessness. In fact, identity-based exclusion from economic and social rights is the source of powerlessness. Such forms of exclusion are suffered by both relatively better-off and worse-off persons belonging to the discriminated groups. Therefore, the basis of preferential policy in favour of the lower castes needs to be based on caste.

Also, this aspect is closely intertwined with the other suggestion that preferential policies should be utilised only for the relatively worse-off sections within the discriminated groups and that the relatively better-off sections should be excluded from the purview of reservations. This view assumes that the relatively better off sections within the discriminated groups possesses enough economic strength to overcome the effects of discrimination faced by them. The better off section can voluntarily withdraw themselves from the reservation opportunities. On the other hand, we should take note of the stipulated quota for the SC/ST is not fulfilled till now. Therefore, 15 % reservation quota should be taken care up in India in first hand.

6.10 Reservation for Better Off

Since caste discrimination is the basis of reservation, the use of the same for relatively better-off sections from the low castes would depend largely on whether they are able to overcome the cumulative impact of discrimination due to their economic strength. Indeed, if that is the case then the relatively better-off sections may not need protection against discrimination in the form of reservation. But if they experience caste-based discrimination, then measures against such discrimination are necessary. As such, there is little research on this issue. It is too early to say whether the relatively better-off sections should be excluded from the purview of the reservation policy. This will require us to identify that critical minimum "economic level", which would enable the lower caste to overcome the discrimination on the basis of economic strength, so that safeguards in the form of reservation against discrimination are not necessary. This will vary from caste to caste depending on the intensity of discrimination.

In the case of the SCs, both the relatively better-off and worse-off sections suffer from discrimination, although in differing degrees and therefore, they require protection against discrimination in the form of both anti-discriminatory laws and equal opportunity policies such as reservations. However, the better-off sections could be excluded from concessionary economic benefits which are already being practised.

6.11 Flexibility in Qualifications

Another issue pertains to the assumptions regarding the adverse consequences of relaxation in qualifications on such aspects as productivity and educational quality. Employers that practise affirmative action have tried to mitigate its potentially negative effects on performance by pre-screening the recruitment and hiring criterion, as well as, by special training and evaluation efforts afterwards.

In case of education, providing admissions to persons with lesser grades does not carry the potential of affecting educational standards. It only provides low caste groups the prospect of accessing education without any significant relaxations in passing grades or marks. But despite this, other writings on these themes have overplayed the issue of merit.

It is necessary to recognise the exclusionary and discriminatory character of our society and economy associated with caste, ethnicity, religion and other group identities and the need to develop remedies. However, to design appropriate policies, an understanding of contemporary forms of discrimination in multiple spheres, and their consequences is quite necessary. It becomes imperative, therefore, to undertake empirical studies on the exclusionary character of our economy, society, and polity, an area which has been neglected in the mainstream social science research so far.

6.12 Inclusive Agenda in 12th Plan

The 12th Five Year Plan has a special focus on the inclusive agenda. The following is an attempt to address the needs of marginalised sections of the population.

Health access to services: Barriers to access should be recognised for disadvantaged people. Among marginalised groups, the SC and ST populations minorities, particularly vulnerable tribal groups (PVTGs), de-notified and nomadic tribes, *Musahars* and the internally displaced shall be given special attention while making provisions for, setting up and renovating sub-centres and *anganwadis*.

Monitoring and evaluation systems: Routine monitoring and concurrent impact evaluations should collect disaggregated information on disadvantaged segments of the population. This is to assess the accessibility of services and their impact.

Representation in community forum: Wherever a community-level forum exists such as Rogi Kalyan Samitis, representation of the marginalised groups should be mandatory. Also, every village health sanitation and nutrition committee should have 50 per cent representation of women.

6.12.1 Education

Address Residual Access and Equity Gaps

Special efforts are needed during the 12 th Plan period for those children who are out of school or who need sustained attention to continue in school. Here the focus has to be on every child in school and learning well.

Focus on SC/ST Children

The Plan document has proposed that at least five per cent of existing government elementary schools in all Educationally Backward Blocks (EBB) with more than 50 per cent tribal population will be converted into residential school complexes (RSCs) having provision for pre-schools, and primary and middle schools. There should be a provision for seasonal hostel facilities for children of migrating families. These hostels will follow norms set out in the Kasturba Gandhi Balika Vidyalaya (KGBV) scheme. In EBBs with over 50 per cent tribal population, government schools would be converted into RSCs and seasonal hostels for migrating tribal children. A few state governments, such as Andhra Pradesh have integrated Ashram Schools (regular residential schools) under the RTE-harmonised SSA. Other states should follow the same approach. Further, convergence with the Ministry of Tribal Affairs for all ashram *shalas* should be forged to achieve adequate pupil teacher ratio (PTR) and acquire infrastructure/ facilities/ teaching–learning equipment (TLE) as per the RTE norms. Special support would be needed to ensure retention and improved learning for children from SC communities. These efforts need to converge with the programmes of the ministry of social justice and empowerment (MSJ&E).

There is a need to review and revise curriculum addressing caste-based exclusion and promoting inclusion. Interventions for SCs include (i) process-based interventions such as curricular review to include discussion on caste based discrimination in textual material; (ii) residential schools run with assistance from the Ministry of Social Justice and Empowerment (MSJ&E) to conform to the RTE norms; (iii) convergence on pre-matric scholarships and incentives provided by Ministry of Social Justice; (iv) partnerships with *Dalit* Civil Society Organisations (CSOs) for support of *Dalit* children.

6.12.2 Focus on Muslims, SC, ST and OBCs for Higher Education

Schemes for establishing model degree colleges, community colleges and polytechnics in the low GER (gross enrolment ratio) districts will be modified to cover districts that have concentration of Muslims. Setting up of women's colleges and hostels in small towns will be given high priority. All these schemes should be included within the ambit of the state strategic plans for higher education.

Targeted schemes will be launched to draw students from Muslims that have low participation in higher education. These schemes will have to combine special incentives to offer to the school pass-outs from these communities. Special scheme will be launched in districts that have sizeable Muslim population. Particularly, educational opportunities for girls will be emphasised.

Despite a number of initiatives in the previous Plan periods, there is a staggering difference among different groups. Hence, a targeted approach with focus on SC and ST dominated regions and convergence of various equity schemes to address the educational needs of the disadvantaged sections will be critical to enhance their inclusion in the mainstream of higher education. Given the co-existence of educational backwardness in both social and location factors, such as their greater presence in rural, hilly, inaccessible terrains, a synergy of efforts to address these factors will be important.

6.12.3 Constitutional Safeguards

The Constitution of India guarantees protection from social injustice and all forms of exploitation (Art. 46). It guarantees equality before law (Art. 14), and enjoins upon the State not to discriminate against any citizen on grounds of caste [Art. 15 (1)]. Untouchability is abolished and its practice in any form is forbidden (Art. 17). The Constitution mandates that no citizen shall be subjected to any disability and restriction on grounds of caste or race [Art. 15 (2)]. It empowers the State to make provisions for reservation in educational institutions [Art. 15 (4) and (5)] appointments for posts in favour of SCs (Art. 16 (4), 16(4A), 16(4B) and Art. 335) (Constitution of India).

Reservation of seats in the Lok Sabha is provided under Article 330, in the State Assemblies under Article 332 and in the Local Self-Governments bodies under Articles 243D and 340T. Besides, Parliament has enacted the Untouchability (Offences) Act, 1955, renamed as Protection of Civil Rights Act, in 1976. Scheduled Castes and the Scheduled Tribes (Prevention of Atrocities) Act, 1989 has also been enacted to check and prevent atrocities against SCs.

6.12.4.1 Scheduled Castes: Strategy for the Twelfth Plan

The principal goals for the Twelfth Plan, towards empowerment of the Scheduled Castes, will be:

1. To ensure the security and dignity of all persons belonging to the scheduled castes, especially women and put a complete end to all forms of 'untouchability' and discrimination against them.
2. To bring members of the SCs—both men and women—at par, to the maximum possible extent, with their non-SC/ST counterparts, in terms of all developmental indices viz.—education, health, asset ownership, food and nutrition, housing, employment and labour force participation.
3. To empower SCs to participate in society and in nation-building, on an equal basis with others.
4. To effectively implement SCSP as the essential instrument for accomplishing inclusive growth.

Constitutional Safeguards

The Constitution of India has made several provisions to safeguard the interests of the STs in Articles 15(4), 16(4), 46, 243M, 243 ZC, 244, the first and second provisos to 275(1), Articles 334, 335, 338A, 339(1), and the Fifth and the Sixth Schedules. Besides these, several laws have been enacted by the Central Government like the Protection of Civil Rights Act, 1955; the Scheduled Castes and Scheduled Tribes (Prevention of Atrocities) Act, 1989; the Provisions of the Panchayats (Extension to Scheduled Areas) Act, 1996; the Scheduled Tribes and Other Traditional Forest Dwellers (Recognition of Forest Rights) Act, 2006 as well as by the State Governments. The Centre has been given the authority of giving directions to the State Governments (Article 339(2), (Para 3 of the Fifth Schedule) in the interest of tribal people. Further, a National Tribal Policy is on the anvil.

Primitive Tribal Groups (PTGs): There are 75 identified Primitive Tribal Groups (PTGs) spread across 17 States/UTs living in utmost destitute conditions. Some of them, in dire straits, also face the threat of extinction. In order to provide focused attention to the survival, protection and development of these PTGs, a special scheme launched in 1998–99 was implemented during the Tenth Plan to provide tribe specific services and support including, inter-alia, housing, land, agricultural inputs, cattle rearing, health, nutritional services and income generating programmes.

Scheduled Tribes (STs) receive similar benefits of reservations as the SCs, i.e. seats in legislatures and local government bodies, government employment and educational institutions. The number of seats reserved for them in each of the three sectors is in proportion to their per cent in the population. However, similar to case of SCs, inclusion in the lists is by executive order and exclusion only through a decision of the Parliament. The communities from different religions, Hinduism, Christianity and Islam as well as indigenous tribal faiths are included.

6.12.4.2 Scheduled Tribes: 12th Plan

The approach of the Twelfth Five Year Plan must be to achieve overall improvement in the socio-economic conditions of the Scheduled Tribes. The plan has recommended following measure towards this end.

a) Relaxing the normative prescriptions about taking up a programme or a scheme in the Tribal majority areas.

b) Preferring engaging people from the tribal community itself in the areas predominantly inhabited by tribals for government efforts at spreading education, health and extension services, nutrition, public distribution, and so on.

c) Reorganising basic services such as nutritional interventions, education, health services, public distribution system, and employment generating activities under MGNREGA.

d) Land acquisition of tribal land to be addressed as required under PESA and displaced tribal population to be resettled and rehabilitated.

e) Tribal communities to have full right to minor forest produce.

Constitutional Safeguards

The Constitution does not make any specific provisions for OBCs, but Article 15 of the Constitution empowers the States to make any special provision for the advancement of any socially and educationally backward classes of citizens.

Article 16 (4) also empowers the State to make provisions for reservations in appointments in favour of any backward class of citizens which in the opinion of the States is not adequately representative in the services under the State. The Directive Principles of State Policy of the Constitution (Article 46) also state that 'The State shall promote with special care the educational and economic interests of the weaker sections of the people.' It also empowers the State to appoint a Commission to investigate into the conditions of socially and educationally backward classes (Article 340).

The forthcoming data of census 2011 on OBCs will help to undertake exact assessment of their population size; literacy rate; employment status in government, private and unorganized sectors; basic civic amenities; health status; poverty status; and human development and HPIs.

Other Backward Class (OBC) group is the most numerous and heterogeneous of all. Over the years their representation in legislatures has vastly increased through the normal processes of competitive politics. It is an account of democratic politics managing inclusion of members of the socially deprived through progressive expansion of affirmative action policies and, thus, preventing the Indian state from acquiring ethno-majority character.

The quantum of reservations for the OBCs has been fixed at 27 per cent which are a little over half to their proportion in the population. Until 1991 several states did not have any provision of reservations for them. Viewed from the national or the State levels, the OBCs today constitute a far more (economically and educationally) heterogeneous category by comparison with the SCs and STs.

6.12.4.3 OBCs and the Twelfth Five Year Plan; the Way Ahead

Educational Development

For ensuring educational development amongst OBCs, schemes for providing scholarships for pursuing Pre-Matric, Post-Matric and other higher education, supported with hostel facilities will be taken up on priority basis.

National Overseas Scholarship Scheme for OBCs could also be formulated similar to those for SCs and STs so that OBC students can also go abroad for educational and professional courses which are generally not available in the country. There is a demand for Rajiv Gandhi National Fellowship (RGNF) scheme on the pattern available to the SC and ST students to be introduced for OBC students during the Twelfth Five Year Plan.

Economic Development

To meet the marketing needs and to facilitate providing a marketing platform for artisans and handicraft persons belonging to OBCs, a Marketing Federation on the lines of TRIFED may be set up.

The main activities of the Federation would include cluster development of the artisans engaged particularly in arts and craft, training for upgradation of their skills, exhibition of their products to showcase their work both in India and abroad, opening of marketing outlets to appreciate, reward and popularise successful models which can be replicated by others

6.13 Muslims

To ensure comprehensive development through a multi-sectoral approach, 90 Minority Concentration Districts (MCDs) covering 34 per cent of the minority population in the country, have been identified on the basis of either human development indicators or basic amenities indicators (Government of India 2012). The effort is to improve the socio economic condition through provision of better infrastructure.

The eleventh plan was the first plan to introduce a number of schemes aimed at improving the conditions of the minorities. As in the case of other disadvantaged communities a three-pronged strategy is needed for Muslims, which will focus on (i) social empowerment; (ii) economic empowerment; and (iii) social justice.

6.13.1 Recommendations for the Twelfth Five Year Plan

The Twelfth Plan has envisaged for the empowerment of minorities through their active participation in the developmental process as participants. The Twelfth Plan document visions for faster and more inclusive growth. The inclusion and empowerment of different socio-religious communities is now critical development imperative. Government of India has envisaged bold measures for inclusion of minorities in to the mainstream. They are listed as under.

a) **Increase allocation**: Increase the scale of key interventions by greater financial outlays across the board to include MSDP and also bringing a larger number of schemes within the scope of the 15 Point Programme, by making educational scholarships demand-driven and by initiating key pilot programmes to develop best practices for the future.

b) **Directly target minorities**: Re-vamp the design, expand the scope and strengthen implementation structures of key initiatives like the MsDP and 15 Point Programme such that minority settlements and people are directly targeted; such direct targeting should be made a condition for approval of all block and district level plans.

c) **Institutionalise robust monitoring**: Create internal accountability and impact-based monitoring systems that go beyond purely physical and financial monitoring. Involve CSOs and peoples' groups in conducting time-bound social audits of schemes and create democratic dialogues between minority groups and state institutions at the grassroots level.

d) **Develop transformative leadership**: Build transformative leadership, through training and capacity building schemes, among minority communities on a large scale, especially among minority women and youth, so that they can themselves create accountability at the local level to help the State provide better neighbourhoods, jobs, education, health, housing, hygiene, skills and incomes.

e) **Focus on skill building for employability**: Develop skills to generate employability among minority youth in all MSDP blocks and towns through direct linkages with the National Skill Development Mission.

f) **Initiate pilot schemes for minorities**: The twelfth plan should institutionalise a 'hub of innovation', through restructuring the Maulana Azad Education Foundation, wherein a range of experiments in educational and livelihood initiatives among minorities can be undertaken. Civil society engagement with Muslims should be revived urgently through grants-in-aid mechanisms.

NSSO data (66th Round) shows that in urban areas, over 88 per cent of Muslim workers in the age of fifteen years and above are in informal employment the highest for any community. Muslims make up just over six per cent of all government jobs, the lowest share of all community and social groups.

RBI data shows that in the 121 districts, average per capita advances to Muslims increased from ₹ 50,000 in 2008 to cover ₹ 100,000 in 2011. But in the same districts advances to Hindus increased from around ₹ 230,000 in 2008 to ₹ 270,000 by 2011. It is good that financial allocation has increased from ₹ 500 crore in 2008-09 to ₹ 3135 crore in 2012-13. The actual per capita expenditure was working out to just ₹ 230 in 2011-12 because 20 per cent of the funds remained unutilised and only about 50 per cent Muslim population could be covered under the scheme (Government of India 2012).

Section II: Social Inclusion in Central Asia

The process of inclusion is not just negating exclusion or undoing discrimination it is strengthening sense of belongingness and bonding within society. It incorporates the marginalised and excluded sections of society into the mainstream community. Inclusion can be considered as comprehensive approach which needs to achieve innovation and integrity. Transition in Central Asia economy has eroded economic benefits such as subsidies and grants meant for the poor. Consequently the poorest section of society has suffered most. The overall analysis of the Central Asian states show that the large segment of society at political, economic and social level is still in flux between the traditional notions of government, Soviet rule, market economy and democratisation. Central Asian states often see contradictory streams within society.

The European Commission (2004) says Social inclusion as "a process which ensures that those at risk of poverty and social exclusion gain the opportunities and resources necessary to participate fully in economic, social and cultural life and to enjoy a standard of living that is considered normal in the society in which they live". Social inclusion involves at least two steps (a) removing barriers to participate and access to resources and opportunities (b) promoting a change in attitudes.

The process of inclusion in Central Asia as strengthening of social bond is at an early stage. These states are undergoing the process of nation-building and as a result many forces are working simultaneously. Analysis of Central Asian history reveals that states are named after a "titular" or "indigenous" nationality. The Soviet policies have organised the region in a manner that each ethnic group has operational autonomy with considerable presence of Russian population. Such strategic presence along with bilingual policies has helped Russia to rule the region. The category 'nationality', referring to one's ethno-national affiliation was recorded as official identity. Dave (2007) in her book on Kazakhstan argues that in the post soviet period the minorities in Central Asian states were not given territorial autonomy and avenues of expressing protest and resistance were taken away. It is most explicit in the language policies of state. For example, in Kazakhstan, after independence, Russian was the second official language and Kazakh being the first. Uzbek and Tajiks are largest minority in Kyrgyzstan and Uzbekistan respectively. Hence both Uzbeks and Tajiks demanded recognition of their languages as second official language. But the demands were rejected (Dave 2007). During implementation of inclusion programmes, Central Asian states have to consider long term economic and comprehensive social interests. During Soviet period various affirmative actions were launched for titular ethnic groups. These include the subsidies, incentives and opportunities for rapid development (Dave 2004).

The transition recession contributed to a deterioration of social protection, social services and, most importantly, triggered high unemployment. The emerging inequality was caused by fundamental changes in the labour market and in the institutional environment. Many experts believe agriculture has the potential to foster social inclusion, primarily by decreasing rural poverty (UNDP 2011).

The initiatives of social inclusion are undertaken by state and civil society. Market is yet to play a crucial role in social inclusion. The government measures of social inclusions are based on welfare, poverty alleviation and equal- opportunity measures as well as general governance. The civil society implements welfare -oriented programmes for the poor, resulting in social inclusion.

6.14 Affirmative Actions

The study title 'Education in Transition' (Kazimzade 2011) defines affirmative action as the policy measures taken by states to address the grievances of minorities and people belonging to lower socio-economic status which are results of past discriminations. The affirmative action in Central Asia has its routes to Soviet period policies. Since independence no direct measures have been undertaken to address grievances of ethnic minorities.

6.14.1 Constitutional Provisions

All Central Asian states have opted for the democratic form of governance after the independence claiming their desire to become developed state. They have adopted the democratic constitutions. While analyzing the constitutional provisions several studies admitted no separate mention or recognition of "minorities" in the constitutions. However, constitutions of these states recognize equal citizenship for all nationalities irrespective of ethnic, racial groups divisions.

6.14.1.1 Kazakhstan

Demographic composition and Kazakh language have served as two salient tools of promoting nationalism and attaining Kazakh ethno national hegemony in the new state since independence in 1991. In this process of nation building many sections of Kazakhstan's society were deprived of their legitimate share of development. These are rural poor, section of Kazakh population Russians, Uzbek, other ethnic minorities and people living in mono company towns. Kazakhstan from time to time has taken measures to recognize and address the need of excluded sections of the society. Kazakhstan's constitution or laws have not mentioned the word minorities or entitlements for such minorities. Thus, special provisions for ethnic minorities are not included in the state policies or programmes. Some of the policies implemented earlier were ad hoc, extra-constitutional and executed informally.

In Kazakhstan, the demographic difference between titular Kazakh ethnic group and Russian minority group is not large. Russians consider Kazakhstan as the extended home and the others including Kazakhs consider Russians as cultural hegemony (superior) groups; as they have made contribution in development of Kazakh ethnic group from pastoral to settled group. There is also a section supporting the claim of cultural hegemony of Russian as former rulers are not reconciling with the minority status.

Right to Participate in the Government

The right to participate in the government and the right to elect and be elected into governmental agencies and institutions of local government are inscribed in Article 33 of the Constitution of the Republic of Kazakhstan. Kazakhstan has set up the structures of ethnic representation in formalistic and ceremonial compliance. Kazakhstan has selectively incorporated safeguards for 'minorities', by stressing the notion of 'malye narody'[46] ('small peoples'), which refers to small ethnic groups, many of whom have no recognisable homeland (Dave 2007).

The Assembly of the Peoples of Kazakhstan represents 300 representatives of different ethnic groups and also has branches at the oblast level. Recently in January 2013, Kazakhstan has revised the rule of ethnic representation to make the assembly a representative body of all ethnic groups. 'Planning Document for the Development of the Assembly of People of Kazakhstan 2020' advocates for monitoring the inter-ethnic situation; conducting research in efforts to improve training programmes, mediation of inter-ethnic problems (Gulmira Kamziyeva 2013).

The significance of social security in the Constitution of Kazakhstan can be comprehended through the various provisions in it. Article 19 underlines freedom about one's national, party and religious affiliation and its clause (2) deals with right to use native language as medium of instruction in education, and also to express and preserve culture. Article 28 ensures economic security of various sections such as pension and social security in the old age, sickness, disability and loss of bread winner. The same article also recommends for voluntary insurance depend on necessity of such provision for society. The Bertelsmann Transformation Index[47] (BTI) examining socio economic condition of society concludes that though affirmative actions have constitutional approvals, the policies of affirmative actions are remaining underfunded and under executed.

---

[46] The term narod (people) presupposes the lack of cultural and territorial concentration and the absence of a homeland.

[47] The report is part of the Bertelsmann Stiftung's Transformation Index (BTI) 2012. It is Global assessment of transition processes in which state of democracy and market economy as well as the quality of political management in 128 transformation and developing countries.

6.14.1.2 Kyrgyzstan

Kyrgyzstan has strained relations between majority Kyrgyz and Uzbek minority group. Such tensions often lead to violent conflict between these groups. The ethnic minorities in Kyrgyzstan are less represented in political sphere. The 2010 ethnic violence has raised the demand for revision of present ethnic quota policies. There are efforts for promoting harmony among the ethnic minorities, helping to develop ethnic cultural centres, strengthen trust, and encourage greater openness in communication between the people of different nationalities and representatives of the government agencies. Despite all these the representatives of ethnic minorities are yet to be incorporated into the government process. The Kyrgyzstan National Assembly has become a representative agency expressing the interests, hopes and protecting the rights of the multitude of ethnic groups residing in the republic.

It can be claimed that the Kyrgyzstan National Assembly is still the only significant platform for managing ethnic relations in the country. That is, the state does not have any special government agencies, such as a state committee or ministry, for solving problems in ethnic interrelations.

Constitutional Provisions

Similar to the constitutional provisions of other countries, Kyrgyzstan constitution advocates integration of various ethnic groups. Ethnic tension in Kyrgyzstan is rooted in economic differences and there is need to adopt systematic policies to eliminate - ethnic tensions. The constitution has provision to protect the rights of ethnic-religious and linguistic minorities. Kyrgyzstan has implemented the affirmative action programme in Uzbek dominated regions of the country. The constitution of Kyrgyzstan has provision for bilingualism. Besides the official language Kyrgyz, Russian is also considered a national language and minorities have the right to preserve their languages. Bilingualism is official policy and the legislation has also been placed to protect its linguistic diversity. In case of education there is provision for four languages as medium of instruction. The right to choose the language of education has been enshrined in the constitution (Article 10). The percentage of language in school roughly matches the ethnic composition of the state.

Inclusion of Minorities in Police and Judicial System

The study conducted by UNHROHC as an assessment of minority participation in law enforcement system notes the decline in the minorities' representations in police and judicial forces. The data shows high underrepresentation of minorities in law enforcement. The study focused on three aspects - representation of minorities in law enforcement agencies, training in inter-ethnic relations and engagement with ethnic groups. It noted that the negative implication developed within ethnic minorities due to lack of fair growth opportunities. The study raised concern about Uzbek under representation in state (Osh oblast) which has more than 50 per cent Uzbek population. The NGOs in Human rights sectors have played significant role in resolving ethnic strife between Uzbeks and Kyrgyz ethnic groups.

6.14.1.3 Tajikistan

Tajikistan also has provision of guaranteeing equal citizenship and equal rights to people of Tajikistan. The provision for language preservation suggests Tajik, Uzbek, Russian, Kyrgyz and Turkmen as regular languages of instruction in the schools. Bozrikova (2004) viewed that equal opportunity at policy level, did not necessarily lead to equal opportunities in practice for minority groups. Civil society has played limited role in social inclusion as they have failed to address poverty and human trafficking. Tajikistan society has seen the rise of influence of Islam in last decade. Presumably, it will be an impediment in the inclusion process.

6.14.1.4 Turkmenistan

Turkmenistan has a disturbed past. Even after independence in 1991, the political instability continued for two decades. In 2010, Turkmenistan political stabilised under the rule of incumbent president Gurbangly Berdymukhamedov. As inclusion measure, he prioritised higher education and health care facilities in rural areas. The country has authoritarian rule and has debarred any kind of criticism of the government. The absence and increased inadequacy of statistical data is a concern for the analysis. Dissemination of information and the means to shape public opinion remain state controlled.

Formally, all citizens have the same civil rights. The structure of society and governance fails to provide members of ethnic minority groups such rights. Often it is reflected in the education and employment policies discriminating Russian, Uzbeks and Kazakhs. Though, as inclusive measure, Mejlis seats increased, under representation three lakh Uzbeks are noticed.

Freedom of assembly and association, though guaranteed in the constitution, hardly exist in reality. Civic self organization remained extremely low. National minorities such as Uzbeks, Russians and Kazaks continue to face discrimination as a result of dominance of Turkish culture in of state, economic and educational institutions. The president continued this policy by controlling ethnic minorities with the help of secret police. Religious freedoms are severely curtailed.

Instead of inclusion, the ethnic minorities, Russian, Uzbek and Kazakh minorities experience social exclusion due to poverty and ethnic discrimination. However, on a good part, rural health institutions were reopened benefitting large mass of rural poor including the ethnic minorities. Similarly, new higher level and specialised education institution was established. Teachers returned to work and students' migration to neighbouring countries for higher education was restricted. Though it has benefitted the excluded groups (ethnic minorities) it will be difficult to quantify the benefit due to dearth of data.

6.14.1.5 Uzbekistan

Uzbekistan's constitution does not refer to the term minority. However, article 4 of the constitution talks about nations and nationalities. The constitution has non-discriminatory provisions with special relevance to minorities in mass media, language and criminal justice. There is a tendency among minority groups to present themselves as titular group in order to get better access to resources. It is particularly observed in Uygurs and Arabs, Tajiks and Kazakh groups (Naumann 2012). The difficulty has arisen in collecting ethnic data as census is not conducted for long period of time since 1989.

Kazakhstan has highest rate of privatization of land. Though the unequal distribution of wealth is much larger, it is feared that unequal distribution of wealth will lead to social exclusion of underprivileged.

6.15 Conclusion

The forces of cohesion and erosion of social bonding are simultaneously at work. However, the process of survival after the independence is reaching some stage of stability. The state and society has started to engage with the social issues, development, deprivation and inclusion. The engagements are at primary stage where state in particular and civil society in general has started recognizing the need of special care for deprived section of society.

Chapter 7

Conclusion and Policy Implications

An inclusive growth has been the main focus of development paradigm during the 12th Five Year Plan. This signifies importance to be accorded to deprived groups for their overall development. Social exclusion exists in various spheres and in many forms. However, race and caste have dominated the debate on social exclusion. As discussed earlier, social exclusion is lack of access to resources and consequent inability to utilize them. It is further aggravated by denial of opportunities which enhances access to resources. Thus, castes, religion, gender, position in social hierarchies are all potential factors of social exclusion.

The societal discrimination and exclusion in multiple spheres and violent opposition by the others reduce venerable groups' freedom and capacity to use civil, political and economic rights and equal opportunities. The failure of entitlement due to caste-based exclusion is in significant magnitude. So the social based exclusion, and discrimination of the disadvantage group continues to be main reason for lower human development and higher deprivations and poverty.

Poverty is a multi-dimensional and multivariate phenomenon; it does not wear uniform face and magnitude across space and time. The review of literature on poverty reveals that most of the studies have not focused on multiple causes of poverty, especially in respect of SCs/STs. It attempts to understand poverty in a holistic manner by examining the vulnerability context, capital assets of the poor, the livelihood strategies to overcome poverty, the policies and programmes which help them to convert their capital assets into livelihood opportunities. Not many studies have attempted to construct vulnerability indices among the social groups.

Against this background, an analysis of some of the exclusion issues may certainly help the policy makers in deciding about the type of the policy intervention needed to tackle the long-standing problem of poverty, especially in respect of SCs/STs in rural areas.

Many empirical studies show that lower access of marginalized groups to resources such as agricultural land and non-farm capital assets. Underemployment, lower daily wages compared with Non SC/ST groups, is linked with the process of exclusion and discrimination. In economic spheres the empirical evidence indicates the exclusion and differential treatment in various markets namely agricultural land, capital, employment, market in consumer goods and the transactions in non-market channels.

Thus the societal exclusion in multiple spheres and violent opposition by the high caste and powerful civil society and also some organs of the state drastically reduced the scheduled caste/tribe freedom and capacity to use civil, political and economic rights and equal opportunities. The failure of entitlement due to caste based exclusion is in significant magnitude. From the empirical evidence, it becomes apparent that among other reasons, the caste based exclusion and discrimination of the Muslims continue to be one of the main reasons for their lower human development and higher poverty.

The approaches of Indian policy makers to overcome the discrimination and address social exclusion include such policy interventions as legal enforcement of anti-discrimination laws, reservation, preferential and general empowering measures which come as part of anti-poverty programmes. These polices have brought positive changes but the rate of improvement has not been fast enough to reduce deprivation and the gap between the excluded group of scheduled caste and tribe and other advanced sections.

The continuing exclusion of disadvantage groups indicates that addressing social exclusion is often a difficult challenge than anti-poverty policy. Social and cultural sources of exclusion (in economic, civil and political spheres) including low self–esteem, stigma, discrimination and denial of citizenship are rooted in informal social structure. Fighting discrimination therefore calls for additional policies complementing antipoverty and economic development programs. But there is also considerable overlap and therefore there is a need to combine and compliment and not to diverse programs against poverty and economic deprivation from policies for equal rights and social inclusion of disadvantage groups.

India's poverty reduction programmes should not overlook social, economic and political inequalities between different social groups. Neither the estimation (NSS) nor the identification (BPL Census) of the poor analyse the causes of poverty or the nature of exclusion. This is partly corrected with an analysis of correlates of poverty; for example, Dalits' deprivation is linked to (landlessness). But this merely shifts the problem, as the causes of these correlates still remain unclear. Though, it is perceived poor land holding of tribals, SC and Muslims coupled with lack of access to forest produce for Adivasis as the causes of exclusion. With the focus on targeted poverty programmes, the nature and causes of deprivation receive little attention.

The affirmative policies that were initially scheduled to exist for ten years have continued for sixty years. The initial focus on most deprived groups has arguably been weakened by the continuous extension of groups of beneficiaries. There is a need to review the implementation of the policies and restructure the programme to target the most deprived groups. There has been assertion of group identity of Dalits with the rise of an English educated urban middle class, due to the result of affirmative action.

The empirical evidence presented in this study proves that caste-based exclusion and discrimination of SCs, STs and minorities attributes to their low level of human development and high level of deprivation. Overall, the incidence of poverty has come down significantly since independence. However, the absolute number of people living below the poverty line was still quite high at 300 million in 2004–5. The incidence of poverty is much higher in case of SCs and STs in both rural and urban areas. The incidence of poverty among SCs and STs was at least thrice as compared to 'Others' in both rural and urban India.

Social exclusion and discrimination are widespread in the private sector and public domain governed by the state. In this context, the inclusion of excluded groups then becomes somewhat different goal than social inclusion of only materially deprived people. Therefore social exclusion framework to study poverty should be taken care to reduce poverty and fight against discrimination. The present policy regime is not addressing the social exclusion. So the inclusive policies should be modified and group focussed. Strategies should be framed in such a manner that improvements in assets and income level of the marginalised community should be enhanced.

Inclusion policies and strategies have been perceived as a powerful instrument in removing barriers blocking excluded groups equal integration. The understating of participation of excluded groups in development process is crucial in the context of globalisation. The disadvantaged groups continue to face a range of multiple challenges relating to access to employment, choice of work, working conditions, employment security, wage parity and discrimination. Barring a few indices, much data are not available on most of the social economic parameters. In this context, social statistics becomes important to substantiate the demand for equal status for disadvantaged groups in various aspects of social, economic and political development. Thus following are recommended for data collection.

a) All the data collection agencies of central and state governments are sensitised to collect and collate data on social group basis, such as SC, ST, OBCs, Muslims, women and people with disabilities.

b) The data collection procedure for social statistics will ensure that social exclusion concerns are regularly included. Such statistics may include political representation at various levels, owing of capital assets, per capita income, employment, health, housing, social security, financial inclusion and people below poverty line etc.

c) The data collection and processing procedure for social statistics programmes will be designed to ensure that measurement method cover and describe all relevant parameters by social group to allow comparisons to be made. Household, institution surveys and administrative sources are valuable and time-use surveys are crucial.

d) The resultant statistics will always be posted as part of regular presentation in a way that will clearly reveal differences and similarities between various social groups in accessing services and the resultant situation of the groups. This can be done by (a) presenting relevant topics in sufficient and relevant detail and by (b) providing statistics according to relevant variables e.g. institutional settings.

The states' policies play a crucial role in the nature of the development process. The inclusive development process is for all the social groups is a reflection of the state's commitment towards dalit upliftment. Thus, the foregoing discussion makes a strong argument for state governments as agents of change. This is supported by the success of social mobilization in states like Tamil Nadu, Kerala, and the north-eastern states, where strong state commitment resulted in the development of the backward castes.

Recent studies suggest that the changes observed by dalits since the economic liberalisation of 1991 have been greater than the institution of reservation for dalits since independence. A study by university of Pennsylvania documented major social and economic shifts among dalits in UP since 1991. Consumerism boosts industrialisation that produces classes to replace caste with rising economic status surpassing social markers. Thus it is believed massive industrialisation will pave for casteless society.

Old school strategies level reservation for government jobs and higher education play a no-win game. One deprived minority gets benefit at the cost of another. But economic growth offers emancipation from clutches of poverty. Freeing up markets coupled with universal education enables Dalits to access market opportunities which can fight the social exclusion.

7.1 Employment

The high LFPR among STs was due to poorer access to education. Rural Muslim participation in education and the labour force were inversely correlated. The Worker Population Ratio for SCs/STs declined marginally as their access to education improved slightly. The open unemployment rate (current daily status) was increasing for Muslims and remained stable for SCs and STs.

Globalisation undoubtedly benefits people, including Dalits, but only a skillful people. The majority being "unskillful" is pushed to suffer insecurities and existential uncertainties. Ideologically, the votaries of globalisation are disposed towards extreme individualism. Social Darwinist contemplates free market as panacea for social mobility. The entire poorer section are comfortable with 'trickle-down theory' is not empirically proved. In last two decades, because of structural adjustment, job opportunities in public sector declined consistently. In 1997, employment in the public sector jobs peaked at 197 lakh, which consistently declined to 180 lakh in 2007 (Chalam 2011). In last two decades, population as well as the job seekers have increased. As the SCs and STs were beneficiaries of public sector jobs owing to reservation, they were the losers in post globalisation era.

7.2 Education

Literacy rate in India has improved from 64.8 per cent in 2001 to 74 per cent in 2011[48] (Census 2011). Recently, female literacy has shown considerable improvement by nearly 50 per cent from 224 million in 2001 to 334 million

---

[48] This indicates literacy rate of population in the age group of 7 and above.

in 2011. The declining trend in overall population growth can be an indirect consequence of rising female literacy level.

Across social groups and religious communities, the problem of illiteracy in both rural and urban areas was most pronounced among SCs, STs, Muslims and females. In rural areas, close to 60 per cent females belonging to the SCs and STs were illiterate in 2007–08. The literacy rate in urban areas is higher than that of rural areas; however, over the years the rural-urban literacy gap has declined from 24 percentage points in 1999–2000 to 17 percentage points in 2007–8. It is good to note that all the three groups (SCs, STs, and Muslims) have been converging towards the national average in terms of literacy rate.

Even though enrolment and attendance in schools have improved over the years, their declining trends at progressively higher levels of education, which was a common feature, though in varying degrees, across all social groups and religious communities, suggests that quality issues remain very serious in the school education system. Further, despite attaining internationally comparable level of the Gender Parity Index, less than half of the girls belonging to Muslims and OBCs were enrolled at primary and upper-primary levels.

The proportion of out of school children is higher among SCs, STs, and Muslims who are the most vulnerable amongst the different socio-religious groups. The proportion of school teachers belonging to these socio-religious groups is also low compared to their share in the total population. Studies have pointed out that under-representation of teachers belonging to these socio religious groups creates a social distance between teachers and students. This is one of the reasons why many teachers have limited commitment towards the educational development of their students (Planning Commission 2011).

Despite making considerable progress during the last six decades, much remains to be achieved in the field of education. Across social groups and religious communities, the problem of illiteracy was much more acute among SCs, STs, and Muslims. More than half of the illiterates in the country were accounted for by SCs (25 per cent), STs (12 per cent) and Muslims (14 per cent).

Though the rate of increase in literacy was higher in rural India than urban India, more than half of the females belonging to the Scheduled Castes (SCs) and Scheduled Tribes (STs) in rural India were illiterate. Muslims had the lowest literacy rate among all religious communities even though there was improvement in their literacy rate over the years. Although literacy rates among SCs, STs, and Muslims were lower, their literacy rates were converging towards the national average.

In India, attendance in private unaided institutions increased significantly, and out of pocket expenditure was higher in such institutions. The high cost acted as a deterrent to participation in higher education particularly for SCs, STs, and Muslims, for whom the incidence of poverty was higher. The participation of STs in higher education was the lowest among all social groups followed by SCs, while Muslims had the least participation among major religious communities.

7.3 Health

On fertility rate status, the SCs, STs, and Muslims suffer the most on account of poor health status. STs and Muslims have the highest Total Fertility Rate (TFR). Only one-third of Muslim and SC women have institutional deliveries, and ST women have even fewer. Also, only around 50 per cent of Muslim, SC, and ST women receive three or more antenatal care. The shortcoming of our public health system has been the failure to provide basic health care to 269.3 million people below poverty line (2011-12).

Regarding immunization of children, not even 50 per cent children received 'all vaccines' in 2005–6. However, there has been an increase in the percentage of ST and Muslim children receiving 'all vaccinations' over the period 1998–9 and 2005–6 (Planning Commission 2011).

7.4 Housing

One-third STs and around half of SCs reside in pucca houses, compared to 66 per cent for all India. Over time, SC and ST households, due to a slower pace in improvement, have experienced a growing divergence from the national average of households residing in pucca houses. Also, a greater proportion of Muslims compared to SCs/STs live in pucca houses, perhaps because a higher proportion of Muslim households live in urban areas.

7.5 Electricity

In terms of using electricity for domestic purposes, the SC and ST households are steadily coming closer to the all India average. Additionally, a higher proportion of Muslim households now have access to electricity for domestic use. It is evident

SC and ST households fare compared to Muslims as well as the national average with respect to the use of electricity. A higher proportion of Muslim households use electricity for domestic use as compared to SCs and STs.

Child Labour: It is quite evident that SC/ST child labour has dropped sharply but is still higher than the national average. There is a need of efforts like the 'Lok Sampark Abhiyan' launched by Madhya Pradesh government (1990s), to see a significant decline in child labour for the SCs and STs.

7.6 Policy Implications

Social inclusion policies are essential to address the issues of social disadvantaged groups. Based on the findings of the study, the following policy implications can be drawn.

a) There is a need to set up an "Equal Opportunity Commission" and bring under its purview all reservation policies related to SCs, STs, OBCs and religious minorities under one umbrella organisation. The main objective of this Commission should be to (a) build up a database on socio-economic profile of these groups; (b) develop policies for each of the groups and sub-groups; (c) monitor the implementation of reservation policy and other policies; and (d) advise the government on a regular basis.

b) The incidence of poverty is a multivariate phenomenon. It was found that the poverty of social excluded groups was mainly due to lack of productive assets like land (endowment failure), lack of human capital— deprivation in capabilities (production failure), greater morbidity rate, limited occupational shift towards non-farm activities, lack of labour migration (exchange failure); high unproductive expenditure (consumption failure) and limited access to the social security benefits (state failure). In order to address all the problems certain strategic steps need to be initiated in the domains of land reform measures and human resource development and management. In the domain of resource endowments of the poor, land reforms should be undertaken, and adopt measures to improve the quality of land in case of non-productive land. The present process for building human capabilities should be streamlined by involving the stakeholders at different stages of delivery.

Health and education affect social outcomes. Social policy directly impacts social outcomes and, through the feedback loops, indirectly impacts economic outcomes.

Since the government formulates the social policies, it has an important role to play in ensuring Government must attach higher priority to provision of health and education services. The performance of each state government is reflected in the HDI of that state, which can guide social policies.

7.7 Restructure Education Delivery System

It is also becoming increasingly important to restructure the education delivery systems from both supply and demand sides. The supply-side measures include provision of adequate educational facilities in remote villages in terms of number of educational institutions, teachers, modern teaching aids and employment-oriented advanced education. The demand side measures include creation of enabling environment, especially for the poorest of the poor by providing adequate scholarships, hostel facilities, clothes, books and fee concessions, especially at the higher levels of education. Although primary education has been made compulsory, the number of dropouts and incidence of child labour continued to be high among SCs, STs and Muslims. This is attributed partly to lack of ineffective supply and demand side measures and partly to poverty of the parents.

Low public expenditure on education, along with the increasing participation of private institutions in imparting education, results in the alienation of the deprived and economically weaker sections from the education system. This issue, however, is receiving high priority with the enactment of the Right to Education (RTE) Act. The Act emphasises both access and quality, in addition to the 'rights' component. It is the responsibility of the Government that the Act is implemented properly in both letter and spirit.

The high incidence of poverty and low participation in higher education are inversely correlated. Establishing publicly funded educational institutions can break this correlation as they can ensure greater participation from poorer sections. At the same time, government may support private funded institutions for technical education. As the enrolment in secondary education increases which in turn increases the demand for technical or professional education.

7.8 Restructure Health Care Delivery System:

Poor spend a lot on health care due to frequent illness. The unhygienic living is the cause of their frequent illness. Private health care is unaffordable for poor. The government health care facilities are grossly inadequate for poor and underprivileged. If government provisioned healthcare facilities are made available adequately and at a lower cost for poor, the poor will utilise the savings for productive activities.

Given the pace of improvement on various health indicators, achieving the health related MDG targets by 2015 is unlikely. Investments in the Twelfth Plan will have to ensure that these problems are addressed.

7.9 Modernise Traditional Occupation:

SC, ST and Muslims are largely concentrated on agricultural activities or traditional occupation of weaving. Agricultural activities and traditional occupation such as weaving need to be modernised to ensure their income. The groups need to be supported by providing adequate credit and credit plus support and equal access to all social groups may address the problems of poverty and social exclusion. Rapid diversification in employment in favour of non-agricultural sector should be the main focus of development programmes.

7.10 Ensure Equal Access of Governmental Benefits

A negative association existed between social security benefits and the incidence of poverty, especially in respect of SCs/STs and Muslims. Due to lack of social security benefits, the incidence of poverty was quite acute and also the chances of the poor remaining poverty-stricken were higher in the case of SC/STs compared to others. Therefore, appropriate measures should be initiated to create awareness of government programmes and ensure equal access to them. If the social security programmes are not streamlined and effectively be implemented, the 'chronic poverty' will not be reduced, in view of several flaws associated with the on-going poverty alleviation programmes combating the problem of income and non-income poverty through a new approach known as direct "cash transfer" to the poor may be an important move.

In this scenario, it is important to reflect on the response of the Indian state in addressing the exclusion and whether the human rights of this group are being protected within a strong policy and legal framework. It is also important to reflect on how SC/STs and Muslims use the democratic space being provided to India's citizens by the Constitution to articulate their demands and defend their human rights.

Though access to banking has grown drastically in the last decade *(from 35.5 per cent households in 2001 to 58.7 per cent in 2011)* more than 40 per cent of households do not use banking services. They are mostly social disadvantaged groups inhabiting in rural areas. Banks and financial institutions need to extend banking services in remote pockets. Some of the banks such as Bank of Baroda have provided mobile banking services in tribal areas in Gujarat through the use of bio-metric machines.[49] Other banks may create such kind of facilities for financial inclusion.

Lessons of the creation of casteless society ought to be included in the school curriculum. This will facilitate evolving of an egalitarian society. This has been already been initiated by the Tamil Nadu government.

7.11 For Scheduled Tribes

The primary reason for the backwardness of the tribals is the failure of the government to reach the STs living in remote areas. The state governments have consistently failed to address issues specific to such deprived section of society. Following measures are recommended for inclusion of tribals.

1. The policy makers must distinguish between the Scheduled Areas that come under the fifth and sixth schedule. Tribals living in the fifth schedule areas are in the disadvantaged position due to scattered locations, dispersal and unorganised character. As a result the development strategies in the fifth scheduled areas, unlike those in the sixth scheduled areas must be different in terms of formulation and administration.

2. Tribals are victims of displacement and large scale industrialisation. Rich resources are available in tribal areas. Thus, all resources available in tribal areas should therefore be declared as Provident Fund (PF) of the tribals. The government can draw from it and like the interest payment made to the depositors in PF; the government should deposit an equivalent amount to the amount of wealth drawn in the name of tribals. As the economists now use contingent valuation as a method to evaluate environmental degradation. The value of tribals wealth utilised by the society should be

---

[49] Bank of Baroda extended this facility to the beneficiaries of Neera cluster of Valsad district in Gujarat. Authors gained this experience while working with the cluster. Neera is a natural hygienic drink.

evaluated so that a proportion of it can be returned for the development of tribals.

3. The social safety net should cover not only the workers but also the loads of migrants from rural to urban areas in search of jobs, particularly the tribals. Programmes such as paucity of fund, mass housing, road building, rapid transport systems, irrigation, drinking water supply, vocational education, medical care, primary education that have direct impact on the socio–economic condition of weaker sections should be brought under new economic strategies by redeployment of funds to counteract the effects of privatisation.

4. National renewal fund should be allotted to state government and it should form part of state capital social welfare budget in order to protect the interests of workers among SC, STs and backward cases. The tribals need to be protected against loss of traditional occupation paid to them in case of encroachment by outsiders.

5. Some part of allocation should be spent on the identified numerically smaller and backward groups of tribals among fifth scheduled areas to remove economic imbalances. Certain new schemes like disability insurance, special programmes for low literacy areas, high infant mortality areas, improvement of nutritional standards among borders, health card schemes, child care centres, mini watersheds, water harvesting stations, community polytechnics need to be introduced to improve the quality of life of STs as well the poor form other social groups.

6. The main aim of special component plan is to ensure maximum coverage of STs under every sector. The present situation indicates that there is difficulty in earmarking requisite percentage of funds under sectors like irrigation and power generation. The situation has to be rectified by the government of India with provision of funds to the extent of 10 per cent. Rural infrastructure development fund specially announced by the government of India should be effectively made use for the economic development of STs.

7. In social welfare budget, the social safety net programmes aimed at improvement in the quality of life of the poor and at mitigation of some of the adverse effects on the poor due to structural adjustment require significant weight. The social safety net programme of the government of India should include quality education and provide at least 50 per cent of the expenditure to the states.

•   The expenditure of the Tribal Sub-Plan (TSP) is 0.22 per cent of GDP in 2011-12, which is exactly the same in 2010-11. Considering the per cent of ST population in 2011 (8.6 per cent) the TSP allotments are short by 20,938 crore (12ᵗʰ Plan). Thus economic programmes that relate to the tribals must be implemented efficiently.

7.12 For Muslims

The Muslim community exhibits deficits and deprivation in all dimensions of development. Programmes to ensure equity and equality of opportunity to bring about inclusion should be such that diversity is achieved and at the same time the perception of discrimination is eliminated. Creation of a National Data Bank (NDB) where all relevant data for various socio religious communities are maintained. It has been recommended along with an Autonomous Assessment and Monitoring Authority (AAMA) to evaluate the extent of development benefits which accrue to different socio religious communities through various programmes. An Equal Opportunity Commission is recommended to look into the grievances of the deprived groups. A carefully conceived nomination procedure should be worked out to increase inclusiveness in governance. The Committee has recommended elimination of the anomalies with respect to reserved constituencies under the delimitation scheme. The state and local government functionaries, responsible for programme implementation should be sensitised to the diversity and the problems associated with social exclusion. A process of evaluating the school curriculum and textbooks needs to be institutionalized. The curriculum should include some chapters on social inclusion process. Teacher training should be compulsory ensuring in its curriculum the components which introduce the importance of social inclusion. The teachers should be sensitized towards the needs and aspirations of Muslims and other marginalized communities. Work out mechanisms whereby Madarsas can be linked with a higher secondary school board so that students wanting to shift to a regular mainstream education can do so after having passed from a Madarsa. The Committee recommended promoting and enhancing access to Muslims in Priority Sector Bank Advances. The real need is of policy initiatives that improve the participation and share of Muslims in the business of regular commercial banks. The community should be represented on the selection panels of credit disbursement. The under-privileged should be helped to utilize new opportunities in its high growth phase through skill development and education.

Section II: Central Asia Aspect

Central Asia is land of diversity. It has many ethnic groups living in five Central Asian states. The territorial spread of these states is uneven where Kazakhstan occupies maximum share to Central Asian land while remaining four tiny states. Though Kazakhstan is large territory of land; Uzbekistan is the most populous country of the region. All the five Central Asian states achieved independence from Soviet regime in early 1990s. They are at the initial state of their statehood. They are undergoing the transition from command economy to market economy. It is carried out with the help of reforms in various levels. The major strategies applied for survival are foreign investment, exploring natural resources, focusing on certain sectors of economy as cash crops or mining, extraction, but it has neglected or failed to distribute the profit earned from these strategies to other areas as education or health. Market economy has produced new inequalities, unemployment and concentration of wealth in the hands of few.

Poverty or economic exclusion only gives partial understanding of social exclusion in Central Asia. Hence, it is essential to analyze this society through the prism of human development. The broader background of transition, shift from command to market economy had defined the context in many ways. Such analysis revealed that Central Asia has higher risk of social exclusion caused due to spatial and structural dimension. Overall rural and semi-urban areas are deprived of development in the sphere of economic, social and civic life. The fruits of development are enjoyed only by urban residents and capital cities or nearby areas. Rural areas in Central Asia have four times higher population than urban areas. The major groups excluded either belonged to ethnic and religious minorities or remote rural and semi urban areas. Above all, common causes for all Central Asia Republics are ethnicity, religion, location, structural and social causes along with country specific variation in the reasons and sphere of exclusion.

7.13 Excluded groups

The analysis clearly reveals that combination of clan (sub-ethnic), ethnicity and class affiliations are major reasons of exclusion in Kazakhstan. Poverty, gender and religion are other factors affecting exclusion. Based on these reasons the excluded group varies within country. Ethnic Kazakhs and other Turkic ethnic groups (Uzbek) are excluded from economic spheres. These groups are largely deprived from economic opportunities due to their historical legacy as minority or non-ruling group or subjected group. They are largely concentrated in southern region of Kazakhstan. While Russian, former ruling class, turned into minority after independence and experienced deprivation in political and cultural spheres. Russian's are residing in northern and western region of Kazakhstan are partially better off than any other regions. The minorties in Kyrgyzstan faced exclusion due to poor governance and poverty. Though the state has made some progress in political front, governance, economic development remained ignored. Kyrgyz, the 'titular' ethnic group experienced exclusion in economic sphere as they largely concentrated in northern rural areas. While the Uzbek ethnic group, mostly residing in south region of Kyrgyzstan experienced deprivation in social, economic and political sphere. Russian though constitutes significant minority in state are economically well off. In Tajikistan poverty, ethnicity and religion are major factors of exclusion. The poor regions are (oblasts) GBAO (Gorno-Badakhshan Autonomous Province), Rasht Valley, and non-cotton growing districts of Sugad and Khatlon regions. Gharmi, one of the Tajik sub-ethnic groups, is most deprived in all spheres of economic, social and civic life. They faced ethnic cleansing duringto civil war and later exclusion. They reside in Rasht Valley of Central Tajikistan and region of western Tajikistan. Traditional social values are strong and plays crucial role in social exclusion especially in gender based exclusion of women and girls from respective avenue of development.

Poverty and ethnicity are major reasons of exclusion in Turkmenistan. Overall analysis reveals Russians, Uzbeks and Kazakhs ethnic minorities are excluded groups. Turkmenistan remained isolated and a closed state within Central Asia. The authoritarian regime curtailed individual freedom and democratic functioning of the institutions. Dissemination of knowledge was state controlled. The statistics provided by the state are highly unreliable and inadequate. Though the country presents a rosy picture about all the communities, the reality might be different. Unreliable information is a serious concern in the country. International interventions and persuasions might bring some solutions.

Economic Exclusion

Social exclusion in Central Asian societies is the product of structures and institutions, values, behavioural pattern and policies. The institutions public and private through their discriminatory practices contribute to exclusion. The policies and growth models led to spatially unbalanced and 'growth pole' based growth. In economy, mining industries, cash crop cultivation, construction and real estate in service sector pulls major state resources leaving other areas of economy deprived of necessary attention. Such growth did not accompany job growth in the region.

Main elements of economic exclusion are unemployment, income poverty, lack of access to assets and capital, informal economy and underemployment. Transition led to skewed distribution of wealth. Economic wealth now is concentrated in the hands of few. The social services, values and behavioural patterns plays exclusionary role in cultural and social sphere of exclusion.

7.14 Poverty in Central Asia

Poverty situation in Central Asia has aggravated in last two decades. It was only since middle of the last decade the situation started improving. Poverty in Central Asia has spatial and structural dimension. Transition from command to market economy and reforms in various sections are major factor influencing the poverty in Central Asia. The immediate cause of poverty in Central Asia was fall in real wages, uneven redistribution of wealth leading to unequal growth among various sections of society. Poverty is largely concentrated in rural areas of Central Asia and certain sections of urban and semi urban pockets.

Absolute, relative, deprivation and subjective are four approaches of poverty measurement in Central Asia. Among them, absolute poverty is widely used and poverty line is based on food consumption. National poverty line is different for each state. Poverty scenario can be compared using common parameter as International Poverty Line and Multi-dimensional Poverty Index (MPI). MPI is composite and mathematical index uses similar indicators as Human Development Index (HDI). The MPI is parsimonious as it uses only three most important dimensions to compare. The analysis of MPI for Central Asia shows that all Central Asian states are facing multi-dimensional poverty.

In rural areas of Central Asia collective farming was major occupation during the soviet period. In the new economy these areas are suffering from high unemployment. Historical legacies have affected rural areas. The differential of demographic ratio resulted into their disadvantages. Besides rural poverty, child poverty is major concern in many states of Central Asia. It is observed that child poverty often works in vicious cycle. Children born and brought up in poverty due to lack of good health and inadequate access to development resources led to become poor parents (weak in health) leading to producing next generation children. Kyrgyzstan, Tajikistan and Uzbekistan were particularly affected by this syndrome. In Kyrgyzstan, 60 per cent rural children under ten year are poverty stricken. In Tajikistan the risk of child poverty is higher than adults. Uzbekistan faces the issue of forced child labour.

The causes of poverty in Central Asia are unemployment and low income. In Central Asia poverty is evolved on the basis of basic subsistence standard of living. In Central Asia such subsistence living is pegged at $1.25 a day. Hunger is another indicator of extent of poverty. Tajikistan has most serious condition of *malnourishment* and under nutrition.

Poverty in Kazakhstan is largely concentrated in remote rural areas and small towns. Poor population is largely concentrated in South Kazakhstan, Karaganda, Kostanay, Zhambyl and eastern Kazakhstan. Mostly Kazakh ethnic groups reside in south Kazakhstan. Highest percentage of poverty is registered in the remotest province of Mangistau. Housing and education are the two major areas affecting poverty. Kyrgyzstan has higher incidence of poverty among the youth of 15 to 29 years. Larger household size, education and migration are major factors affecting poverty.

Like other central Asian states Tajikistan has high incidence of poverty in rural areas. Poverty in Tajikistan is function of poor governance, high unemployment rate, lack of access to quality education and degradation of land resources. Tajikistan shows intrinsic poverty and has developed multidimensional understanding of poverty. Turkmenistan does not have poverty indices (BTI Turkmenistan 2012). Uzbekistan has around 6.8 million people deprived of basic consumption needs. It is caused due to structural problems. Poverty in Uzbekistan is based on location, employment status and attainment of education. The most affected group is farmers.

7.15 Entitlements in Central Asia

As the Central Asian states are at the early stage of statehood, government plays significant role in three key areas – (a) employment, (b) education, (c) health and nutrition. In Central Asia, social benefits systems were severely hit by the global financial crisis. Unemployment increased and unemployment benefits expired. Kazakhstan has registered steady decline in labour force in 1990s (UNDP 1995). However situation improved in last decade. The employment of labour resources varied across regions primarily due to distribution of industrial facilities. The highest rate of employment was registered in Northern and Western Kazakhstan dominated by Russians and Kazakhs signifying high employment of these two communities. In Kyrgyzstan, agriculture accommodates maximum labour force followed by trade and allied services. Private sector dominates in urban area jobs such as trade and other services (UNDP 2010). In Tajikistan, the agriculture provides employment to nearly two third of population. Since 2000, Uzbekistan's labour force experienced new job opportunities in service sector and lesser dependence on Agriculture. Across the region, the employment situation has rather worsened in last two decades.

While on labour force participation, Kazakhstan has highest participation rate followed by Tajikistan and Kyrgyzstan, while the lowest is marked in Uzbekistan. Uzbekistan has relatively small industrial base as against large trained human resource contributing to low participation.

Of late, all Central Asian states have recognized the importance of education as a key area for betterment of society and are taking efforts to improve education scenario. All countries have provision for free education. Many reports suggest that urban areas get privileged in receiving the resources, facilities and finance in education. Rural children are deprived of education and better opportunities. Central Asia has high adult literacy rates. Over all the literacy rate and access to education is relatively better off with some intra and inter-country variations. At present Uzbekistan and Kazakhstan have highest year of schooling (10 years) in the region. The Central Asian countries has maintained better enrolment ratio. However, achievement of universal education and reduce dropout of children in school are two major challenges.

Kazakhstan has well developed higher education system. Kyrgyzstan has managed to survive the transition from command education to market based education system with strong negative impact of poverty and unemployment on the education sector. Its higher education system is based on two principles, achieving and maintaining past successes and innovative reforms to allow national educational institutions to integrate into the international educational community. Girl's education is a matter of concern in Tajikistan. The country provides presidential quota reservation for girls. Access for low income groups to tertiary education is difficult in Uzbekistan. The major hurdles are affordability of education due to high tuition fees, distance of higher education institute makes it difficult to rural students. Above all, in Central Asia, the decline in quality of education is a matter of concern. The teacher quality, class size and equipment have worsened in recent years.

Health care system is in transition from command and control model to decentralized and pluralistic model in Central Asia. The major limitation and challenges were inherited from soviet regime. Central Asian states have undertaken several health reforms. The major difficulty was lack of institutional capacity and insufficient trained man power due to outmigration of existing skilled personals. The counties have the biggest challenge of establishing health care system on a financial viable basis and reduce out of pocket expenditure. During reforms period, Uzbekistan has focused child and maternal care, promoting privatization, improving health care services, minimizing optimum cost and decentralization of health service management.

In Central Asia male mortality rates are higher than female mortality. This is evident in all the surveys. This unusual finding needs further investigation. Tajikistan's people have poor access to drinking water. Specifically, 89 per cent urban and 60 per cent rural population have access to safe drinking water. Central Asian states have relatively better access to basic sanitation facilities. Uzbekistan reports 100 per cent houses have sanitation facilities. Contrary to India, in the region, LPG natural gas is used for cooking, followed by biogas and electricity and other solid fuels. LPG constitute around 95-97 per cent of use.

7.16 Inclusion in Central Asia

Transition in Central Asia economy has eroded economic benefits meant for the poor such as subsidies and grants. Consequently the poorest section of society has suffered most. The overall analysis of the Central Asian states show that the large segment of society at political, economic and social level is still in flux between the traditional notions of government, soviet rule, market economy and democratization. Central Asian states often see contradictory streams within society. Inclusion in Central Asia as strengthening of social bond is at early stage. These states are undergoing the process of nation-building and as a result many forces are working simultaneously. Analysis of Central Asian history reveals that states are named after a "titular" or "indigenous" nationality. Soviet government has ensured operational autonomy of different ethnic minority groups. It has maintained the balance between autonomy and centralization (national integration) through the provision of bilingual policies. While in post independent the minorities in Central Asian states were not given such territorial autonomy and avenues of expressing protest and resistance were taken away. This further resulted in exclusion of minorities. It is most explicit in the language policies of states. Barring Russian, all other minorities' languages were derecognized in the state. While implementation of inclusion programmes, Central Asian states have to consider long term economic and comprehensive social interests. During Soviet period various affirmative actions were launched for titular ethnic groups.

These include the subsidies, incentives and opportunities for rapid development. The initiatives of social inclusion are undertaken largely by state and civil society. Market is yet to play a crucial role in social inclusion. The government measures of social inclusions are based on welfare, poverty alleviation, equal opportunity measures and general governance. The unequal distribution of wealth is much larger; it is feared that unequal distribution of wealth will lead to social exclusion of underprivileged.

All Central Asian states have opted for democratic set up. Though constitution talks of equal citizenship for all nationalities irrespective of ethnic or racial groups divisions, no mention of minorities is marked in the constitution. The UN study on minority participation in law enforcement system notes the decline in the minorities' representations in police and judicial forces. Tajikistan society has seen the rise of influence of Islam in last decade. Presumably, it will be an major challenge to the inclusion process.

Turkmenistan has a disturbed past. The country has authoritarian rule and has debarred any kind of criticism of the government. The absence and increased inadequacy of statistical data is a concern for the analysis. Dissemination of information and the means to shape public opinion remain state controlled. The ethnic minorities, Russian, Uzbek and Kazakhs minorities experience social exclusion due to poverty and ethnic discrimination.

To sum up, liberalisation of economy commenced in India in 1991. Due to the impact of liberalisation, socio-economic situation changed for the better. Many hitherto excluding groups showed remarkable improvement in socio-economic indices. Though the social inclusion task is yet to be completed; it is certainly on right path. On the contrary Central Asian states achieved independence from soviet regime in early 1990s. Immediately after independence, ethnic situation worsened in all the Central Asian states. It has shown marginal improvement in last decade. Though majority community has been benefitted by the economic advancement, this has resulted in larger social exclusion of ethnic minorities. International community and international organisations have to mobilise the state authorities for inclusion of minorities in the region's development process.

Reference

Agency on Statistics Republic of Kazakhstan (2011), *Statistical Indicator,* Astana: Kazakhstan.

Agrawal, Grisrish and Gonsalves, Colin (2005), 'Dalit and the Law', Human Right Law Network: Delhi.

Ainur Elebaeva (2004), 'Kyrgyzstan', Working Paper No. 4, Presented in Sub-Regional Seminar on Minority Rights: Cultural Diversity and Development in Central Asia, United Nations Office of the High Commissioner For Human Rights: Bishkek.

Akiner, S. (1997), 'Central Asia: Conflict or Stability and Development?' No. 6, Minority Rights Group: London.

Alagh, Y.K. (2010), 'The Poverty Debate in Perspective: Moving Forward with the Tendulkar Committee', *Indian Journal of Human Development,* 4 (1): 33-44.

Alkire, S. and Foster, J. (2007), 'Counting and Multidimensional Poverty Measurement', Oxford Poverty & Human Development Initiative, Working Paper 07,

Alkire, S. and Santos, M. (2010), 'Acute Multidimensional Poverty: A New Index for Developing Countries', Human Development Research Paper 2010/2011, UNDP.

Alkire, Sabiana and Foster, James (2011), 'Understanding and Misunderstanding of Multidimensional Poverty Measurement', *Journal of Economic Inequality,* 9 (2): 289-314.

Al-Samarrai, S., Bella, N., Liebnitz, M. P. B., Buonomo, M., Cameron, S., Clayson, A., & Watkins, K. (2010), *Reaching the Marginalized,* UNESCO: Paris.

Appasamy, P., Guhan, S, Hema R. *et al* (1996), 'Social Exclusion from a Welfare Rights Perspective in India', International Institute for Labour Studies and United Nations Development Programme, Research Series, 106, ILO Publications: Geneva.

Atkinson, A. and Hills, J. (1991), 'Social Security in Developed Countries: Are There Lessons For Developing Countries' in Ahmad, E., Dreze, J., Hills, J. and Sen, A. (eds.) *Social Security in Developing Countries:* Oxford University Press.

Atkinson, A. B. (1998), 'Social Exclusion, Poverty and Unemployment' in Hills, J. (ed.) *Exclusion, Employment and Opportunity, Centre for Analysis of Social Exclusion* (CASE), London School of Economics and Political Science: London.

Babajanian, Babaken V. (2006), 'The Social Exclusion Framework and Policy Reduction Strategy in Tajikistan', *Central Asia Survey*, 25 (4): 403-418.

Bachev, Hrabrin (2012), 'Farm Diversification and Market Inclusion in Central Asia in East Europe and Central Asia', in *Institute of Agricultural Economics*, Sofia, Munich Personal Repec Archive, MPRA Paper No. 38683, Online at http://mpra.ub.uni-muenchen.de/38683/.

Bandara, A.; Malik H. M. and Gherman, E., (2004), 'Poverty in Countries of Central Asia', in *Bulletin on Asia-Pacific Perspectives, 2004/05: Asia-Pacific Economies: Living with High Oil Prices?*, United Nations and ESCAP, pp. 117-129.

Banerjee, Abhijit and Rohini Somanathan (2001), 'Caste, Community and Collective Action: The Political Economy of Public Good Provision in India', Department of Economics, MIT, and Department of Economics, University of Michigan.

Banerjee, Biswjit and Knight J.B. (1985), 'Caste Discrimination in Indian Urban Labour Market', in *Journal of Developing Economics,* 17(3), pp 277-307.

Barry, B. (1998), 'Social Exclusion, Social Isolation and the Distribution of Income', CASE paper 12, Centre for Analysis of Social Exclusion, London School of Economics.

Baru, R., Acharya, A.; Acharya, S.; Kumar, A.K.S. and Nagaraj, K. (2010), 'Inequities in Access to Health Services in India: Caste, Class and Region' in *Economic and Political Weekly*, 45 (38).

Bassiuoni, S. (2011), 'Briefing Note on the Situation of Women in Central Asia', Working Paper, Division of Gender Equality, Office of the Director General, UNESCO, available at http://www.unesco.org/new/fileadmin/

MULTIMEDIA/HQ/BSP/GENDER/Working Paper_BriefingWorking Paper_S Bassiuoni_Situation of Women in Central Asia.pdf.

Bassouk, E. L. and Donelan, B. (2003), 'Social Deprivation', in Green, B.L. (ed.), *Trauma Intervention in War and Peace*, Kluwer Academic Publishers: New York City.

Baulch, Bob (1996). The New Poverty Agenda: A Disputed Consensus. IDS Bulletin, 27 (1): 1-10

Benn, Melissa,. (2000), New Labour and Social Exclusion. *Political Quarterly*, 71(3).

Bertelsmann Stiftung, BTI (2012), *Kazakhstan Country Report*, Gütersloh: Bertelsmann Stiftung, 2012.

Bertelsmann Stiftung, BTI (2012), *Kyrgyzstan Country Report*, Gütersloh: Bertelsmann Stiftung, 2012.

Bertelsmann Stiftung, BTI (2012), *Tajikistan Country Report*, Gütersloh: Bertelsmann Stiftung, 2012.

Bertelsmann Stiftung, BTI (2012), *Turkmenistan Country Report*, Gütersloh: Bertelsmann Stiftung, 2012.

Bertelsmann Stiftung, BTI (2012), *Uzbekistan Country Report*, Gütersloh: Bertelsmann Stiftung, 2012.

Bhalla, A. S. and Lapeyre, F. (1999), 'Poverty and Exclusion in a Global World', St. Martin's Press; New York and Macmillan Press: London.

Bhalla, Ajit. and Lapeyre, Frederic. (1997), Social Exclusion: Towards an Analytical and Operational Framework. *Development and Change*, 28

Birdar R. R. (2008), 'Multiple Facts of Social Exclusion in Rural India: Emerging Evidence', *South India Journal of Social Sciences II* (2): 30.

Birdar R. R. (2012), 'Incidence of Poverty among social Groups in Rural India', Social and Economic Change Monographs No. 24, Institute For Social and Economic Change: Bangalore.

Bozrikova, T.N. (2004), 'Problem of Ethnic Minorities in Tajikistan', working paper no 1, presented in Sub-regional Seminar on Minority Rights: Cultural Diversity and Development in Central Asia, United Nations Office of the High Commissioner for Human Rights: Bishkek.

Bramley, Glen and Tania Ford (1999), 'Social Exclusion and Lack of Access to Services: Evidence from the 1999 PSE survey of Britain', *Poverty & Social Exclusion Survey: Working Paper 14.*

Bravi, A. and Solbrandt, N. (2011), 'Food Security Challenges facing Central Asia', online at: http://europeandcis.undp.org/uploads/public1/files/vulnerability/publications/The Status and Challenges of Food Security in Central Asia.pdf.

Breman, J. (2010), 'A poor Deal', *Indian Journal of Human Development*, 4 (1): 133-42.

Buckley, C. (1998), 'Rural Urban Differentials in Demographic Processes: The Central Asian States', in *Population Research and Policy Review, 17* (1):71-89.

Burchardt, T., Grand, J. and Piachaud, D. (1999), 'Social Exclusion in Britain 1991-1995', *Social Policy and Administration*, 33(3): 227-244.

Burgess, R. and Stern, N. (1991), 'Social Security in Developing Countries: What, Why, Who, and How?' in Ahmad, E., Dreze, J., Hills, J. and Sen, A. (eds.) *'Social Security in Developing Countries'*, pp41-80, Clarendon Press: Oxford.

Buvinic, Mayra (2005), 'Social Inclusion in Latin America' in Mayra Buvinic and Jacqeline Mazza, (eds.), *Social Exclusion and Economic Development*, pp. 3-32, Johns Hopkins University Press: Berkeley.

Census (2011), Government of India, Ministry of Home Affairs, Office of the Register General: India.

Cerami, A. and Stubbs, P. (2010), *'The Political Economy of Child Poverty and Exclusion in Countries in Transition', Draft* study for UNICEF CEE/CIS region.

Chalam, K. S. (2011), *Economic Reforms and Social Exclusion, Impact of Liberalisation on Marginalised Groups in India*, Sage: New Delhi.

Chambers, R (1983), Rural Development: Putting the Last First, London: Longman.

Chambers, R (1988), Poverty in India: Concepts, Research and Reality, Discussion Paper 241, Institute of Development Studies: Brighton, UK.

Chandhoke, N. (2012), 'Why People Should not be Poor', *Economic and Political Weekly*, 47 (14): 41-50.

Christine, J. and Revenga, A. (2000), 'Making Transition Work for Everyone: Poverty and Inequality in Europe and Central Asia', World Bank: Washington DC.

CIA World Fact Book (2013), available at: http://www.indexmundi.com/tajikistan/economy_profile.html, accessed on June 2013.

Clert, C. (1999), 'Evaluating the Concept of Social Exclusion in Development Discourse', European *Journal of Development Research*, 11(2): 176-199.

Collins, Kathleen (2006), *'The Logic of Clan Politics in Central Asia: The Impact on Regime Transformation'*, Cambridge University Press: Cambridge.

Constitution of India (2007), Ministry of Law and Justice, Government of India.

Constitution of Republic of Kyrgyzstan (2010), Online Available At: http://www.gov.kg/ page_id 263, accessed on February 2013.

Constitution of Republic of Tajikistan (2003), Online Available At: http://www.tajik-gateway.org/index.phtml lang en id 874, accessed on April 2013.

Constitution of the Republic of Uzbekistan, available at http://www.gov.uz/en/constitution

Cornia A.G. D. and Kotz, M. Spoor and McKinley, T. (2003), 'Growth and Poverty Reduction in Uzbekistan: An Overall Strategy for Pro-Poor Growth', UNDP: Tashkent.

Country profile TrnasMonEE, (2012), online at www.transmonee.org.

Dandekar, V. M., and Rath, N. (1971), 'Poverty in India-I: Dimensions and Trends', *Economic and Political Weekly*, 6(1): 25-48.

Darity Jr., William and Steven Shulman (1989), *Question of Discrimination—Racial Inequality in the US Labour Market*, Wesleyan University Press: Middletown, Connecticut.

Dasaratharamaiah, K. and Y V Ramanaiha (2006), 'Socio-Economic Well Being of Scheduled Caste and Scheduled Tribes: A Microlevel Analysis, *The Asian Economic Review*, 48(2): 309-16.

Datta, K. L. (2010), 'Index of Poverty and Deprivation in the Context of Inclusive Growth', *Indian Journal of Human Development*, 4 (1): 45 -70.

Dave Bhavana, (2004), 'Minorities and Participation in Public Life', Working Paper No. 5 Presented in Sub-Regional Seminar on Minority Rights: Cultural Diversity and Development in Central Asia, United Nations Office of the High Commissioner for Human Rights: Bishkek.

Dave, Bhavana (2007), *Kazakhstan Ethnicity Language and Power*, Routledge: New York.

Deaton, A. and Dreze, J. (2008), 'Food and nutrition in India Facts and interpretations', *Economic and Political Weekly*, XLIV (7): 42-65.

Desai, S.; Dubey, A.; Joshi, B. L.; Sen, M.; Shariff, A. and Vanneman, R. (2010), Human Development in India challenges in society in transition' A Report prepared by NCAER: New Delhi.

Deshi, A. K. and Singh H. (1995), 'Education, Labour Market Distortions and Relative Earning of Different Religious - Caste Categories in India', *Canadian Journal of Development of Studies*, December 21.

Deshpande, A. (2005), 'Affirmative Action in India and the United States', Background Paper for 'Equity and Development', *World Development Report 2006*, World Bank: Washington, DC.

Deshpande, S. and Yadav, Y. (2006), 'Redesigning Affirmative Action: Castes and Benefits in Higher Education', *Economic and Political Weekly*, June 17.

Dev, Mahendra, S. (2000), 'Economic Reforms, Poverty, Income Distribution and Employment', *Economic and Political Weekly*, 35 (10).

Dev, Mahendra, S. (2013), *India Development Report 2012-2013*, Indira Gandhi Institute of Development Research, Oxford University Press: New Delhi.

DFID (2005), 'Reducing poverty by tackling social exclusion' A DFID policy paper, Department for International Development., Online available at: http://www2. ohchr.org/english/issues/development/docs/socialexclusion.pdf.

District Information System for Education (DISE), (2010), Op Cit. in *India Human Development Report 2011 Towards Social Inclusion*, Institution of Applied Manpower Research, Planning commission and Government of India, 2011: New Delhi.

Dowling, M., & Wignaraja, G. (2006), 'Central Asia's Economy: Mapping Future Prospects to 2015', in Silk Road paper, *Central Asia and Caucasus Institute, Silk Road Studies Program*.

Dreze, J. and Sen, A. (1991), 'Public Action for Social Security: Foundations and Strategy' in Ahmad, E., Dreze, J., Hills, J. and Sen, A. (eds.) *Social Security in Developing Countries*, Pp 1-40, Clarendon Press: Oxford.

Dubey, Amaresh, Hasan, Zoya, Prakash, Louis, Xaxa, Thorat, S.K. (2003), Social Exclusion and Poverty in India in Arjan de Haan (ed.), papers prepared for DFID India, DFID Globalisation and Social Exclusion Unit, University of Liverpool, London.

Duclos, Jean-Yves (2002), 'Vulnerability and poverty Measurement Issues in Public policy', *Social Protection Discussion Paper Series No. 0230*, Social Protection Unit Human Development Network, World Bank., online available at: http://siteresources.worldbank.org/SOCIALPROTECTION/Resources/SP-Discussion-papers/Safety-Nets-DP/0230.pdf

Duffy Katehrine (1995), 'Social Exclusion and Human Dignity in Europe: Background Report for the Proposed Initiative by the Council of Europe', Council of Europe: Strasbourg.

Dumont, L. (1980), *Homo Hierarchicus: The Caste System and its implications*, University of Chicago Press.

Elebaeva, Ainura and Omuraliev, Nurbek (2002), 'Problems of Managing Ethnic Relations in the Kyrgyz Republic', in *Central Asia & Central Caucasus Press AB/* Institute for Central Asian and Caucasian Studies in Sweden and the Institute of Strategic Studies of the Caucasus in the Republic of Azerbaijan. Online at: http://www.ca-c.org/journal/2002/journal_eng/cac-01/18.eleben.shtml.

Elster, J. (2000), 'Cycling and Social Inclusion', Centre for Analysis of Social Exclusion.

Embassy of Republic of Kazakhstan, Online at: http://www.kazakhembus.com/

Erica Marat (2013), 'Nations in Transit Kyrgyzstan', Freedom House Report, available at: http://www.freedomhouse.org/sites/default/files/NIT2012Kyrgyzstan_final.pdf, accessed April, 2013.

ESRC (1999), 'Persistent Poverty and Lifetime Inequality: The Evidence' *CASE report 5* Centre for Analysis of Social Exclusion, Centre for Analysis of Social Exclusion an ESRC LSE, London.

European Commission (2004), 'Joint Report on Social Inclusion 2004, European Commission Directorate-General for Employment and Social Affairs: Luxembourg.

European Training Foundation, (2013), *ETF Key Indicator for 2012 Overview and Analysis*, online at: http://www.etf.europa.eu/webatt.nsf/0/4091C214695FAC D2C1257B640062A3E5/$file/Key 20indicators 202012.pdf.

Falkingham J. (1999a), 'Welfare in Transition: Trends in Poverty and Well-being in Central Asia', Centre for Analysis of Social Exclusion: London.

Falkingham, J. (1999b), 'Central Asia 2010 Prospects for Human Development', Regional Bureau

Falkingham, J. (2000), 'A Profile of Poverty in Tajikistan' CASE paper 39, Centre for Analysis of Social Exclusion, London School of Economics: London.

Falkingham, J. McKee, M., Healy, J. (eds.), (2002), Health *Care in Central Asia,* Open University Press: Buckingham.

FAO (2003), 'Fertilizers use by crop in Uzbekistan', FAO Corporate Document Repository, Online available at: http://www.fao.org/DOCREP/006/Y4711E/Y4711E00.HTM.

Fields, Gary S. (2001), 'Distribution and Development, A New Look at the Developing World', Russel Sage Foundation: New York, and the MIT Press:Cambridge, Massachusetts, and London).

Fisman, R. and Gatti, R. (2002), 'Decentralization and corruption: evidence across countries', *Journal of Public Economics*, 83 (3): 325-345.

Food and Agriculture Organization (2011), 'The Status and Challenges of Food Security in Central Asia,' Food and Agriculture Organization Regional Office for Europe and Central Asia: Budapest.

Gaidar, Y. (2007), 'Collapse of an Empire: Lessons for Modern Russia', The Brookings Institution: Washington D.C.

Gassmann, F. (2011), 'Background Paper on Social Protection in Central Asia', online at: http://europeandcis.undp.org/uploads/public1/files/vulnerability/Senior 20Economist 20Web 20site/SP_in_CA_Paper_v31mar2011_11_04.pdf.

Gentile, M. (2005), 'Population Geography Perspectives on The Central Asian Republics', *Working Paper, 16, Institute for Futures Studies*: Stockholm.

Ghurye, G.S. (1957), *Caste and Class in India,* Popular Book Depot: Bombay.

Giddens, A. (1994), *Beyond left and right: The future of radical politics,* Stanford University Press.

Government of India (1979), *Report of the task force on projections of minimum needs and effective consumption demand,* Perspective Planning Division, Planning Commission.

Government of India (2000), *National Family and Health Survey (NFHS-2),* 1998-99, International Institute of Population Sciences: Mumbai.

Government of India (2006), 'Social, Economic and Education status of Muslim Community of India' a report prepared by Rajendra Sachar et al, Government of India: New Delhi.

Government of India (2007), *National Family Health Survey (NFHS-3), 2005–06,* International Institute of Population Sciences: Mumbai.

Government of India (2008a), *Eleventh Five Year Plan,* Planning Commission, Government of India, Oxford University Press: New Delhi.

Government of India (2008b), *Report of the Committee on Financial Inclusion*, Report prepared by expert committee under the chairmanship of C Rangrajan, SIDBI.

Government of India, (2009), *Report of the Expert Group to Review the Methodology and Estimation of Poverty'* Planning Commission: New Delhi.

Government of India, (2012), *Twelfth Five Year Plan (2012- 2017), Volume III: Social Sectors*, Planning Commission: New Delhi.

Government of Republic of Tajikistan (2012), *Tajikistan Demographic Health Survey 2012*, Ministry of Health of Republic of Tajikistan.

Grant, U., Hulme, D., Moore, K., & Shepherd, D. (2004), 'Understanding Chronic Poverty In Transitional Countries,' In Grant, U., Hulme, D., Moore, K., & Shepherd, D. (eds), *The Chronic Poverty Report 2004-05*, University of Manchester, Institute For Development Policy & Management (IDPM), Chronic Poverty Research Centre (CPRC).

Gugushvili, A. (2011), 'Material Deprivation, Social Class and Life Course in the Balkans, Eastern Europe and Central Asia', in *Studies of Transition States and Societies, 3 (1)*: 39-54.

Guhan, S. (2001), 'Comprehending Equalities', reprinted in S Subramaniam (ed), *India's Development Experience*, Oxford University Press: New Delhi.

Gupta, K., Arnold, F. and Lhungdim, H. (2009), 'Health and Living Conditions in Eight Indian Cities', National Family Health Survey (NFHS-3), 2005-06, International Institute for Population Sciences: Mumbai; USA: ICF Macro: Calverton, Maryland.

Haan, A. (1999), 'Social Exclusion: Towards a Holistic Understanding of Deprivation', Social Development Department, Dissemination Note No. 2, Department for International Development: London, U.K.

Haan, A. (2000), 'Social Exclusion: Enriching the Understanding of Deprivation', *Studies in Social and Political Thought*, 2(2): 22-40, University of Sussex: United Kingdom.

Haan, Arjan (1997), 'Poverty and Social Exclusion: A Comparison of Debates on Deprivation' *Working Paper No. 2*, Poverty Research Unit, Sussex University: Brighton.

Haan, Arjan and Amaresh Dubey (2003), 'Poverty in Orissa: Divergent Trends? With Some Thoughts on Measurement Issues', Paper Presented at Monitoring of Poverty in Orissa, 26-27 Feb. 2003, at Bhubaneswar (mimeo).

Halis, Akder (1994), 'A Means to Closing Gaps: Disaggregated Human Development Index', UNDP Occasional Paper, Human Development Report Office (HDRO), United Nations Development Programme (UNDP).

Hashim, S R (2009), 'Economic Development and Urban Poverty' in *India: Urban Poverty Report* United Nations Development Programme: New Delhi.

Haughton, J. H., & Khandker, S. R. (2009), *Handbook on Poverty and Inequality*, World Bank Publications: Washington DC.

Hills, J.; Grand, J. and Piachaud, D. (2002), (eds) *Understanding Social Exclusion*, Oxford University Press: New York.

Hulme David, Moore Karen, Shepherd Andrew (2004), 'Chronic Poverty: Meanings and Analytical Frameworks WP1', I.I.P.A and CRPC: New Delhi.

Human Development Report (2013), *The rise of the south: Human Progress in diverse world*, Republic of Kazakhstan, Kyrgyzstan, Tajikistan, Turkmenistan, Uzbekistan.

IFPRI (2012), 2012 Global Hunger Index *The Challenge of Hunger: Ensuring Sustainable Food Security Under Land, Water, and Energy Stresses,* International Food Policy Research Institute/Welthungerhilfe/Concern Worldwide, Bonn/Dublin/Washington DC.

International Council on Human Rights Policy (2001), *Racial and Economic Exclusion Policy Implications*, Imprimerie ATAR: Geneva, Switzerland.

International Food Policy Research Institute (2010), 'Global Hunger Index-The Challenge of Hunger: Focus on the Crisis of Child Undernutrition', New Delhi.

International Food Policy Research Institute, (2010), Global Hunger Index–*The Challenge of Hunger: Focus on the Crisis of Child Under Nutrition*, International Food Policy Research Institute, Washington, D. C.

Ivanov, A. and Peleah, M. (2010), 'From Centrally Planned To Human Development', Background paper 38 for the GHDR 2010, http://hdr.undp.org/en/reports/global/hdr2010/papers/HDRP_2010_38.pdf.

Jafferlot, Christophe and Laurent and Gaynor, (ed.) (2012), *Muslims in Indian Cities: Trajectories of Marginalisation*, Columbia University Press: New York.

Jayadev, A., Motiram, S. and Vakulabharanam, V. (2011), 'Patterns of Wealth Disparities in India: 1991-2002' in Ruparelia, S.; Reddy, S. Harriss, J. and Corbridge, S. (ed.), *Understanding India's New Political Economy: eat Transformation?*, Routledge: London.

Jha, R., and Dang, N. (2009), 'Vulnerability to Poverty in Selected Central Asian Countries,' in *The European Journal of Comparative Economics,* 6 (1):17-50, Online available in DSpace on 2010-12-20T06: 06: 03Z (GMT). No. of bitstreams: 1 Jha_Vulnerability2009. pdf: 364148 bytes, checksum: 8e1e289f8d6e4d49ebac09d9d8a2cc44 (MD5) Previous issue date: 2009-11-09T02: 29: 57.

Jogdand, P.G. (ed.) (2000), *New Economic Policy and Dalit,* Rawat Publication: Delhi.

Julian Le Grand (2003), 'Individual Choice and Social Exclusion' CASE paper 75, Centre for Analysis of Social Exclusion, London School of Economics Houghton Street: London.

Kamziyeva, Gulmira (2013), 'Assembly of People of Kazakhstan to Monitor Inter-Ethnic Situation', in Central Asia Available at http://centralasiaonline.com/ en_GB/articles/caii/ v features/main/2013/05/10/feature-01.

Kanan, K.P. (2010), 'Estimating and Identifying the Poor in India', *Indian Journal of Human Development,* 4 (1): 91-98.

Kandiyoti, Deniz (1999), 'Poverty in Transition: An Ethnographic Critique of Household' in *Development and Change,* 30 (3): 499-524.

Karen Dawisha and Parrot (Eds.) (1994), Conflict, Cleavage, and Change in Central Asia and the Caucasus Series: Democratization and Authoritarianism in Post-Communist Societies (No. 4) University of Maryland, College Park.

Kasenov, U. (2003), 'Post-Soviet Modernization in Central Asia: Realities and Prospects', in B. R. Zhukov, *Central Asia: The Challenges of Independence,* Aakar Books: New Delhi, pp. 28-53.

Kaser, M. (2005), 'Labour Market Policies and Central Asian Poverty', in *Central Asian Survey,* 24 (4):351-371.

Kathuria, Preeti, (2012), 'Incidence and Co-relates of Chronic Poverty in Remote Rural Areas: A Study of Dhar District (Madhya Pradesh)', Anmol Publications: New Delhi.

Kazakhstan, United Nations Development Programme (2004), *Poverty in Kazakhstan: Causes and Cures, UNDPKAZ,* 8, 122.

Kazimzade, Elmina (2011), 'In the Margins: Minority Education in Central Asia', *Khazar Journal of Humanities and Social Sciences, 14 (1),* pp 5-20. [Published by Khazar University Press (Baku, Azerbaijan)] available at http:// hdl.handle.net/123456789/1307.

Kenneth J. Arrow, (1998), 'What has Economics to Say about Racial Discrimination?' *The Journal of Economic Perspectives*, 1 (2): 91-100.

Ketkar, S.Y. (1909), *The History of Caste in India,* Taylor and Carpenter: Ithaca.

Khan, Mumtaz Ali, (1995), 'Human Rights and the Dalits', Uppal Publishers: Delhi.

Kishwar, M. (2002), 'Working Under Constant Threat: Some Setbacks and Some Steps Forward in Sewa Nagar', *Manushi* 130 (May–June).

Kohli, A. (2001), *The Success of India's Democracy,* Cambridge University Press: Cambridge.

Kothari, R. (1970), *Caste in Indian Politics,* Orient Longman: Delhi.

Krishna, Anirudh (2006), 'Pathways Out of and Into Poverty in 36 Villages of Andhra Pradesh, India', *World Development*, 34 (2): 271-88.

Krishna, Anirudh, M Kapila, M Porwal, and V Singh (2003), 'Falling into Poverty in a High-Growth State: Escaping Poverty and Becoming Poor in Gujarat Villages', *Economic and Political Weekly*, 38 (49):5171-79.

Kudat, A.; Peabody, S. and Keyder, C. (2000), Social Assessment and Agriculture Reform in Central Asia and Turkey', World Bank - Technical Papers in its series Papers with number 461.

Kumar, Anand (1989), *State and Society in India*, Radiant: New Delhi.

Kundu A. (2009), 'Access to Basic Amenities and Urban Security: An International Analysis With A Focus on The Social Sustainability of Cities' In *India Urban Poverty Report 2009,* Ministry of Housing And Urban Poverty Alleviation, and UNDP: New Delhi And Washington, DC.

Kundu, A. and Sarangi, N. (2007), 'Migration, Employment Status and Poverty', *Economic and Political Weekly*, XLII (04),

Kuzio, T., (2001), 'Transition in Post-Communist States: Triple or Quadruple?' *Politics*, 21 (3): 168-177.

Laderchi, C. R., Saith, R. and Stewart F., (2006), 'Does the definition of poverty matter? Comparing four approaches', in *Poverty in Focus: What is Poverty? Concepts and Measures*, International Poverty Centre, UNDP: Brazil, Online available at: www.ipc-undp.org/pub/IPCPovertyInFocus9.pdf.

Lal Deepak (1984), *Hindu Equilibrium: Cultural Stability and Economic Stagnation*, Vol. I Carendor: Oxford.

Lazreg, M. (2000), *Making the Transition Work for Women in Europe and Central Asia,* World Bank Publication: Washington DC.

Levitt, Theodore, (1993), *The Globalization of Markets,* Harvard Business Review.

Lister, R. (2004), *Poverty Key Concepts,* Polity Press: Cambridge.

Luhman Niklas (1990), *Political Theory in the Welfare State.* Berlin, New York: Walter de Gruyter.

M.B Dhanya, Samantroy Elina (2012), 'Engendering Gender Statistics: An Analysis of Gender Differentiated Statistics in India', NLI Research Studies Series, No. 101/2012, V V Giri National Institute, 2012, NOIDA, U.P.

Malhotra, Devika (2010), 'Governance Initiatives for Inclusive Growth: An Efficient Policy Model for India', Unpublished Research Paper Presented At National Law University Jodhpur (NLUJ), Faculty of Policy Sciences, Accessed at Social Science Research Network http://papers.ssrn.com/sol3/papers.cfm abstract_id 1728442, April 2013.

Marcus R.et al (2004), 'Childhood Poverty in Kyrgyzstan Initial literature review', in Childhood Poverty Research and Policy Centre, online available at: http://r4d.dfid.gov.uk/PDF/Outputs/ChildhoodPoverty/CHIP_Report_1_ (English).pdf.

Marshall, J. (2003), 'Children And Poverty—Some Questions Answered," *CHIP Briefing Paper,* 1.

Mayra Buvnic (2005), 'Social Exclusion in Latin Aamerica', in Mayara Buvinic and Jacqueline Mazzaand Ruthanne Deutsch (eds.) *Social Inclusion and Economic Development in Latin Aamerica,* Inter-Aamerican Development Bank: New York.

McKee, M. (2007), *Health: A Vital Investment for Economic Development in Eastern Europe and Central Asia,* WHO and European Observatory on Health System and Policies: Denmark.

McKinley, Terry (1997), 'Beyond the Line: Implementing Complementary Methods of Poverty

Mearns, R. and Sinha, S. (1999), 'Social Exclusion and Land Administration in Orissa, India', Policy Research Working Papers, 2124, World Bank, South Asia Regional Office, Rural Development Sector Unit: Washington, D.C.

Measurement', UNDP Discussion Paper.

Meenakshi, J V, R Ray and S Gupta (2000), 'Estimates of Poverty for SC, ST and Female - Headed Households', *Economic and Political Weekly,* 35 (3): 2748-55.

Mehta, Asha Kapur and Amita Shah (2001), 'Chronic Poverty in India: Overview Study', CPRC Working paper No. 7. Manchester: IDPM, Chronic Poverty Research Centre (CPRC).

Mehta, P. B. (2006), 'Democracy, Disagreement and Merit', *Economic and Political Weekly*, June 17.

Milanovic, B. (1999), 'Explaining the Increase in Inequality during the Transition', in *Economics of Transition*, 7(2): 299-334.

Ministry of Education Republic of Kyrgyzstan (2006), *Education Development Strategy of the Kyrgyz Republic 2007-2010*, Ministry of Education, Science and Youth Policy Republic of Kyrgyzstan: Bishkek.

Ministry of Health and Medical Industry, Turkmenistan (2001), *Turkmenistan Demographic and Health Survey 2000*, Ministry of Health and Medical Industry: Turkmenistan.

Mitra, Pradeep (2008), *Innovation Inclusion and Integration from Transition to Convergence in Eastern Europe and the Former Soviet Union*, The World Bank: Washington.

Mohanty, Mritiunjoy (2006), 'Social Inequality, Labour Market Dynamics and Reservation', *Economic and Political Weekly*, September 2.

Motiram, S. and Naraparaju, K. (2013), 'Growth and Deprivation in India: What does recent data says?', Indira Gandhi Institute of Development Research, Working Paper No. 2013-005.

Motiram, S. and Vakulabharanam, V. (2012), 'Understanding poverty and inequality in urban area since reforms bringing qualitative and quantitative approaches together', *Economic and Political Weekly*, XLVII (47- 48): 44-52.

Moya, Flynn (2004), "Migrant Resettlement in The Russian Federation: Reconstructing 'Homes' and 'Homelands'" P.15. ISBN 1-84331-117-8, Online at: http://books. google.co.in/books id YLeAxHLmgR8C pg PA15 dq hl en redir_esc yv onepage q f false

Muddiman, D. (2000), 'Theories of Social Exclusion and The Public Library', *Open to All?: the Public Library and Social Exclusion*, 1-15.

Munshi, Kaivan and Rosenzweig, Mark (2003), 'Traditional Institutions Meet the Modern World: Caste, Gender and Schooling Choice in Globalizing Economy'.

Mutatkar, Rohit (2005), 'Social Group Disparities and Poverty in India', Working Paper Series No WP-2005-004, Indira Gandhi Institute of Development Research: Mumbai.

Muthalagu, K. (2007), 'Poverty Eradication in India under Anti-Poverty Programmes: Some Observations, *Kurukeshtra*, 56 (2): 4.

Nanchariah G. (2000), 'Economic Development of Scheduled Caste' in Chandu Subba Rao and D. Francis (ed.) *Development of Weaker Section,* Rawat Publication: Delhi.

Nancy Birdsall and Richard Sabot (1991), 'Unfair Advantage - Labour Market Discrimination in Developing Countries', World Bank Studies.

National Commission for Scheduled Castes and Scheduled Tribes (2003), Sixth Report 1999-2000 and 2000-2001, Government of India: Delhi.

National Sample Survey (1975), *28th Round Report, 1973–74,* Ministry of Statistics and Programme Implementation, Government of India: New Delhi.

National Sample Survey (1982 and 1992), Report on Land and Livestock Holding Survey, 37th 48th Rounds, Ministry of Statistics and Programme implementation, Government of India.

National Sample Survey (2001), *55th Round Report, 1999-2000, Report no 468,* Ministry of Statistics and Programme Implementation, Government of India: New Delhi.

National Sample Survey (*2006), 61st Round Report, 2004-2005, Report no 508, 517, Report on Status of Education and Vocational training in India 2004-2005,* Ministry of Statistics and Programme Implementation, Government of India: New Delhi.

National Sample Survey (2011), *66th Round, Report No 551 – Status of Education and Vocational Training in India 2009-10,* Ministry of Statistics and Programme Implementation, Government of India: New Delhi.

National Sample Survey Organization (NSSO) (1997), *50th Round Report (1993-94), Report No 422, Differences in Level of Consumption among Socio –Economic Groups; 1993-94,* Department of Statistics, Government of India: India.

National Sample Survey Organization (NSSO) (2006), *59th Round Report (2002-03), Report no 503. Household Assets Holdings, Indebtedness, Current Borrowings and Repayment of Social Groups in India (as on June 30, 2002),* Ministry of Statistics and Programme Implementation, Government of India.

National Sample Survey Organization (NSSO) (2006), *61st Round Report (2004-05), Report no 516, Employment and Unemployment Situation among Social Groups in India, 2004-05 (Part I and II),* Ministry of Statistics and Programme Implementation, Government of India.

National Sample Survey Organization (NSSO) (2007), *61st Round Report (2004-05), Report No 514 Household Consumer Expenditure among Socio-Economic*

Groups, Ministry of Statistics and Programme Implementation, Government of India.

National Sample Survey Organization (NSSO) (2012), *66th Round Report (2009-2010), Report no 542, Energy Sources of Indian Households for Cooking and Lighting*, Ministry of Statistics and Programme Implementation, Government of India.

National Sample Survey Organization (NSSO) (2012), *66th Round Report (2009-2010), Report no 543, Employment and Unemployment Situation among Social Groups in India*, Ministry of Statistics and Programme Implementation, Government of India.

National Sample Survey Report (1983, 1993 and 1999-2000), Report on Employment and Unemployment situation among social groups in India, *38th, 50th and 55th Round,* Ministry of Statistics and Programme implementation, Government of India.

National Statistical Committee Kyrgyz Republic (NSCKR) (2010), Online available at: http://stat.kg/index.php option com_frontpage Itemid 1 lang english.

National Statistical Committee of Kyrgyz Republic (2010), available at, http://unstats.un.org/unsd/dnss/docViewer.aspx docID 38start.

Naumann, Mathew (2012), A Section on Central Asia, in *State of the World's Minorities and Indigenous People 2012,* Minority Rights Group: London.

Nayak, P. (1994), 'Economic Development and Social Exclusion in India', Chapter 2 *in 'Social Exclusion and South Asia'*, Labour Institutions and Development Programme, DP 77, International Institution.

Nilekani, N. (2008), *Imagining India: Ideas for the New Century*, Penguin: New Delhi.

Nussbaum, M. (2000), *Women and Human development the capabilities approach,* Cambridge University Press: UK.

Panarin, S. (1996), 'Political Development Paradigm for the Newly Independent States in Central Asia: The Consequences of Migration', RAND Corporation, Online available at: http://www.rand.org/content/dam/rand/pubs/conf_proceedings/CF130/CF130ch8.pdf.

Pathak, D. C. and Mishra S. (2013), Poverty in India and its Decompositions: A Critical Appraisal of the New Method, in S. Mahendra Dev (ed.) India Development Report: 2012-2013, India Gandhi Institute of Development Research, Oxford University Press: New Delhi.

Pathak, D.C. and Mishra, S. (2011), 'Poverty Estimates in India: Old and New Methods, 2004-05,' Working Paper No. WP-2011-015, Indira Gandhi Institute of Development Research: Mumbai.

Patwardhan, V. and V. Palshikar (1992), 'Reserved Seats in Medical Education: a Study', *Journal of Education and Social Change*, 5: 1-117.

Peimani, H. (1998), *Regional Security and the Future of Central Asia: The Competition of Iran, Turkey, and Russia*, Praeger Publishers: Westport, CT.

Petrovsky, V. (2005), 'Human Development and Human Security in Eurasia', in *International Journal on World Peace*, 22(4): 17-75.

Pierson, J. (2002), *Tackling Social Exclusion*, Routledge: London.

Planning Commission (1992-1997), *Eighth Five Year Plan*, Planning Commission, Government of India: New Delhi.

Planning Commission (1997-2002), *Ninth Five Year Plan*, Planning Commission, Government of India: New Delhi.

Planning Commission (2006), *Scheduled Caste Sub Plan, Guidelines for Implementation*, Government of India: New Delhi.

Planning Commission (2008), *Eleventh Five Year Plan*, Government of India: New Delhi.

Planning Commission (2011), *India Human Development Report 2011 Towards Social Inclusion,* Institute of Applied Manpower Research, Government of India: New Delhi..Planning Commission (2012), *Twelfth Five Year Plan*, Planning Commission, Government of India: New Delhi.

Planning Commission (2013), 'A Press note on Poverty estimates 2011-12', Government of India, Online available at: http://planningcommission.nic.in/news/pre_pov2307.pdf

PROBE (1999), *Public Report on Basic Education in India*, Oxford University Press: New Delhi.

Putnam, R. et al (1993), *Making Democracy Work: Civic Traditions in Modern Italy*, University Press: Princeton.

Radhakrishnan and Ray (2005), *Handbook of Poverty in India: Perspectives, Policies and Programs,* Oxford University Press: New Delhi.

Ramanjaneyulu, M. (2007), Trends and Influences on the Incidence of Poverty in India. Particulary Social Influences' (mimeo).

Rao, V.M. (2010), 'Upward Revision of the Poverty Line: Some Implications for Poverty Analysis and Policies', *Indian Journal of Human Development*, 4 (1): 143-55.

Ravenendran, G. (2010), 'New Estimates of Poverty in India: A Critique of Tendulkar Committee Report', *Indian Journal of Human Development*, 4 (1): 75-89.

Rawls, John (1999), *Theory of Justice*, Harvard University: USA.

Reddy, B.P. Jeevan, (1999), The Perils of Globalisation-Part I, *The Hindu*, dt.20-1-1999 and Part-II dt.21-1-1999.

Risley, H. (1915), *The People of India*, Thacker, Spink and Co.: Calcutta and Simla.

Rose-Ackerman S. (2001), 'Trust, Honesty and Corruption: Reflection on the State-building Process', *European Journal of Sociology*, 42: 526-570.

Rumer, B. and Zhukov, S. (2003), 'The Geo-economic Significance of Central Asia', in B. R. Zhukov, *Central Asia: The Challenges of Independence*, Aakar Books: New Delhi.

Runciman, W. G. (1966), 'Relative Deprivation and Social Justice: A Study of Attitudes to Social Inequality in Twentieth-Century', University of California Press: Berkeley, England.

Sabine Bernabè and Alexandre Konev (2003), *Identifying Vulnerable Groups in the Kyrgyz Labour Market: Some Implications for the National Poverty Reduction Strategy* CASE Paper 71 Centers for Analysis of Social Exclusion London School of Economics Houghton Street London.

Scoville, James G.L. (1996), 'Labour Market Under Pinnings of a Caste Economy-Failing the Caste Theoream,' in *The American Journal of Economics and Sociology*, 55 (4).

Sen, A. (1981), Poverty and Famines: An Essay on Entitlement and Deprivation, Oxford University Press: New York.

Sen, A. (1985), *Commodities and Capabilities*, Elsevier Science Publishers: Oxford.

Sen, A. (1997), *Inequalities Re-examined*, Harvard University Press: Cambridge.

Sen, A. (1998), 'Social Exclusion: A Critical Assessment of the Concept and Its Relevance', Paper Prepared for the Asian Development Bank: Manila.

Sen, A. (1999), *Development as Freedom,* Oxford University Press: Oxford.

Sen, A. (2000), 'Social Exclusion: Concept, Application and Scrutiny, Social Development Papers No. 1', Asian Development Bank: Manila: Philippines.

Sen, A. (2009), *The Idea of Justice*, Harvard University Press.

Sen, Abhijit (2000), 'Estimates of Consumer Expenditure' *Economic and Political Weekly,* 35 (51):

Sen, Amartya (1976), 'Poverty: An Ordinal Approach to Measurement', *Econometrica,* 44: 219-231.

Sen. A. (2005), 'Human Rights and Capabilities', *Journal of Human Development,* 6(2): 151-66.

Shagdar B. (2006), 'Human Capital in Central Asia: Trends and Challenges in Education', *Central Asian Survey,* 25(4): 515-532.

Shah, Ghanshyam (ed.) (2001), *Dalits and the State*, published for Centre for Rural Studies, Mussoorie, Concept Publishing Company: New Delhi.

Shariff, Abusaleh (2012), 'Inclusive Development Paradigm in India, a Post Sachar Perspective', Us India Policy Institute, Development, Democracy and Diversity, USIPI Occasional Paper no 1, NCAER: New Delhi.

Shepherd, Andrew (2010), 'Tackling Chronic Poverty', Chronic Poverty Research Centre, December, Available at: http://www.chronicpoverty.org/uplads/publication_files/Tckling 20chronic 20poverty 20webcopy.pdf.

Sheth D. L. (2004), 'Caste, Ethnicity and Exclusion in South Asia: the Role of Affirmative Action Policies in building inclusive societies', Background paper.

Silver, H. (1994), 'Social Exclusion and Social Solidarity: Three Paradigms,' IILS Discussion Papers 69, International Labour Office: Geneva.

Singh, Katar (2009), *Rural Development, Principles, Polices and Management*, Sage: New Delhi.

Smailov, A. A. (2011), *Results of the 2009 National Population Census of the Republic of Kazakhstan: Analytical Report*, The Agency on Statistics of The Republic of Kazakhstan: Astana.

Sonowal C.J (2008), Indian Tribes and Issue of Social Inclusion and Exclusion, *Centre for Studies of Social Exclusion & Inclusive Policies, Tata Institute of Social Sciences,* Stud Tribes Tribals, 6(2), *Mumbai*

Spoor, Max (2011), 'Multidimensional Social Exclusion and the 'Rural-Urban Divide' in Eastern Europe and Central Asia', Keynote Speech delivered at Congress of the European Society of Rural Sociology, Inequality and Diversity in European Rural Areas, Chania, Greece.

Srivastava, R. (2005), 'Economic Change and Social Groups in Uttar Pradesh, 1983-2000', Mimeo, Centre for Studies in Regional Development, School of Social Sciences, Jawaharlal Nehru University, Delhi, paper presented at a seminar 'Uttar Pradesh in the 1990s: Critical Perspectives on Society, Polity and Economy' held on March 10-11, 2005 organized by Centre for Political Studies, School of Social Sciences, Jawaharlal Nehru University.

Starr, S. Frederick (1999), 'Civil Society in Central Asia', in M. Holt Ruffin, Daniel Clarke Waug (eds.) *Civil society in Central Asia,* Washington: University of Washington Press.

Statistics Agency of Kazakhstan and UNDP (2004), *'The Expanded UN Theme Group on Poverty Alleviation, Employment and Social Safety',* UNDP.

Stoltzfus, R. J., Mullany, L., & Black, R. E. (2004), 'Iron Deficiency Anemia', In *Comparative Quantification of Health Risks: Global And Regional Burden of Disease Attributable to Selected Major Risk Factors,* pp. 163-209, World Health Organization: Geneva.

Streeten, P.; Burki, Haq, M. and Stewart, F. (1981), *'First things first meeting basic human needs in developing countries,* Oxford University Press: New York.

Subramanain, S. (2010), 'Identifying the Income-Poor: Some Controversies in India and Elsewhere', Discussion Paper, Courant Research Centre, November.

Sundaram, K (2001), 'Employment and Poverty in 1990s: Further Results from NSS 55th Round Employment-Unemployment Survey 1999- 2000', *Economic and Political Weekly,* 36 (32): 3039-49.

Suryanarayan, M. (2011), 'Policies for the Poor Verifying the Information Base', *Journal of Quantitative Economics,* New Series 9 (1): 73-88.

Swaminathan, M. (2010), 'The New Poverty Line: A Methodology Deeply Flawed', *Indian Journal of Human Development,* 4 (1): 121-25.

Swinnen, J. and Kristine Van Herck (2011), 'Food Security and The Transition Region, FAO Investment Centre', Working Paper Prepared Under The FAO/EBRD Cooperation For Presentation At EBRD's Grant Planning Meeting, At London, FAO and EBRD: Rome.

Teltumbde, Anand (2013), 'FDI in Retail and Dalit Entrepreneurs', *Economic and Political Weekly,* 2013, Vol XLVIII (3): 10-11.

The Constitution of the Republic of Kazakhstan (1995), Available online at: http://www.akorda.kz/en/category/konstituciya accessed on January 2013.

The Constitution of Turkmenistan, (2003), online at http://www.refworld.org/cgi-bin/texis/vtx/rwmain docid 3df0739a4, accessed on April 2013.

Theodore, Levitt (1984), 'The globalization of Markets', *The Mckinsey Quarterly*, summer 1984, Pp. 1-20.

Thorat, S. (2004a), 'Persistence of Poverty: Why is Scheduled Castes and Scheduled Tribes Stay Chronically Poor?', IIPA for Centre for Studies on Chronic Poverty: London.

Thorat, S. (2004b), 'Remedies against Economic Discrimination – International Experience of Reservation Policy in Private Sector' in Bibek Debroy and Shyam Babu (eds.) *The Dalit Question-Reforms and Social Justice*, Globus: Delhi.

Thorat, S. (2004c), 'On Reservation Policy for Private Sector', *Economic and Political Weekly*, XXXIX (25): 2560-2563.

Thorat, S. and Deshpande, R.S. (1999), 'Caste and Labour Market Discrimination' in *Indian Journal of Labour Economic*, Conference Issue, November.

Thorat, S. and Mahamallik, M. (2005), 'Persistent Poverty: Why do Scheduled Castes and Scheduled Tribes Stay Chronically Poor?', a Paper Presented at the CPRC-IIPA Seminar on Chronic Poverty: Emerging Policy Options and Issues, organised by Indian Institute of Public Administration, New Delhi during September 29-30, 2005, Indian Institute of Public Administration: New Delhi.

Tilly, C., (2007), 'Poverty and the Politics of Exclusion', in Narayan, D. and Petesch, P. (eds.), *Moving out of Poverty*, World Bank Publications: Washington DC.

Townsend, P. (1979), *Poverty in the United Kingdom*, Allen Lane and Penguin Books: London.

U.S. Department of Health and Human Services for CDC (2003), 'Fertility', in *Reproductive, Maternal and Child Health in Eastern Europe and Eurasia: A Comparative Report*, U. S. Department of Health And Human Services, Centers for Disease Control and Prevention (CDC): Atlanta, pp.21-34.

UNDP (1997a), 'Human Development Report 1997', Oxford University Press: New York.

UNDP (1997b), *Uzbekistan Human Development Report*, UNDP: Tashkent.

UNDP (1999), Uzbekistan Human Development Report, The Challenge of Transition, UNDP, available at http://hdr.undp.org/en/reports/national/ europethecis/uzbekistan/name,2952,en.html.

UNDP (2001), *HDR Republic of Kazakhstan 2000 Fighting Poverty for Better Future*, United Nations Development Programme, Republic of Kazakhstan: Almaty.

UNDP (2002), *Rural Development in Kazakhstan: Challenges And Prospects*, Republic of Kazakhstan: Almaty.

UNDP (2003), *Human Development Report 2003,* Oxford University Press: New York.

UNDP (2004a), 'Cultural Liberty in Today's Diverse World', *Human Development Report 2004*, Published by United Nations Development Programme, Oxford University Press: New Delhi.

UNDP (2004b), *Kazakhstan Human Development Report, Education for All: The Key Goal for a New Millennium*, Almaty, Kazakhstan, available online at http://hdr.undp.org/en/reports/national/europethecis/kazakhstan/name,3286,en.html.

UNDP (2005), *Uzbekistan Human Development Report, Decentralization and Human Development*, Tashkent: UNDP Uzbekistan and Centre for Economic Research, available at http://hdr.undp.org/en/reports/national/europethecis/uzbekistan/name,3294,en.html.

UNDP (2007, 2008), *Uzbekistan Human Development Report, Education in Uzbekistan Matching Supply and Demand*, UNDP Uzbekistan: Tashkent, available at http://hdr.undp.org/en/reports/national/europethecis/uzbekistan/name,9015,en.html.

UNDP (2008), 'Living with HIV: The Human Cost of Social Exclusion', UNDP Regional Bureau for Europe and the CIS: Bratislava, http://europeandcis.undp.org/rhdr.

UNDP (2009), National Human Development Report 2009 From Exclusion to equality: realizing the rights of persons with disabilities in Kazakhstan', Almaty, Kazakhstan online available at:

UNDP (2010), *Kyrgyzstan Human Development Report, Kyrgyzstan: Successful Youth Successful Country*, available at http://hdr.undp.org/en/reports/national/europethecis/kyrgyzstan/name,8941,en.html.

UNDP (2011), *Beyond Transition, Regional Human Development Report: Towards Inclusive Societies*, Regional Bureau for Europe and CIS: Brastilava.

UNDP (2013), *Tajikistan Human Development Report*, Oxford University Press: New York.

UNDP, (1995) *Kazakhstan Human Development Report 1995*, Oxford University Press: Almaty, Kazakhstan.

UNESCO (1999), *Country Report on Education for All*, Kyrgyzstan: Bishkek.

UNESCO (2006), *Literacy for Life*, EFA Global Monitoring Report: Paris.

UNESCO (2009), Regional Overview of Central and Eastern Europe and Central Asia, No- ED2009/WS/25

UNESCO (a) (2000a), Republic of Uzbekistan Final Report, Tashkent, Uzbekistan, (Report on Education for All).

UNESCO (c) (2000c), Education for All 2000 Assessment Kyrgyzstan, available at: http://www.unesco.org/education/wef/countryreports/kyrgyz/rapport_3. html, accessed on 18 June 2013.

UNESCO, (b)(2000b), Education for All 2000 Assessment Kazakhstan, available at: http://www.unesco.org/education/wef/countryreports/kazakhstan/ contents.htmlcont.

UNHROHC (United Nations Human Rights office of the High Commissioner) (2012), *Effective participation of persons belonging to minorities in law enforcement: Building an inclusive and responsive police force and judiciary,* United Nation Human Rights: Bishkek, available at: http://www.ohchr.org/ Documents/Events/Minority2012/Bishkek2012Report.pdf.

UNICEF (2010), 'School Drop Outs in Kyrgyz Republic', in Paper Series Out of School Children in Central and Eastern Europe and Common Wealth of Independent, States, Paper 7, pp 115-136.

UNICEF (2009a), 'Innocenti Social Monitor 2009 – Child Well-Being at a Crossroads: Evolving Challenges in Central and Eastern Europe and the Commonwealth of Independent States', UNICEF Innocenti Research Centre: Florence.

UNICEF (2009b), *The State of World's Children, Maternal and New Born* Health, UNICEF: New York, available at: http://www.unicef.org/sowc09/docs/ SOWC09-FullReport-EN.pdf.

UNICEF (2011), Regional Analysis 2010, Regional Office for Central and Eastern Europe and Commonwealth of Independent States (CEECIS): Geneva.

UNICEF (2012), Country Profile TrnasMonEE, available at www.transmonee.org.

UNICEF and WHO (1999), Report of the UNICEF/WHO Regional Consultation, Prevention and Control of Iron Deficiency Anaemia in Women and Children, Geneva, Switzerland.

United Nations (2005), 'Summary of the discussion at the Sub-Regional Seminar on Minority Rights: Cultural Diversity and Development in Central Asia', in *Fifty-seventh session Working Group on Minorities,* Bishkek: Commission on Human Rights.

United Nations (2010b), *The World's Women 2010, Trends and Statistics*: New York.

United Nations (2012), 'Economic and Social Council, Committee on Economic, Cultural and Social Rights, Implementation of the International Covenant on Economic, Social and Cultural Rights', Second periodic report submitted by States parties under articles 16 and 17 of the Covenant, Uzbekistan, accessed on June 5, 2013.

United Nations Data, A World of Information, United Nations Statistical Division, available at: http://data.un.org/.

United Nations Department of Economic and Social Affairs, (2010a), *Rethinking Poverty: Report on The World Social Situation 2010*.

United Nations Development Group (2004), 'The United Nations System in Turkmenistan, Common Country Assessment', Online available at: https://docs.google.com/viewer?url http 3A 2F 2Fwww.undg.org 2Farchive_docs 2F5471-Turkmenistan_CCA.doc.

United Nations, Department of Economic and Social Affairs, Population Division (2012), *World Contraceptive Use*, available at: http://data.un.org/DocumentData.aspx id 314.

USAID (2003), Reproductive Maternal and Child Health in Eastern Europe and Eurasia: A Comparative Report, U.S Department of Health and Human Services, Centre for Disease Control and Prevention: Atlanta.

V.R. Charyeva, E.Y. Samarkina, and J.M. Sullivan (2001), *Demographic and Health Survey 2000*, Ministry of Health and Medical Industry, Turkmenistan and ORC Macro, USA: Ashgabad, Turkmenistan.

Vakulbharanam, Vamsi, Motiram, Sripad (2007), 'Understanding Poverty and Inequality in Urban India since Reforms: Bring Qualitative and Qualitative Approach Together', *Economic and Political Weekly*, XLVII (47 & 48), Dec 1, 2012.

Velaskar, P. R. (1986), 'Inequality in Higher Education: A Study of Scheduled Caste Students in Medical Colleges of Bombay', unpublished PhD dissertation, Tata Institute of Social Sciences, Mumbai.

Vizard, Polly (2005), 'The Contributions of Professor Amartya Sen in the Field of Human Rights Centre for Analysis of Social Exclusion', London School of Economics: Houghton Street.

Walker, A. (1997), 'Introduction: The Strategy of Inequality' in A. Walker and C. Walker, (eds.), *Britain Divided: The Growth of Social Exclusion in The 1980s and 1990s,* Child Poverty Action Group: London.

Weisskopf, T. E. (2004), 'The Impact of Reservation on Admissions to Higher Education in India', *Economic and Political Weekly,* September 25.

Weisskopf, T. E. (2006), 'Is Positive Discrimination a Good Way to Aid Disadvantaged Ethnic Communities?' *Economic and Political Weekly,* February 25.

Weitz-Shapiro, Rebecca, Winters, Matthew, (2008), *Political Participation and Quality of Life,* Columbia University, Inter,-American Development Bank: Washington.

William Darity Jr. (1997), 'Reparations' in Samuel L. Myers, Jr. (Edited), *Civil Rights and Race Relations in the Post Reagan-Bush Era,* Praeger: London.

William Darity Jr. (Edit) (1995), Economics and Discrimination Vol. I, an Elgar Reference Collection (U.S.)

William Darity Jr. with Steven Shulman, (1989), 'Question of Discrimination – Racial inequality in the U.S. labour market', Wesleyan University Press: Middletown, Connecticut.

World Bank (2000a), *India: Reducing Poverty, Accelerating Development,* The World Bank, Oxford University Press: Washington, D.C.

World Bank (2000b), *Republic of Tajikistan Poverty Assessment Program report No. 20285-TJ,* World Bank, Online at: http://www-wds.worldbank.org/servlet/ WDSContentServer/WDSP/IB/2000/08/14/000094946_00080105305244/ Rendered/PDF/multi_page.pdf.

World Bank (2003), *Uzbekistan Living Standards Assessment: Policies to Improve Living Standards, (in two volumes) Vol. II Report No. 25923-UZ,* World Bank, accessed online at: http://www-wds.worldbank.org/servlet/ WDSContentServer/WDSP/IB/2003/06/17/000160016_20030617131238/ Rendered/PDF/259230UZ.pdf.

World Bank (2004), *Kazakhstan Dimensions of Poverty in Kazakhstan (in two Volumes) Volume I Policy Briefing, Report no. 30294-KZ,* World Bank: accessed online at: http://web.worldbank.org/WBSITE/EXTERNAL/TOPICS/ EXTPOVERTY/EXTPA/0,,contentMDK:20455713~menuPK:435735~page PK:148956~piPK:216618~theSitePK:430367~isCURL:Y~isCURL:Y,00.html.

World Bank (2005), 'Growth, Poverty and Inequality, Eastern Europe and the Former Soviet Union', The World Bank: Washington.

World Bank (2006), Development Policy Review, 'India Inclusive Growth and Service Delivery: Building on India's Success', Report No. 34580-IN, May 29, 2006.

World Bank (2007a), 'From Red to Gray: The 'Third Transition' of Ageing Populations in Eastern Europe and the Former Soviet Union', http:// siteresources.worldbank. org/ECAEXT/Resources/publications/454763-1181939083693/full_report.pdf.

World Bank (2007b), 'Republic of Uzbekistan: Living Standard Assessment Update, Report No. 40723-UZ, Online available at: http://www-wds. worldbank.org/external/default/WDSContentServer/WDSP/IB/2007/10/05 /000020439_20071005095235/Rendered/PDF/407230UZ.pdf.

World Bank (2007c), *Kyrgyz Republic Poverty Assessment (in two Volumes), Volume II: Labour Market dimension of poverty, Report No. 40864-KG*, World Bank, accessed online at: http://web.worldbank.org/WBSITE/EXTERNAL/TOPICS/ EXTPOVERTY/EXTPA/0,,contentMDK:21571661~menuPK:435735~page PK:148956~piPK:216618~theSitePK:430367~isCURL:Y~isCURL:Y,00.html.

World Bank (2010), 'Uzbekistan Climate Change: A country note', Online available at: http://www.worldbank.org/eca/climateandagriculture.

World Bank (2012), Available at, http://data.worldbank.org/.

World Bank Development Indicators, (2013), World Bank, available at http://data. worldbank.org/data-catalog/world-development-indicators.

World Bank Uzbekistan snapshot (2012), 'World Bank – Uzbekistan Partnership: Country Program Snap shot', World Bank, October 2012, Online available at: http://www.worldbank.org/content/dam/Worldbank/document/Uzbekistan-Snapshot.pdf.

World Bank, (1998), 'Income, Inequality, and Poverty during the Transition from Planned to Market Economy', The World Bank: Washington, DC.

World Bank, (2007d), 'Higher Education in Central Asia The Challenges of Modernization, Case Studies from Kazakhstan, Tajikistan, Kyrgyz Republic and Uzbekistan', In Jose Joaquin Brunner and Anthony Tilett (Eds), *Higher Education in Central Asia; The Challenges of Modernization An Overview*, Washington: *The World Bank*

World Health Organization (2010), *Poverty, Social Exclusion and Health Systems in the WHO European Region*, WHO Regional Office for Europe: Copenhagen.

Xaxa, Virginius, (2001), 'Protecting Discrimination: Why Scheduled Tribes Lag Behind Scheduled Castes, *Economic and Political Weekly*, XXXVI (29): 2765-2772.

Yarkova, T. et al. (2004), 'Child Poverty in Kyrgyzstan Initial Literature Review', Childhood Poverty Research and Policy Centre.

Yitzhaki, S. (1979), 'Relative Deprivation and the Gini Coefficient', *Quarterly Journal of Economics*, 93, pp 321—324.

Zajda, J. (2005), *Minorities, Indigenous Groups and Identity Politics in Education and Policy: The Central Asia*, in Joseph Zadja (ed.) *International Handbook on Globalization*, Australian Catholic University, School of Education: Melbourne.

Zeitlyn, Sushila (May 2004), 'Social exclusion in Asia – some initial ideas', DFID: London.

Zoninsein, Jonas, (2001), 'GDP Gains and Long-Term Discrimination against Blacks: The Inverse Relationship', in Charles V. Hamilton, et al. (eds.), *Beyond Racism: Race and Inequality in Brazil, South Africa, and the United States*, Boulder, CO: Lynne Rienner.

*　　*　　*

Printed in the United States
By Bookmasters